John Deere
Snowmobiles

John Deere Snowmobiles

Development, Production, Competition and Evolution, 1971–1983

RONALD K. LEONARD *and*
RICHARD TEAL

McFarland & Company, Inc., Publishers
Jefferson, North Carolina

LIBRARY OF CONGRESS CATALOGUING-IN-PUBLICATION DATA

Leonard, Ronald K., 1934– author.
John Deere snowmobiles : development, production, competition and evolution, 1971–1983 / Ronald K. Leonard and Richard Teal.
p. cm.
Includes bibliographical references and index.

ISBN 978-0-7864-7837-8 (softcover : acid free paper) ♾
ISBN 978-1-4766-1355-0 (ebook)

1. John Deere snowmobile—History.
2. Deere & Company—History.
I. Teal, Richard, 1941– author. II. Title.
TL234.2.L46 2014 338.7'62922042—dc23 2013048975

BRITISH LIBRARY CATALOGUING DATA ARE AVAILABLE

Front cover: A 1980 John Deere Trailfire cuts a path (courtesy Roger Tesch)

Manufactured in the United States of America

McFarland & Company, Inc., Publishers
Box 611, Jefferson, North Carolina 28640
www.mcfarlandpub.com

Table of Contents

Introduction

In 1971, after 134 years in the same business, the oldest agricultural company in the United States decided to manufacture snowmobiles to enter a recreation market. This was a major departure from their long successful history of manufacture and sale of agricultural machines. At that time, Deere & Co. was the largest agricultural equipment manufacturer in the world. The profitable success of the company throughout its history was based in agriculture. Loyal customers expected John Deere products to perform well and be dependable. Thousands of customers, dealers and company employees were excited by this news. This book explains why this decision was taken and how the snowmobile business influenced consumer products marketing and manufacturing in Deere to drive the growth of the profitable lawn and garden tractors and related homeowner products. The book arose from the personal knowledge and experiences of the authors, from interviews with employees involved with all aspects of the venture, and from materials published or obtained by Deere & Company.

In Casey's *Daily Dispatch*, David Galland's analogy "The Tracks of Mankind" theorized that people, like animals, leave tracks that enable others to easily identify them. The experiences that thousands of Deere customers, dealers, and employees had during the years Deere manufactured and marketed snowmobiles made tracks as easily identified as those left by a snowmobile. There are thousands of human and snowmobile tracks in this book that we obtained from many who willingly shared their memories, photos and documents. Without their help this book would have been as obscure as footprints in the snow after a strong wind. At the start of our research we thought of Deere snowmobile tracks as something that had passed out of existence; the reality is that thousands of John Deere snowmobiles are still in barns, sheds and garages, ready to ride at the first snowfall.

The market changed rapidly during the years 1971 to 1983, when Deere was in the business. The industry endured the first U.S. energy crisis in 1973 and 1974, and twice there were two consecutive years of low snowfall in the traditional snow-belt regions in North America. In the 1980s, resorts in snow areas were renting sleds and snowmobile gear. This lowered the annual cost of snowmobiling for the occasional rider who didn't have storage or a trailer to haul sleds to a snow area. As a result, homeowners, especially in marginal snow regions, didn't buy as many machines. These influences combined to cause extreme fluctuation of annual sales, prompting many companies to exit the business after Deere began production; thus, new snowmobiles migrated into the market at bargain basement prices.

The authors received a pleasant invitation to attend the 20th annual Vintage Snowmobile Club two-day event held at Waconia, Minnesota, in late January 2010. Several thousand people attended, and families with young children came to enjoy riding and racing all makes of snowmobiles in weather that hovered around zero. Vintage Snowmobile organizations are located across North America, their members reliving experiences from riding their older sleds, manufactured from the mid–1960s until the mid–1980s. Owners of snowmobiles made by other manufacturers in the era that Deere was in the business were present at Waconia. Race drivers and mechanics of Enduro Team Deere, the last Deere race team, attended and participated. Deere race sleds were featured that year during a special evening program conducted by Jon Carlson and other members of the Deere race teams. Brian Nelson, who won the 1976 I-500 cross-country race riding a John Deere Liquidator sled, was the featured speaker. Deere consumer snowmobiles from every year of production were displayed outdoors and judged for best original or restored condition. This event rekindled our memories of the challenging and satisfying experiences we had in design and manufacture of snowmobiles and gave a substantial boost to our motivation to perform the research to tell the story of Deere in the snowmobile business. The research was strongly reinforced by the extensive records that Jack Hoffman, Jr., generously contributed; these were informative about the origin and development of the snowmobiles from his work at the Horicon Works.

Deere Corral Waconia 2010 (Richard Teal collection).

What Is Snowmobile Fun About?

"If you've ever ridden on a snowmobile, you know there's no feeling quite like it. To travel in the winter in a world that's clean, fresh and quiet. Where the winds don't feel as cold and your limit is the edge of the snow." These words, located on the inside cover of the Big John album that Deere produced for dealers to promote the 1975 models, conveyed the message that riding a John Deere snowmobile would be a different experience from anything offered by other Deere machines. Snowmobile fun can be found anywhere there is snow. A snowmobile provides a powered vehicle for off-road outdoor recreation in the coldest part of the year from Maine to California and from Nova Scotia to British Columbia. Snowmobiles expanded the winter sport choices beyond ice skating, downhill and cross-country skiing, and in winter they replaced the outboard motor and boat of summer. Adrenaline starts to build as the engine roars after pulling the rope or turning the key to start. With helmet secure, coat zipped, and mittens on, you are ready for a ride that is the best experience imaginable. As you travel the sound is left behind, and you sense the powerful engine vibration tremors in your hands and feet and hear the air rushing over your helmet. Nothing else feels like gliding on a motorized sled over the winter landscape.

From a humble beginning in 1960, the sport of snowmobiling rapidly grew in popularity and dozens of manufacturers rushed into the business. The sleds, as they were commonly called, provided outdoor recreation during winter for millions of people in the snow belt of the U.S. and Canada. Snowmobile trails were built across almost every type of terrain imaginable. Every ride is different depending on the trail, the weather and your mood. Families could be found on leisurely rides through the countryside, going where they had never been. Friday night visits to a local tavern for a fish fry were often made riding a snowmobile. Snowmobile clubs organized fund raising and competitive events throughout the snow-belt areas. Families hauled their sleds to scenic locations for vacations. Snowmobiles are used for other purposes beside recreation: Ski resorts use them as work vehicles, park rangers ride them to inspect the vast spaces in the national parks, law enforcement agencies conduct search and rescue missions where other vehicles can't operate, and in Northern Canada, Eskimos use them for transportation as modern day dog sleds.

Today, manufacturers make snowmobiles that improve rider comfort and expand the limits of performance. The 2012 American Snowmobiler Buyers Guide listed 109 models produced by four manufacturers. The engine displacements range from 123cc to 1200cc and the price varied from $2,599.00 to $17,499.00. The heaviest machine weighed a robust 730 lbs. dry weight. The snowmobile suspension is now based on motorcycle dirt bike technology for long vertical travel of the skis and up to 18 inches of lift for the track suspension. The machines are tailored to fit the needs of riders from a child to a race driver. Deere snowmobiles used a leaf spring to support the ski and a track suspension that would move vertically about two inches. The typical weight was about 400 pounds without the operator and prices ranged from $1500 to $2500. In today's snowmobile market, customers can select sleds to match their performance needs from the wide range of features and cost.

Racing Snowmobiles

Snowmobile races provide entertainment for thousands of spectators during winter months. An oval race is like watching Olympic speed skating. Sleds roar down the straightaway, and each driver leans to the inside and hopes the track and skis hold the machine going around the curve. Many don't make it and skid sideways into a snowbank. In cross-country racing, sleds seem to fly over the road ditch crossings, landing on the other side with a couple of rebounds. Hopefully the rider doesn't lose control. It is ironic to watch the machines run 60 or 70 mph in a roadside ditch, going faster than the vehicle speed limit on the road. Racing became popular in winter during the decades of the '60s and '70s and drag racing was done on dirt tracks in summer. The Horicon Works drag racing team provided performance input to product engineers from their experiences and enjoyed the competition at the same time. Racing snowmobiles was an exciting and valuable part of the Deere snowmobile experience.

Winter racing venues were of many types. Oval races were held typically on lakes

Ed Kruel, John Orvis, Bill Borth and Bob Hoffman, John Deere drag team (courtesy Ed Kruel).

and fairgrounds. Cross-country races could be organized in many different venues throughout the snow regions, where combinations of challenging terrain could include road ditches, lakes, riverbeds and snowmobile trails. The racecourse is mile after mile of endless ditches, forests, cold weather, snow, ice and almost anything else. Cross-country races were and still are the ultimate measure of human endurance and durability of the race machine in bitter cold.

As engine power increased, sleds ran faster and the race associations set longer race routes. The crown jewel of cross-country races was the legendary Winnipeg to St. Paul International 500 mile race (WSP I-500), which grew to be a four-day event held in late January. Several manufacturers fielded company race teams and numerous dealers sponsored independent drivers who were most of the race entrants. Bragging rights went to the driver and the manufacturer who won. Deere chose to concentrate on cross-country racing as the ultimate verification of superior performance and durability. A typical midwinter race often started in the early morning in subzero weather but for the drivers it was just another day at the racetrack.

Deere and Company Enters the Scene

In the 1960s, vast economic, social, and technological forces drove changes in the U.S. and Canada that exerted powerful influence on decisions made by U.S. manufacturers and marketers. The growth of the U.S. economy spurred the rapid expansion of the suburbs that created a large market for homeowner machines for yard maintenance. Social changes were dramatized by Woodstock and the emergence of the hippie movement that spread across the country. Technological forces were driven by events like the launch of *Sputnik* in 1957 and the Cuban missile crisis, which produced industrial expansion that brought advancements in materials and products. From these industries new materials and technology were spun off to products for consumer markets. The Japanese challenge emerged as their industries designed and manufactured a broad number of products like motorcycles, stereos and a vast assortment of other consumer goods. Manufacturers in Japan began to supply small engines that were designed with advanced technology to achieve more power with easier-starting engines than U.S. manufacturers. These products were quickly accepted in the U.S. market. By the end of the 1960s, Honda was marketing walk-behind mowers, and Kubota was selling small compact utility tractors.

Deere and Company began the decade of the 1960s with a dramatic advancement in technology with the design and manufacture of the New Generation Tractors that rapidly advanced the growth of Deere agricultural machine sales and market share. This event was a visible symbol of the new leadership by Bill Hewitt, who was determined to drive growth and expansion of Deere not only in the U.S. market but worldwide. Hewitt commissioned the design and manufacture of a homeowner garden tractor first manufactured in 1963, and in 1967 Horicon Works began to investigate the snowmobile market. All new ventures required considerable discussion and debate among Hewitt and his board of directors. The conservative culture of making decisions was their heritage from John Deere's humble beginning in 1837 as the company continued to grow and develop with its focus on agriculture. By the 1960s, Deere had evolved into a publicly owned company with its major focus still on the agricultural market.

The book *John Deere's Company* by Wayne G. Broehl, Jr., explains in detail the growth of the company from the founding in 1837 until Hewitt's retirement in 1982. In the present book, Chapter 1 provides a summary of the growth of Deere during the Charles Wiman era, from 1928 until 1954, and how William Hewitt, Wiman's son-in-law, as president and CEO from 1955 to 1982, continued Wiman's growth initiatives and extended them beyond expectations. The conservative culture of the company strongly influenced the decisions both men made. When Hewitt retired, the five successive generations of Deere family leadership of the company ended.

Chapter 2 discusses why and how the decision was made to enter the consumer products market. Our research uncovered some surprising details of the internal working of the company as this decision was made. The first consumer product was the lawn and garden tractor manufactured in 1963, followed by the snowmobile in 1971. Snowmobiles provided the impetus to establish a network of independent dealers separate from agriculture for the consumer product market. The consumer products required a separate internal marketing organization in Deere and established the Horicon Works as the factory that produced consumer products.

Chapter 3 looks in detail at how other Deere growth initiatives interacted with and influenced the timing of decisions about the manufacture of consumer products. It covers the major internal product snowmobile meetings and the information used to make specific decisions about the snowmobile design and manufacturing processes. It concludes with a description of the first production John Deere Model 400 and 500 snowmobiles. Chapter 4 then delves into the market reaction to the new snowmobiles and how chaotic the environment was at the factory as they designed and manufactured 36,990 snowmobiles in the second year.

Chapter 5 describes the changes implemented for people and work processes in the engineering department and factory. The title connotes that major overhauls of the engineering capability and factory operations were needed to be a strong competitor in the market. Why they were needed and how they were implemented in both factory and engineering follows in Chapter 6, describing the period when the Horicon Works concentrated on design and manufacture, as well as on corrections to the first two years of snowmobile production. All models produced in the first four years were built on the mid-engine chassis. The chapter also describes how the JD 340/S snowmobile for racing was designed and how well it performed in competition.

Chapter 7 goes into detail about new front engine chassis machines that improved performance and durability. The Cyclone and Liquifire sleds produced as 1976 models established Deere as a major competitive force with the leaders in the industry. This design program verified the value of a product design schedule with one year to operate the engineering test sleds in winter to obtain the correct performance calibration before production.

Chapter 8 provides a complete history of the factory and Deere race teams, their machines and race team results. The influence of racing wasn't limited to the factory race teams; however, a discussion of independent dealer and private owners is beyond the scope of this book. Web sites like JD Sleds provide numerous videos of John Deere snowmobiles in all types of racing venues.

Chapter 9 explains how the Horicon Works expanded its available market with the design of new concept snowmobiles marketed as the new breed of Deere Spitfire and Trailfire snowmobiles, and how their manufacture became profitable. Kawasaki emerged as the engine supplier.

Chapter 10 relates how the snowmobile business drove internal changes in the Horicon factory operations in support of new product engineering designs for the grounds-care markets. Horicon Works entered new market segments of commercial mowers and compact utility tractors, as well as providing vastly improved rear-engine riding mowers, lawn tractors and garden tractors. A new strategy for purchasing engines and drive trains in new product programs was developed and successfully implemented. The factory made major productivity advancements during that period by implementation of a flow-through manufacturing system that was modeled after the Toyota manufacturing processes in Japan — but adapted to the Horicon Works culture and location. Its effectiveness was magnified by the installation of an Automatic Vehicle Guidance system in assembly. A new paint building was installed that synchronized parts flow through the paint system, as triggered by the demands for daily assembly.

The final chapter details how the design of new products was incorporated into a team-based organization that improved the productivity of the factory by doing concurrent design of the product with the manufacturing personnel at the Horicon Works or at suppliers of major components. The Horicon Works factory and the sales branch marketing effort became a major contributor to the survival of Deere and Company during the agricultural recession that began in 1982, as Horicon was winding down production of snowmobiles. Fortune 500 rankings that began in 1955 are displayed throughout the book at significant times to illustrate the effect of new initiatives on Deere's financial performance.

1

Origin and Growth of the John Deere Company

Deere and Company was founded in 1837 when John Deere made his steel plow and began to manufacture and sell it to farmers. His company continued to manufacture agricultural equipment, improving and adding new products as needed for changing farming practices. In 1971, after 134 years, Deere began to manufacture snowmobiles at the former Van Brunt factory in Horicon, Wisconsin, that Deere had purchased in 1911. Entering a sport vehicle market was a significant departure from Deere's history of manufacturing and marketing agricultural machines. A brief summary of the development of Deere and Company helps to understand why Deere entered the snowmobile business. For a detailed history of the five generations of John Deere and his descendants, who led the company from 1837 until 1982, see *John Deere's Company: A History of Deere & Company and Its Times* by Wayne G. Broehl, Jr. His book describes each era in five sections, as follows:

Part I. Opening the Prairie: The John Deere Years (1837–59)
Part II. Marketing and Manufacturing in an Expansionist Age: The Charles Deere Years (1860–1907)
Part III. Consolidation and Control: The William Butterworth Years (1908–27)
Part IV. From Retrenchment to Expansion: The Charles Wiman Years (1928–54)
Part V. Worldwide Corporation: The William A. Hewitt Years (1955–82)

Upon returning to Deere & Co. in 1944, after serving as a colonel in the Ordnance Corps of the U.S. Army and then as the director of the farm machinery and equipment division of the War Production Board, Charles Wiman, who had served as president of Deere since 1928, reestablished control of the company. The leadership had been distributed among three men while he was on leave during World War II, when Burton Peek served as president. Wiman reaffirmed and strengthened the Deere policy of decentralized management. He supported strongly that the units should have control of their businesses—yet he could intervene if they were not actively addressing changing markets.

Throughout his years as president of Deere, Wiman was a strong supporter of developing new products. He first voiced support of product development after his election to the Deere board of directors in 1919. To provide for new products outside the scope of factory unit managers, Wiman created an Experimental Department, later renamed the Development Department, and located it in Moline. It was tasked with the design of developing machines for new or changing farm practices. The concern that had plagued Deere management throughout its history was the tendency for unit managers to be too slow in responding to changing farming practices— a likely consequence of decentralized management.

In 1945 Deere contracted with the Ordnance Corps of the U.S. Army to produce 75mm shells in Dubuque, Iowa. Wiman then bought the ordnance factory and enough land on which to build a new tractor factory. In January 1945, the Deere board of directors approved an expenditure of $9.4 million for the factory and a new small tractor, the Model M, to be manufactured in Dubuque. Deere was authorized to continue engineering work on it during the war, as permitted by the allocation of scarce resources. The Model M was a low-cost tractor rated at 14.4 drawbar horsepower. Wiman also bought Lindeman, a manufacturer of small crawler tractors in Seattle, and later manufactured them in Dubuque. This small crawler tractor was the start of Deere's manufacture of industrial equipment at Dubuque, Iowa.

Wiman purchased the Des Moines Ordnance plant at Ankeny, Iowa, in 1947 from the U.S. government for $4.15 million. Several farm machines were transferred from Moline factories to provide work for the John Deere Des Moines Works. By 1950 production began there of the John Deere Model 8 self-propelled cotton picker. Farmers were anxious to replace the hard manual labor required to pick cotton by hand. Development of a John Deere cotton picker was discontinued during the war due to materials and people needed for the war effort. After the war ended, Wiman authorized an aggressive program to get back into the cotton-picker market, as International Harvester in Chicago and Rust in Pine Bluff, Arkansas, were rapidly increasing their production. The Des Moines Works cotton picker soon became the most successful product for that factory by the commitment to make product improvements needed in the market to adapt to changing farming practices. The Deere cotton picker work was resumed at the Development Department in Moline after World War II ended. While working there, Arthur "Blackie" and Wally Hubbard conducted field tests of the experimental pickers on Wiman's ranch in Arizona. During the 1960s on test trips for the Des Moines Works, they often talked about the focus to get the cotton picker into production. "Wiman walked behind the test pickers and helped to glean the missed cotton so we could weigh it to determine the machine's efficiency," Wally said.

Other Deere plants were allocated capital to expand their operations. As a result, from 1945 to 1948 Deere sales tripled from $94 million to $293 million. With this sharp upturn in sales and profits, Wiman secured board approval to build a factory in Scotland. It was to be the first Deere factory in Europe. Another growth venture was a plan to manufacture nitrogen fertilizer on a new site in Oklahoma. Wiman had learned about nitrogen fertilizer during a meeting in 1951 with the U.S. Department of Agriculture. He was convinced that farmers would rush to buy nitrogen fertilizer when they learned, by applying it to growing crops, they could produce 100 bushels of corn per acre rather than 40. Wiman believed the fertilizer business would be profitable and complement Deere machinery sales. After endless delays by the British government, the Scotland project was scuttled. Due to a sharp decline in farm equipment sales in the U.S. in 1953 and 1954, the fertilizer program was also terminated.

Internal growth of the company's combine harvester, cotton picker, and most other farm implements was going well. The major weakness was the tractor business. The aged two-cylinder "Poppin' Johnny" was hard to sell against strong competition like IHC and also from tractors made by Allis Chalmers, Oliver and JI Case. They had modern designs of four-cylinder engines and were more powerful and versatile tractors. Deere tractors needed a larger, more powerful engine and all-new drive train components to replace the horizontal two-cylinder engine, which had been manufactured since 1924. Wiman understood that the aged two-cylinder tractor had to be replaced. The Deere board was strongly in favor of concentrating on the tractor business instead of other growth ventures like fertilizers and international operations. In 1953 the Deere Board of Directors authorized an engineering project for an all-new tractor. In his book, Broehl states there is no record of the date when this was decided, as the project was so secret no board minutes were kept.

For this project Wiman departed from the Deere policy of decentralized management that gave authority to make new product decisions to the factory managers. The project personnel were located in an abandoned grocery store in Cedar Falls, Iowa, separate from the Waterloo Tractor Works and reported to a vice-president at Deere and Company rather than the Waterloo factory manager. Other than the project employees, nobody was permitted access. During World War II, Wiman well may have been aware of the famous Skunk Works organization used to design the P-38 fighter plane— and later other airplanes—at Lockheed Martin Aircraft Company, in a location walled off from the factory. That successful design in record time of the world's fastest fighter airplane likely influenced him to separate the design and manufacturing engineering from the Waterloo factory that had produced the two-cylinder engine tractors since 1923.

William (Bill) A. Hewitt became president of Deere & Company in 1955, succeeding his father-in-law, Charles Wiman. In 1954 Wiman learned he had a fatal illness that gave him only a short time to live. This caused him to review the succession plan and to recommend Bill Hewitt to the board of directors as the next president. Hewitt, a California native, had obtained a degree in economics from the University of California Berkeley after service in the U.S. Navy on the battleship *California* during World War II. After graduation he worked as a territory manager for a Ford-Ferguson distributor in the farm equipment business. He met Patricia, Charles Wiman's daughter, and soon they married. Within a few months he began work for Deere in the San Francisco sales branch. He progressed rapidly to become the branch manager. After six years he transferred to the Deere headquarters in Moline. From these experiences he was judged to be the best qualified person to succeed Charles Wiman as president of Deere. Upon his election as president in 1955, he continued the uninterrupted succession of five generations of Deere descendants as head of the company.

Broehl's book describes the challenges Wiman faced with the board of directors to get approval of Hewitt for the job. Some of the members of the board of directors were descendants of the family and voted different blocks of stock that represented personal holdings and those of family trusts, and their support was required to elect a new president. As the new president, Bill Hewitt embraced the growth initiatives that Wiman had begun, and propelled the company to greater levels of success than anyone expected. Charley Wiman's untimely death in 1955 launched Hewitt, then forty years old, as the business leader of the most respected company in the business, with a new tractor design already underway. Since 1837, four generations of leadership by John Deere and his descendants had left a long record of steady and profitable growth. Now it was Hewitt's job to lead the company.

The Fortune ranking of the top 500 companies in the U.S. first appeared in 1955 and has been published annually since then. In 1955, Deere & Company ranked 104th with annual sales of $303.4 million and profits of $20.6 million. (The complete list is in the Appendix). In 1915 Wiman started to work at Deere in the shop and earned $0.15 per hour. Since his election to the board of directors in March 1919 and as president in 1928, Wiman had guided the company through two depressions, the dust bowl drought in the '30s and World War II. Deere was still in business after 118 years and going strong.

The culture of Deere was strongly influenced by the values of the founder, John Deere. Hewitt and his predecessors stressed the core values were honesty and hard work. A John Deere machine had to be dependable and perform to the satisfaction of the customer. Every employee in the company needed to perform his job correctly to ensure the customer received a good machine. A satisfied John Deere customer would develop loyalty to the brand. In all human interactions, loyalty develops from trust. Trust is founded on integrity and it had to be there when one worked for John Deere. These values continued to be stressed to all employees throughout the company. During the years the plows were manufactured in Grand Detour, Illinois, John Deere stated to his business partner Tate, "I will never put my name on a product that does not have in it the best that is in me." While the enterprise had to earn a profit to stay in business, the company first had to do the right thing in design and manufacture of its products. Another way of expressing this is the machine speaks clearly, whether or not it operates to the satisfaction of the customer. The customer's experience determines his willingness to purchase another John Deere product in the future. This customer loyalty has sustained the growth of Deere throughout its history.

Hewitt's tenure as president and later CEO can best be characterized as "driving growth." He began immediately to grow the business more aggressively than Wiman. The new tractors required a huge investment for all new manufacturing equipment at

Waterloo and Dubuque. Likewise significant investments were planned at all the other Deere farm equipment factories for new and larger equipment to match the more powerful tractors. Hewitt was determined to seek growth in the international markets. He assigned several of his senior management in Moline to investigate the major agricultural producing countries in the world where Deere could enter the market. Once it was determined that a market would need John Deere products, the focus shifted to determine an economical plan to supply products for that market. By that time the economic recovery from the carnage caused by World War II was well underway; however, some countries protected their domestic manufacturers with tariffs and other national regulations.

The most significant new growth venture occurred in 1956 with the purchase of the Heinrich Lanz tractor factory in Mannheim, Germany—a well-established German company that opened the door for Deere to set up a marketing organization in Europe. Located close to the Rhine River in the heart of the Mannheim industrial region, the Lanz factory had been rebuilt following its destruction during World War II. Mannheim

Mannheim Tractor Factory, circa 1950s (courtesy Julia Piesker).

was chosen as the site of the European headquarters located near the tractor factory. That same year, international growth continued with the start of a sales branch in Mexico, and later a manufacturing operation located near Monterey. A few years later Deere began manufacturing operations in France and Spain. Even though many markets had tariff restrictions, Deere was able to begin limited operations in South Africa, Brazil and Argentina. Deere was already well established in Canada. Hewitt directed the start of the Industrial Equipment Division for markets in North America. Industrial products were manufactured in plants in Moline as well as Dubuque, Iowa.

Under Hewitt's direction, the product introduction of the New Generation Tractors in 1960 became the signature product event of the growing company. They were shown to dealers at an event named Deere Day in Dallas. Selective factory and Deere personnel were invited to witness firsthand the dealer reaction to the new tractors. This was the most dramatic product introduction ever held for John Deere dealers. Over 6000 dealers from all over North America were flown to the introduction in Dallas. Nothing of this magnitude had ever been done before in the industry.

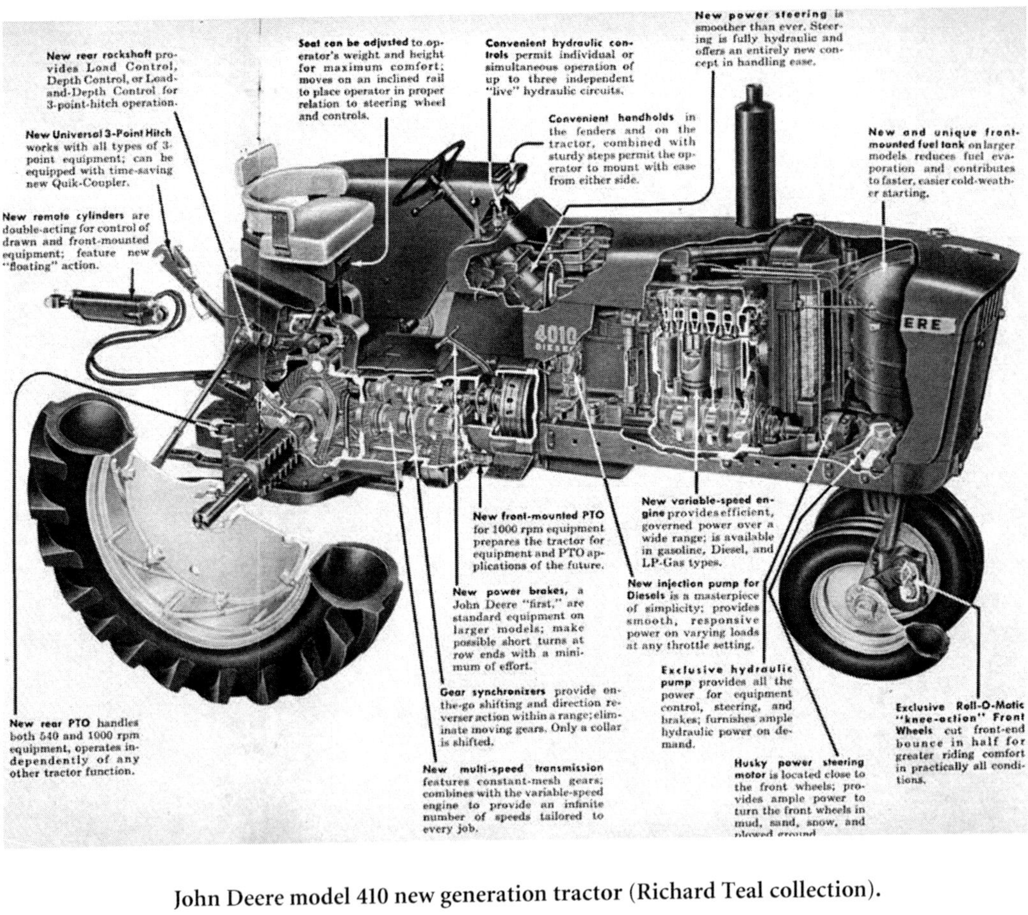

John Deere model 410 new generation tractor (Richard Teal collection).

Hewitt's keen flair for marketing was evident in the product introduction. The new 4010 tractors were showcased in the Neiman Marcus Department Store in Dallas. The tractor was in a large gift box located in the jewelry department. It was wrapped with a diamond-studded velvet ribbon. Patricia (Tisch) Wiman Hewitt cut the velvet ribbon with a large pair of scissors. Stanley Marcus pulled away the wrappings to reveal the gleaming green and yellow tractor inside. Diamonds were attached to a banner on the hood that twinkled the name John Deere; a diamond cornet was affixed to the exhaust pipe, and that night Al Hirt entertained at a Texas style barbeque with fireworks. This was not the usual foot-in-the-furrow agricultural dealer new product introduction.

In anticipation of the success of these new tractors, Hewitt directed the Deere implement factories to develop larger implements to utilize the higher horsepower in the new tractors. These included a number of wider and larger planters, tillage tools and harvesters. In all meetings with company personnel, Hewitt stressed that the corporate goal was to overtake International Harvester Company (IHC)—to enable Deere to become number one in market share in North America and in the world. IHC had long held this position. President Wiman had made a huge bet on the success and growth of Deere with the new tractors. His decision to form a Skunk Works-type organization was rewarded handsomely with the rapid acceptance in the market of the all-new tractors. In 1963 a new engineering center was built in the Waterloo area where all future tractor and engine design and test work would be performed. It was named the Product Engineering Center (PEC). Although built for tractor engineering, it would later become involved with engine engineering for the snowmobile. The Fortune 500 ranking published in 1960 listed Deere at number 78 with sales of $542.5 million and profits of $48.5 million. In Hewitt's first five years as president of Deere, sales increased 79 percent and profit more than doubled. Not a bad start for a relatively young CEO of an agricultural company. Expectations were high for even better financial performance with the new tractors and implements. They were an immediate success in the market.

During those years Ron Leonard attended the Product Review Meetings at the Des Moines Works factory. The Des Moines Works manufactured cotton harvesters, tillage tools, corn pickers and corn heads for mounting on combines. Mr. Hewitt urged the factory to make better machines than competition so John Deere dealers would have a marketing advantage. These requests sounded the theme that the founder, John Deere, had repeated throughout his tenure that he would improve his plow whenever he could. They were repeated many times at similar meetings all over the company. Most of those meetings closed with the words, "The best days of Deere and Company are ahead." The values that had enabled the founder to be successful were stressed skillfully to all employees. The products were to do the intended job and be durable and long-lasting in order to be worthy of the John Deere name. The same company logo was on every machine and publication. To reinforce these values, Hewitt wrote a series of Green

Bulletins that all department managers in the company were required to read and discuss with their employees.

By 1963 Deere overtook IHC as the market leader in sales in North America and the world. The new Deere tractors and other Deere products experienced a growing reputation of excellent performance and durability. The Deere dealer organization became stronger throughout all market regions in North America. Numerous new dealers were established in the major markets. Deere continued to design advanced features for the New Generation Tractors. Noteworthy was the upgrade to the JD3020 and JD4020 models in 1963. Increased power levels, a power shift transmission that provided shift-on-the-go under power, and later the Sound-Gard body (the cab enclosure for the operator) all were major innovations that the market accepted readily. The Dubuque Works continued to produce and upgrade the agricultural Model 1010 and 2010 New Generation Tractors that had also been introduced in Dallas in 1960.

While the success of Deere's North American agricultural operations was good news, all was not going well with the international and industrial ventures. The new businesses were taking time and money that reduced the profits earned by the North American agricultural operations. In 1963 Deere Industrial formed a joint venture company with Hitachi. This venture added larger, more powerful products needed to expand the product line for the Deere Industrial Division dealers. In Germany the outdated Lanz Bulldog had lost market share in the European markets to more modern tractors from Ford, Fendt, IHC, Massey Ferguson and Deutz. In 1960, Deere discontinued manufacturing the Lanz Bulldog tractor that had been in production for forty years—the same number of years that John Deere manufactured two-cylinder tractors at Waterloo, Iowa. The John Deere/Lanz tractor factory had large losses in 1956, 1957 and 1958. The European business broke even in 1959; obviously, becoming profitable at this factory was key to successful growth in the European market.

Coinciding with the 1960 New Generation Tractors made at the Waterloo Tractor Works, a new tractor design began production in Mannheim. It was intended to provide new, modern tractors to the European market. European countries had strict regulations for all vehicles used on the roads and highways—including tractors. Tractors required different lighting, higher capacity hitches, stronger brakes, different tires and faster transport speeds than tractors used in the North America markets. Importing agricultural machines from the U.S. was not profitable, as the national governments protected their domestic manufacturers with tariffs.

In 1961 Mannheim produced two new tractor models, JD300 and JD500, with two more models, JD100 and JD700, added the next year. They were designed jointly at the Product Engineering Center in Waterloo and Tractor Engineering at Dubuque. The high hopes for successful marketing them were doomed from the start, as they did not have the features required by European farmers; key components were based upon specifications generally accepted by the market for small agricultural tractors in the U.S. Consequently another major redesign was commissioned that began production

Lanz bulldog tractor, circa 1956 (courtesy Julia Piesker).

in 1965. Both of these tractor ventures were costly in human resources and capital investment. To further improve their tractor business for European markets in 1965, Deere transferred the engineering for small agricultural tractors from the Dubuque, Iowa, industrial factory to the Mannheim factory. It took until 1982 for the European business to turn a profit.

In North America during the 1960s and 1970s, Deere made rapid market share gains with new agricultural products. With record sales, the agricultural division was very profitable. Let's return again to the Fortune 500 rankings. In 1964, the first year of sales of 1000 garden tractors, Deere ranked 81st with sales of $639.1 million and profits of $45.7 million. By 1971 the ranking slipped to 103rd while sales grew to $1,137.70 million and profits were still $46.0 million! This sales growth was a substantial increase of 78 percent since 1964. The low profit margins or losses from the international and industrial ventures eroded the strong financial performance of the agricultural business. In *John Deere's Company*, Broehl states, "It was hard for Deere to take, and by the fall of 1970 there was a siege mentality in Moline about the troubles."

These financial results had a major influence on Deere and Company's management decisions on when or whether to enter another new business like snowmobiles. The debate vacillated between sales volume growth in new businesses or improved margins from the existing businesses. Hewitt was determined to continue growth of the company with garden tractors and later snowmobiles, which were the products that enabled Deere to establish the consumer products division of the company.

2

Start of Deere Consumer Products Business

Bill Hewitt's Vice-President for Agricultural Equipment Marketing in North America, C.R. Carlson, and his son R.J. Carlson, were influential in starting and building the Deere Consumer Products business. Hewitt had convinced the energetic, enthusiastic, and strong-willed C.R. Carlson to transfer to Moline in 1957 as his vice-president of marketing. C.R.'s long record of successful work at Deere included factories and marketing. In 1931 he was the factory manager at the Deere Works in Welland, Ontario, and later was the general manager of the Minneapolis sales branch. In 1945, in his new position, C.R. became a member of the Deere board of directors.

Jon Carlson, R.J.'s son, recalls a story told often at his family dinner table, about a meeting Hewitt convened at his home on a Friday night in 1960 with some of his key operations staff. Jon's grandfather, C.R. Carlson, attended this meeting along with Woody Curtis and George French. Thus marketing, finance and manufacturing were all represented. A bottle of aged Chivas Regal was on the table. Hewitt's agenda was how to overtake IHC as the worldwide market leader. With the New Generation Tractor and larger implements, he wanted "Ag" marketing to be more aggressive to grow Deere sales faster. Hewitt was well aware that some IHC sales were obtained from small retail stores in rural towns across NA. Not only did IHC have a garden tractor, they also sold products like cream separators and refrigerators. Deere dealers and sales branch marketing were lobbying Deere to make a garden tractor. Hewitt agreed that Deere needed a garden tractor and other homeowner lawn maintenance products. The discussion focused on how Deere Marketing could establish consumer products dealers without diverting dealer sales effort from the Ag business, and where Deere should manufacture the garden tractor.

At the conclusion of the meeting, Hewitt made it clear that the next growth business for Deere would be consumer products. His staff should plan how to market and where to manufacture garden tractors. But marketing them could only begin after Deere overtook IHC in worldwide sales, and then his staff would give full attention to the aged Chivas. This meeting was the launching point for the company to prepare to manufacture garden tractors. In the mid–1950s and continuing in the 1960s, the market for homeowner maintenance equipment was growing rapidly in North America. IHC and dozens of other companies were manufacturing walk-behind mowers, riding mowers and garden tractors. These products were being sold in a wide variety of rural and urban retail outlets.

Horicon Works' service manager Wayne McClellan said, "I attended the Harrisburg, Pennsylvania, farm show in 1958 where I first saw garden tractors." With the foundry production dying at Horicon, Al Hyland, chief engineer, and Elmer Quick, foreman of the engineering shop, cobbled together a mockup of a garden tractor. "This tractor was discussed with some of the Moline management but no specific action was started," Wayne said. In 1961 the Development Department in Moline was authorized by Hewitt to design a garden tractor. It was located in the former Wagon Works factory in Moline. Theo Brown, who was chief engineer there for many years, directed the design activities at the Development Department. Since there was no manufacturing at the Wagon Works, the Industrial Works factory in Moline was chosen to manufacture the garden tractor, along with industrial products.

In 1962, Martin Berk worked as an engineer at the Deere Spreader Works in East Moline. His neighbor was Wayne Kellums, who was a division engineer in the Product Engineering Department at the Industrial Works in Moline. Wayne was responsible for the production design of the garden tractor that had been designed at the Development Department. One summer night they were talking and Wayne asked Martin if he was interested in working on the project. He answered yes and Martin transferred to the industrial factory in July.

The Wagon Works, where the Development Department was located, was not used for any production. Jack Hoffman, Jr. grew up in Moline, Illinois, where his father worked for many years as the general manager of the Deere Planter Works. In 1967 Jack worked as a design engineer at the Deere Spreader Works with Martin Berk. Later Jack transferred to Horicon, where his assignment was division engineer for lawn and garden equipment. He was quite familiar with all of the Moline Deere factories. "The Wagon Works was where the Velie automobile was made in the early 1900s. The car was not a Deere product. However, Mr. Velie was a son-in-law of John Deere and held a block of Deere stock so that he voted as a member of the Deere Board of Directors," Jack said.

Henry Dreyfus Associates (HDA) did the styling of the garden tractor. Initially Martin worked to improve the design of the variable-speed belt drive. This innovation enabled the operator to speed up or slow down without stopping to shift gears. With this feature Deere dealers would have a major advantage over competitors, as most industry garden tractors had to stop mowing to change gears. "Two prototypes had been built in the Industrial Works engineering shop," Martin said. "I became familiar with the Industrial Works factory where the tractors were to be manufactured, and made several trips to visit suppliers who would make some of the components." Just before Thanksgiving in 1962, the company officers held a meeting at the Moline Industrial factory. Wayne Kellums came to Martin's design board and asked him to see Jack French, the chief engineer for the Industrial Works, after the meeting ended. Jack told

Martin the company had decided to manufacture garden tractors at the Horicon Works. Martin met with Horicon Works' factory manager Bob Hendrix and chief engineer Al Hyland about transferring there, and he accepted the invitation. With a briefcase full of drawings, he began work at Horicon on December 1, 1962. In July of 1963, Horicon Works made the first year's production of 1000 garden tractors. Al Hyland retired that year and Martin succeeded him as chief engineer.

In 1962, upon his return from active duty with the U.S. Navy, Ralph Muenchow was one of the factory employees who assembled the tractors. Ralph recalls they worked in an area of the factory where the grain drills were produced. Employees who made the parts helped to rework or modify them to make assembly easier. Martin and Wayne McClellan often worked late at night to make changes needed to assist the first production. "Everyone was very helpful to us to make the assembly easier," Ralph said. Nothing creates more excitement in a factory than startup of a new product. The enthusiasm results from more jobs that provide opportunity for personal growth. For the engineers it is the culmination of several years of work. After the upfront investment of engineering and the factory cost of people, materials and machine tools, the company expects a profitable return on its investment.

The decision to manufacture consumer products at Horicon had profound implications. Within Deere, the Horicon Works, not the Industrial Works, was designated as the base for consumer product engineering and manufacturing. The success of the first major consumer product — garden tractors — was squarely in the hands of the agricultural management in the company for engineering, manufacturing and marketing. C.R. Carlson had decided to market the Deere garden tractors through the established agricultural dealer organization, and the reception by dealers and customers was excellent. The second year the factory produced 15,000 garden tractors, so the Deere consumer products business was off to a successful start.

Horicon is located in southern Wisconsin near numerous other manufacturers. Garden tractor manufacturers Bolens, Ariens, Simplicity and JI Case, as well as engine manufacturers Kohler, Tecumseh, and Briggs and Stratton, were nearby. Other manufacturers of outboard motors, motorcycles and machine tools were located in Fond du Lac, Hartford, Oshkosh and Milwaukee. The Horicon factory site was alongside the Rock River upstream from the dam that created the vast Horicon Marsh. Covering 32,000 acres it is the largest cattail marsh in the U.S. The marsh is a stopover for the migration of Canada geese on the Mississippi flyway.

The Horicon factory had manufactured grain drills and companion tillage machines since Deere purchased the Van Brunt Grain Drill factory in 1911. It had a sterling reputation of good working relations with its employees, both salary and wage. The Van Brunt family owned the business and treated their employees well, and Deere continued to nurture that environment. When garden tractor production began at Horicon Works, third-generation family members worked there. The population of 3500 people in Horicon and others in Dodge County welcomed the jobs the new prod-

John Deere Horicon Factory, circa 1960s (courtesy Bob Strassmann).

ucts brought to the factory. Horicon employees were widely recognized throughout Deere for their work ethic and skills. Many employees lived in Horicon or on nearby farms. With the agricultural machines, the factory provided seasonal employment for production employees. Since production was very low in the spring and summer months, employees who farmed went home in the spring to plant their crops and returned in the fall after the harvest. This positive working relationship was very helpful to the successful launch of new products in the factory.

In 1960 Hewitt commissioned the design of a new headquarters building that was located in East Moline, Illinois. It was to be a symbol of a modern progressive company.

Broehl's book describes how this was done. Designed by the world-famous architect Eero Saarinen, it was sited in the rolling hills in East Moline that overlooked the Rock River valley. The sturdy Core-ten steel and glass structure conveyed Hewitt's vision of a strong and growing company with its corporate offices housed in a world-class structure. Its opening in 1964 coincided with the marketing of the Model 110 and 112 lawn and garden tractors, which were the first non-agricultural products made by Deere for many decades.

John Deere model 110 (courtesy Bob Strassmann).

The Trail to the Decision to Manufacture Snowmobiles

The market liked the Deere garden tractors and sales grew steadily. The agricultural dealers concentrated on selling garden tractors to the farm market. The rapid growth of the garden tractor market in the 1960s was driven by suburbanites who wanted machines to reduce the time to mow large lawns. Deere added smaller and larger garden tractors to appeal to all segments of the market. As garden tractor sales grew, dealers began to ask JD to make snowmobiles, as some Deere dealers were selling snowmobiles manufactured by other companies. The snowmobile business grew rapidly in the 1960s. Many suppliers of components for lawn and garden tractors also supplied parts for snowmobiles, so it was logical for suppliers to urge Deere to get into the business.

C.R. Carlson retired in 1967 after serving as Hewitt's vice-president of marketing for worldwide agricultural products. His son R.J. (Bob) Carlson had worked in sales branch marketing and was a sales branch manager before transferring to Deere & Company in Moline. R.J. was very familiar with the growth of the company in the agricultural market. As described earlier, the 1960s were boom years for Deere agricultural equipment sales. Farm sizes were increasing and farmers wanted more powerful tractors with larger implements. By 1968, R.J. held the position of Director of Marketing in Moline at Deere's worldwide headquarters.

John Deere World Wide Headquarters (Richard Teal collection).

The Carlson family owned a vacation home at Balsam Lake, Wisconsin, where they spent the 1968 Christmas holiday. "I begged my Dad to rent a snowmobile for us to ride," Jon said. "I had seen the lights at night going past our house and heard the roar of the machines." Jon was then 13 years old. R.J. resisted, but finally agreed to rent one for two hours—and then kept it for two days. After that, R.J. embraced the opportunity to grow the consumer products business with snowmobiles.

Riding a snowmobile in the winter provided thrills and adventure for both rural and urban people in the snow belt in North America. Trails were built across farms to link towns. The vast lake areas in the northern regions of the country, the mountains, and the Midwest prairies provided remote areas to explore while riding a snowmobile. Riding a powered sled in snow was the winter counterpart of a boat and outboard motor in the summer. Boats with outboard motors and snowmobiles provided year-round utility and recreation for many customers who lived in the snow regions of North America.

The debate continued in Moline on whether to enter the snowmobile business. Some argued that Deere had no experience in a sport recreational vehicle market. The lack of profits from the Industrial Equipment Division and the International ventures supported their argument. The lawn and garden tractor business was growing and was profitable. Shouldn't the company just concentrate on growing the business with garden tractors and homeowner maintenance equipment? The shadow of this concern hovered over snowmobiles during all the years Deere was in the business. Finally the supporters who wanted to grow the consumer products business with snowmobiles were rewarded. They had a strong argument on how to restructure Deere sales branch marketing to access the total market in North America.

Factory Snowmobile Investigations

All Deere factories were treated as profit centers. In addition to manufacturing personnel, each factory had its own staff of accounting, human resources, product engineering, marketing and product support. An annual Product Review Meeting (PRM) was held at each factory, with management people in attendance from the corporate headquarters in Moline, and Horicon was no exception. Martin Berk, as engineering manager at Horicon, recalls that he proposed Deere manufacture snowmobiles at these meetings in 1967 and 1968. He was supported in this discussion by Horicon marketing manager Ray Davis and factory manager Jack Moore. However, no formal approval was given to proceed by the Moline management. Suppliers continually suggested that Deere was missing out by not being in the snowmobile business. "Horicon began to investigate the snowmobile market anyway and to evaluate competitive snowmobiles in 1967," Martin said.

The decentralized management that Charles Wiman had redefined after resuming control of the company in 1945 reinforced the factory manager's authority and responsibility for new products related to that factory's business, since the Horicon Works was the only consumer products factory within Deere. The success of garden tractors justified Hewitt's direction for growth in consumer product markets and provided a positive environment for investigation of other products. The decision to study the snowmobile market was clearly within Horicon Works manager Jack Moore's broad scope of authority.

Kohler supplied garden tractor engines to Horicon and many other manufacturers, and they also made snowmobile engines. Kohler invited Horicon factory personnel to attend a competitive snowmobile evaluation in Winter Park, Colorado, in the winter of 1968. "I, Jack Moore, and Jack Hoffman were flown there in the Kohler company airplane with Art Kross, Kohler engine manager, to observe and participate," Martin said. After the trip to Colorado with Kohler, Horicon purchased several competitive snowmobiles for evaluation of machine design concepts. From this work, Horicon PED learned that one important decision was whether to mount the engine in the middle of the chassis or in front between the two skis.

Jack Hoffman's March 1968 Product Engineering Department Monthly Report (MR) stated that the factory and PED had completed a cost study of a Polaris snowmobile on March 27, 1968. This was one of several competitive machines that the department had been authorized to purchase to determine the desired design direction for a JD snowmobile. This activity was initiated at the factory after the trip Martin Berk and others had made to Winter Park earlier that winter with the Kohler Company to ride representative industry sleds. Horicon PED continued to evaluate the design direction during the summer of 1968. This project was discussed again informally during the June 1968 Horicon Works PRM.

In early fall of 1968, Jack Hoffman and Gerry Buelow were back in Winter Park with the competitive sleds to determine the design direction for a JD snowmobile. Jack's reports do not identify the specific models of competitive sleds, but he recalls that one was a front-engine chassis sled. Following this evaluation, Horicon Works issued an Engineering Order (EO) to begin the design of a JD snowmobile. Prototypes were built in the PED experimental shop for field performance testing that began during the winter of 1968–1969. Jack Hoffman recalls that Bob Trapp from OMC was hired to assume responsibility for design of the JD snowmobile in the fall of 1969. Jack's PED Monthly Report (MR) November 1969 states he and HDA associates Jim Conner and Chuck Pelly were at Winter Park to familiarize themselves with riding a snowmobile.

Another key component was the type of suspension. Most competitive machines were made with a rubber track that traveled over spring-retained bogie wheels to cushion the sharp jolts when the machine traveled over the frozen terrain. In 1970 Edgar Hetteen's new development of the front-engine chassis and slide-rail suspension was also manufactured by Polaris. When the slide rail suspension was combined with the front-engine position, the sled performance improved. The slide suspension was supe-

4.3.2 Snowmobile Design Types

4.3.2.1 Engine Mounted Forward in Chassis

EXAMPLE: Arctic Cat

4.3.2.2 Steering Linkage Mounted Forward in Chassis

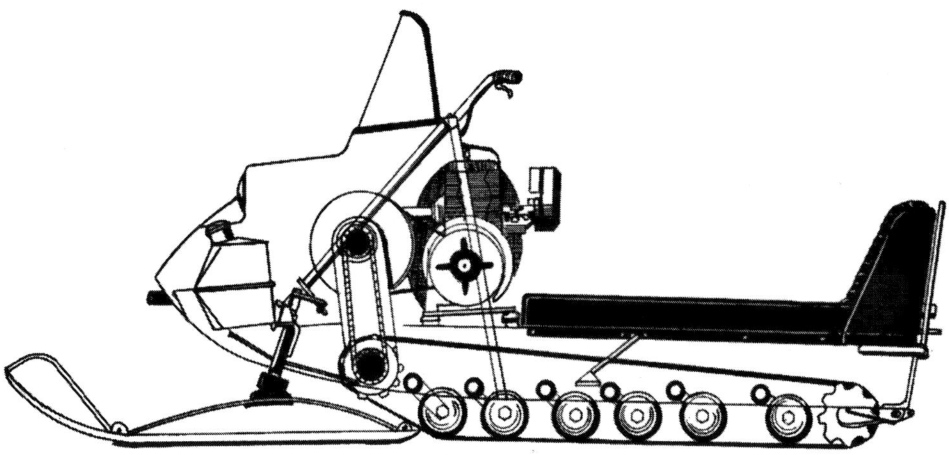

EXAMPLE: Ski-Doo

4.3.2.3 Snowmobile Suspensions

Slide Bar Track Support
Bogie Wheel Suspension
Hybrid Slide Bar and Bogie Wheel System

Front-engine vs. mid-engine (courtesy Jack Hoffman).

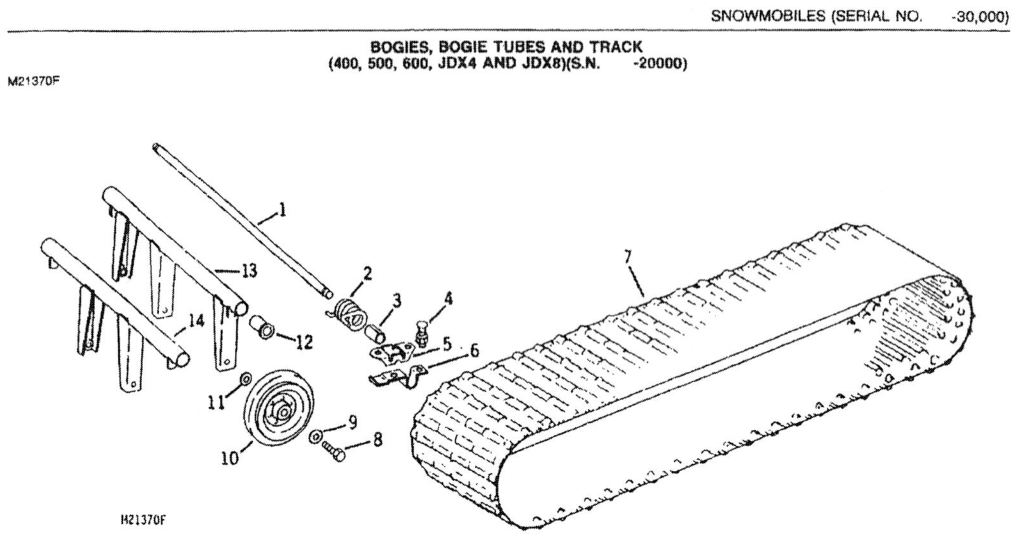

1972 JD model 400 and 500 bogie wheel suspension (courtesy Roger Tesch).

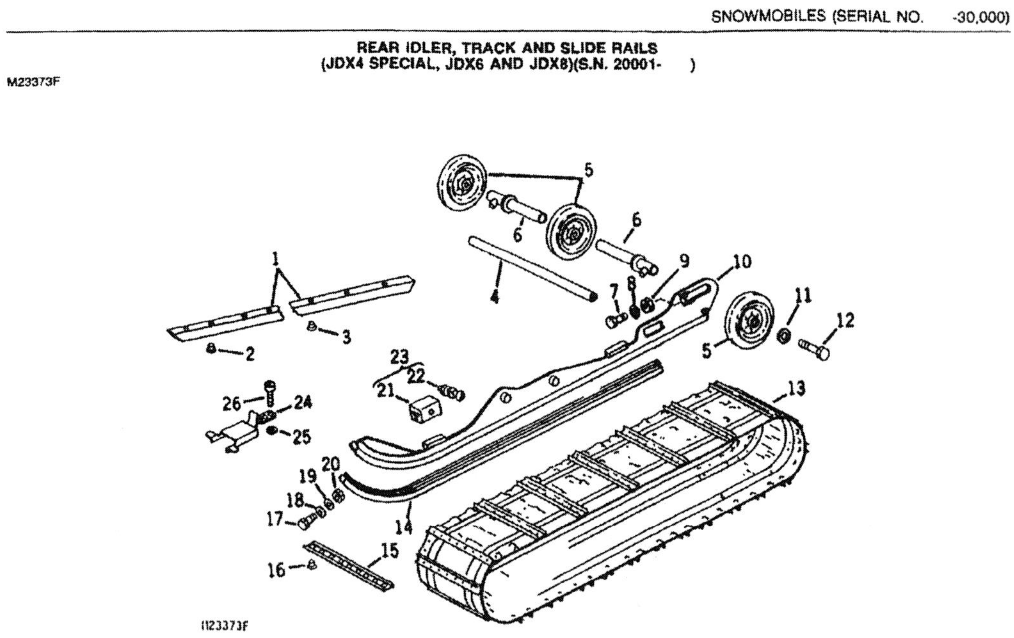

1973 JD model JDX8 slide rail suspension (courtesy Roger Tesch).

rior in deep snow, as the front-engine position lowered the center of gravity and moved it forward. Customers who enjoyed riding at high levels of performance were buying these machines. As is often the case, there were numerous durability problems with the new configurations, especially the track for the slide-rail suspension.

Machine Styling

Since the successful restyling of the JD Model A and B two cylinder tractors in 1938, Wiman had contracted industrial design services for all Deere products from HDA. From the beginning of his tenure as CEO, Bill Hewitt insisted that Deere continue to improve the styling and appearance of its products. HDA supplied industrial design services to a number of other large U.S. corporations. They were the keeper of the Deere corporate image for styling that included shape, color and graphics. After HDA personnel made the rounds of the Deere factories, they were required to stop in Moline and brief Bill Hewitt on the results of their work. Horicon had requested styling concept sketches from HDA as they began to design a Deere snowmobile. The engine location had a major influence on appearance. The mid-engine position required a higher profile than the front engine; thus, it was more difficult for stylists and engineers to achieve the goal of a low sleek look. At that time the front-engine chassis configuration was gaining in popularity with race and high-performance riders.

"I took a call at home on a Friday afternoon in late 1969 from Bill Hewitt," Jon Carlson said. "Mr. Hewitt asked me to tell my dad we were to meet him Saturday morning at the maintenance building at the company headquarters." R.J. had arranged for competitive snowmobiles and one Horicon prototype to be shipped to Moline for such a meeting with Hewitt. Hewitt brought his twin daughters and R.J. and Jon met them there. Jon recalls Hewitt was well dressed, wearing a White Stag jacket — not snowmobile gear. The competitive machines were models from Arctic Cat, Ski-Doo, Polaris and Grand Prix to compare with the Horicon Works prototype. The Horicon prototype demonstrated in the meeting was similar to the snowmobiles made by many companies during the growth of the market in the 1960s. The engine was in the middle of the chassis. Bumps were cushioned with spring-retained bogie wheels inside of a rubber track. The rolling hills of the Deere campus were an excellent site to showcase the machines. Jon drove them with Hewitt's daughters riding separately on each machine. This was a comfortable assignment for Jon, as he had attended birthday parties for the Hewitt daughters at the Hewitt home in Moline; thus he knew them well. After Jon demonstrated a machine, it was returned to the building, where they discussed the merits of each. The HDA styling concept sketches that Horicon had requested earlier were used in the discussion. "Mr. Hewitt asked about the different engine locations," Jon said. Hewitt liked the styling of the Grand Prix best. He emphasized the machine appearance should be appealing and reflect the company's image of quality products. He disliked particularly the white color, as he believed the machine should be easily visible in snow.

At the end of the demonstration Hewitt authorized R.J. to develop a comprehensive plan to enter the snowmobile business. Our research did not reveal any Horicon personnel attended this meeting. "Following this meeting there was no more indecision. Horicon was authorized to design and manufacture snowmobiles," Jon said.

3

Deere Prepares for Snowmobiles

When the demonstration of industry snowmobiles was held in Moline, Bill Hewitt was well underway expanding Deere from its strong North American agricultural base into an international company. In the late 1960s in the Ag organization, there were about twelve sales branches and ten factories in the U.S. and Canada. Sales branches and factories were the operating arms of Deere & Co. Like the tentacles of an octopus, all units were part of the main body and were structured the same everywhere. Although they were managed as separate profit centers, there was only one Deere. Financial data from all units were consolidated at the corporate headquarters in Moline, Illinois. This template of the Deere organization developed for agriculture was used to structure the Industrial Division, so the same model was applied to the sales branch organization for consumer products.

John Deere moved his plow company to Moline in 1848, leaving Grand Detour, Illinois, where he started his company by making the first successful plow that worked in the tough prairie soil. The company grew during its first 134 years by building factories in Moline, then later by buying farm implement companies in Moline and other locations. In William Butterworth's era as president (1908–1927), Deere bought the Dain hay harvesting business in Ottumwa, Iowa, in 1910; the Van Brunt grain drill factory in Horicon, Wisconsin, in 1911; and the Waterloo Boy tractor factory in Waterloo, Iowa, in 1918. With these purchases Deere became a full line company with tractors and implements. To establish Deere as a national company, Butterworth and his board of directors bought the independently owned sales branches. Several of the branch managers obtained seats on the Deere & Company board of directors as part of the purchase agreement. No more significant purchases were made until Wiman resumed control of the company after World War II. Broehl named the Butterworth era: "Emergence of the Modern Company."

Deere dealers operated their JD dealerships under a contract with Deere sales branches that determined the number and location of the dealerships in their region. Dealers' sales and service personnel were supported through their sales branch, with Deere product sales and service information generated at each factory. Deere dealers administered the company's warranty policy with their customers; thus dealers were directly involved with strengthening the customer loyalty engendered by the reputation of John Deere products. Centralized control of all operations was enforced by decisions made in Moline. Deere senior management set the prices for the products each year and approved the annual production schedule for each factory quarterly. At the time the decision was made to manufacture snowmobiles, Deere financed dealer inventory for up to 15 months. Territory managers monitored the retail sales activity of the dealers in their respective territories. This information was consolidated at each sales branch and then compiled for the quarterly schedule meetings, which determined the factories' production schedule. The results from these schedule meetings were implemented promptly by each factory in order to adjust factory and field inventory to the desired level. All factories used the same Economic Order Quantity (EOQ) calculation to minimize the annual cost of inventory. When a change was required, purchasing personnel were on the phone or traveling to a supplier to negotiate the terms of the change, which often increased the cost to the factory. The effect of a schedule cut could take months to implement.

Hewitt and his staff set the company-wide annual capital budget for investments. Each unit submitted its request for investment capital annually. These were pared down until the total amount equaled the Deere budget. When the decision was made to manufacture snowmobiles, there were some enthusiastic supporters—but others saw this as a threat to their factory's ability to get capital for new products, factory equipment and new facilities. Factory accounting staff prepared the same Authority for Expenditure (AFE) document for all capital expenditures. One of the key calculations was the return on investment (ROI). Horicon Works—the only consumer products factory—was in competition with the agricultural factories for its investment capital.

Sales Branch Marketing and Service

With Hewitt's approval to manufacture snowmobiles, the debate was over. Now the task in sales branches and the Horicon Works was to implement his direction to manufacture and market snowmobiles. Since the sales branches had evolved over time with the agricultural market, major changes were required to focus on the consumer market, where large numbers of customers were located. Garden tractors were off to a good start, marketed by agricultural dealers; however, most of those dealers were located in sparsely populated rural locations. This limited that dealer's access to the major markets for homeowner yard and maintenance equipment. Hewitt recognized that the Deere marketing organization would need a different focus to reach the growing consumer grounds-maintenance market when he held the Friday night meeting with his staff before Deere entered the garden tractor market. C.R. Carlson had elected to market the garden tractors with the agricultural dealers, as the major focus in 1960 was to overtake IHC in the agricultural market. Since that goal had been achieved, Deere now needed to embolden its sales branches with a marketing plan for consumer products dealers. Making their own brand of snowmobiles was the key for Deere to set up independent consumer product dealers separate from agricultural dealers.

In the snow belt regions of the country, many John Deere dealers were selling other manufacturers' snowmobiles. Locating retail outlets close to the high population markets would generate more sales. The new products were required to provide enough income to support a separate retail business. Snowmobile dealers would have snowmobiles for the winter market and garden tractors to sell for the summer. In southern branches, where grounds-maintenance work was done during most of the year, more grounds-care products would serve the same purpose for independent dealers in those markets. Deere sales branches hired additional territory manager staff to select new consumer product dealers. Territory managers helped identify desirable locations near suburban residents and trained the new dealers in Deere business practices. In sparsely populated areas, they worked with existing agricultural dealers to increase their sales of consumer products. This took months of work in all the sales branches, and in some locations even longer to select the dealer and the desired location for the business. The sales branch managers were charged with the responsibility to avoid disrupting the agricultural dealers.

Bill Lee was an Ag territory manager for the Moline Branch who lived in Burlington, Wisconsin. "In 1971 Deere decided to realign the sales territories by switching this area to the Minneapolis Branch. When I started with Deere this territory was in the Moline Sales Branch and was an agricultural territory," Bill said. The Minneapolis Branch, as did other branches, researched the sales potential for garden tractors and snowmobiles to determine where they should establish new dealers. The Minneapolis Branch could best support this area in northern Illinois and southern Wisconsin. Deere expected good snowmobile and lawn-mowing product sales there. "I was asked if I wanted to transfer to the Minneapolis Branch as a consumer products territory manager and my family and I could stay right where we were," Bill said. "I was excited about the snowmobiles and growth opportunities for consumer products sales."

Horicon Factory Preparation

All departments at the Horicon Works were involved in preparing for snowmobile production. Since products drive everything within factory operations, the Product Engineering Department had to lead the effort. Engineering developed and published the product specifications for part geometry and material required for the factory to make the new machines. Design and verification was an iterative process that balanced key issues: design of the product; working with manufacturing, engineering and purchasing to obtain quality manufacturing processes; verification of the design; and meeting the planned schedule — all of this within the cost goals so the company could profit from the business. The factory accounting department coordinated financial data with Deere accounting in Moline, and human resources and industrial relations departments hired and trained new personnel.

The Horicon Works marketing and service department wrote the machine operators' manuals and service manuals and determined the supply of service parts required for distribution to sales branches and dealers. Before each sales season the Deere and Company advertising department determined the national advertising campaign with factory marketing. Factory marketing obtained performance comparisons of competitive snowmobiles with Deere machines by working with the PED. The marketing publications for snowmobiles, like all other machines, became the company's communication with dealers and customers.

How the Snowmobile Progressed from Concept to Production

R.J. Carlson acted quickly to focus sales branch marketing and factory plans following the approval by Hewitt. He convened a special meeting on February 23, 1970, at Horicon with key Deere personnel who would be needed to support the new snowmobile business. At this meeting, Factory Manager Jack Moore introduced the snowmobile discussion, and Bob Trapp presented the Horicon Works plans to design and manufacture the sleds. Since Horicon had no in-house snowmobile design expertise, they hired Bob Trapp from Outboard Marine Company (OMC) to develop the snowmobile market and product information for the special meeting. After this meeting he was assigned responsibility for the design of Deere snowmobiles. Horicon PED used a process to define specifications for the Deere snowmobile that was similar to the procedure used in all units at Deere. The first step was market research by the engineering and marketing departments. Horicon's evaluation of competitive machines in 1968 and 1969 provided the data for the machine specifications presented in the Special PRM.

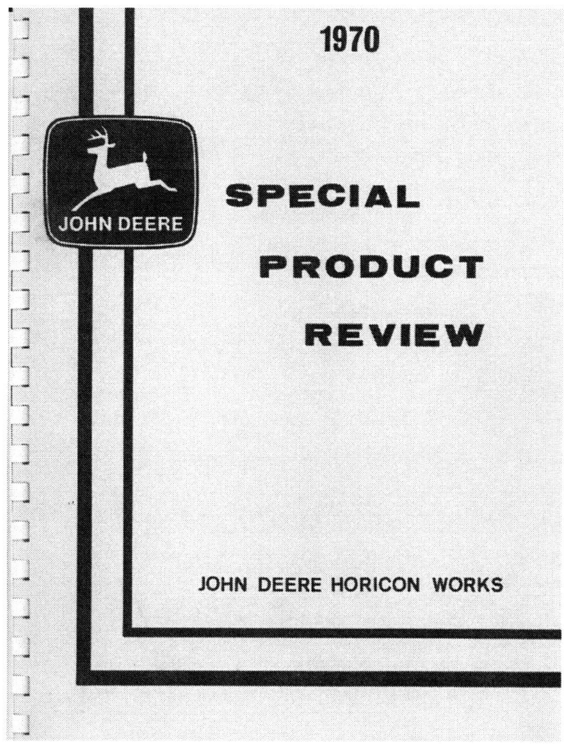

Special Product Review book (courtesy Jack Hoffman).

Of course, the focus for the

Special PRM featured snowmobiles, but also it included discussion of new garden tractors and walk-behind machines. Myron McCunn and Jack Hoffman, division engineers, presented those design programs. Deere planned to provide a full line of products for winter and summer homeowner needs in addition to snowmobiles. Without doubt, though, the snowmobile was the major topic in the meeting, as it was the key product for the sales branches to recruit consumer products dealers independent from the agricultural dealers.

Bob Trapp was supported in the presentation of snowmobile information by engineer Bob Bishop and designer Ernie Schnell, along with Gerry Buelow, the PED test manager. Both types of machine chassis were described and information was presented about the performance of the Deere test machines. This caused significant discussion about the most suitable chassis type for Deere to use for their first products. The industry leader in total machines sold was Bombardier, Ltd. (Ski-Doo), who began in Canada and continued to increase their dealer numbers in the U.S. The Ski-Doo Snowmobiles

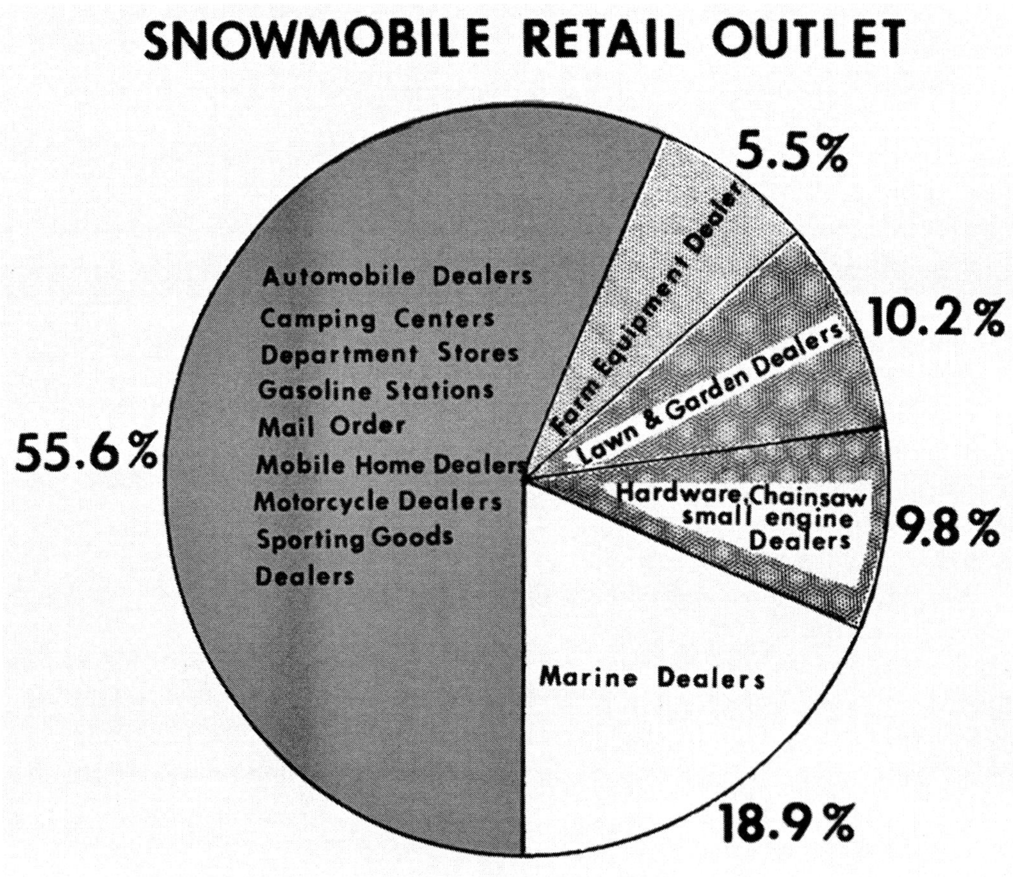

Snowmobile retail outlet location chart (courtesy Jack Hoffman).

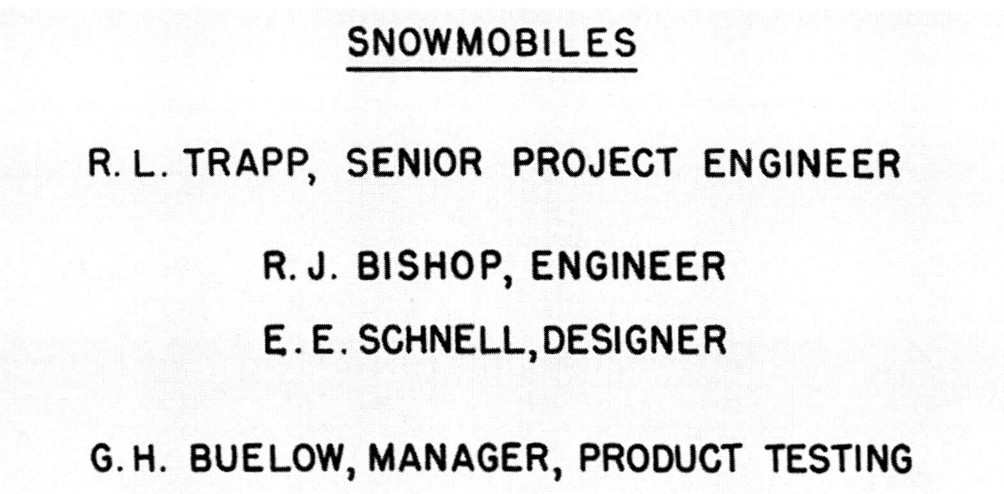

Engineers assigned to first snowmobile (courtesy Jack Hoffman).

were on a mid-engine chassis and sold in a variety of retail outlets that included automobile dealers, marine dealers, hardware stores and farm equipment dealers who only sold 5.5 percent of the market. Our research did not produce any information on whether or not the small sales by Ag dealers were considered to be significant.

Ski-Doo was the dominant market leader, with Arctic Cat and Polaris leading the next group of higher volume producers. With the industry sales data presented in this meeting, strong growth in the market was projected, with 1970–71 industry sales estimated to be 390,000. The sales season was understood to extend from October until April in most areas. It is easy to understand why Horicon promoted entering the business during those years. Based upon this information, Deere planned to make rapid market share gains and soon equal Polaris and Arctic Cat in unit sales. Deere sales were estimated to reach 60,000 in 1974–75, which would result in 13 percent market share. Although characterized as sales, they were actually shipments. The industry sales data were generated after contacting component suppliers who had intelligence on the OEM manufacturers' production volumes. The International Snowmobile Industry Association (ISIA) data shown later in this book are much lower than the estimates used in the Special PRM; ISIA did not have the total annual sales since many small manufacturers were not dues paying members.

Which Style of Chassis Did Deere Choose?

Edgar Hetteen, who founded both Polaris and later Arctic Cat, is considered to be the father of the business. He built the first snowmobile in 1954 in his welding shop in Roseau, Minnesota, powered by a 10 hp Briggs engine. Numerous improvements followed during the next several years. When he began production in 1960, the business was named Polaris. To promote sales of the first production of over 600 machines in 1960, he rode a snowmobile 1,200 miles across the Alcan wilderness, but his absence from Polaris did not please their board of directors. Hetteen soon left the company and worked as a bush pilot in Alaska until he started another snowmobile company, Arctic

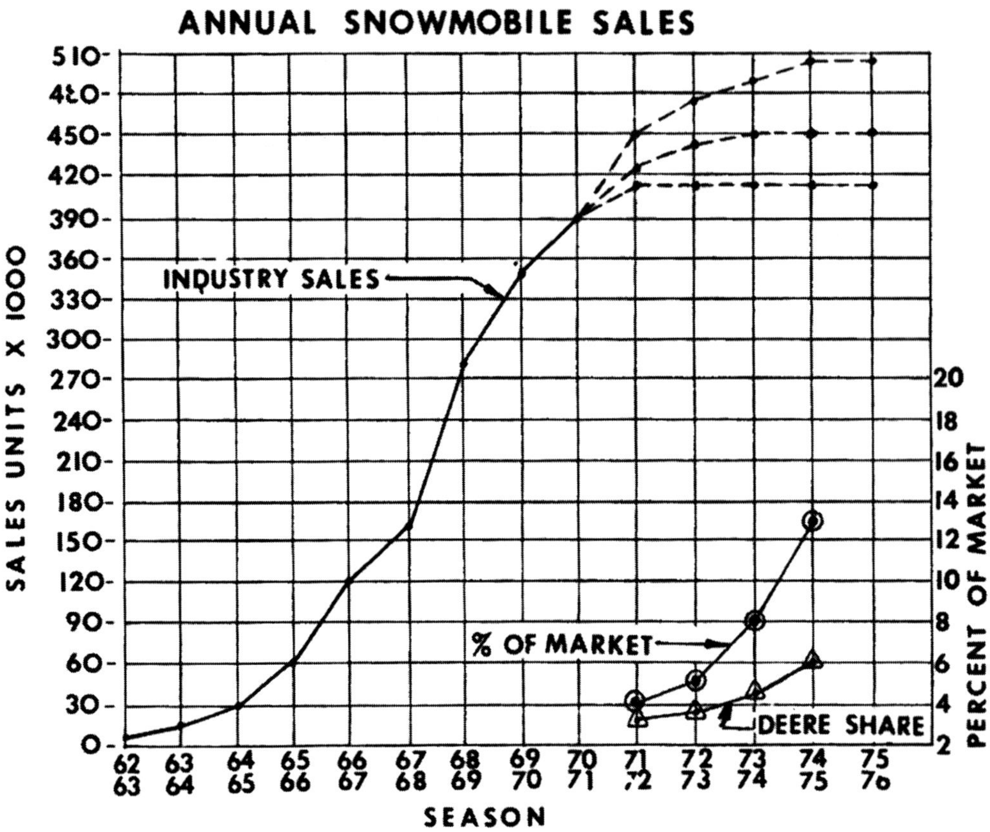

Projected Deere Sales

Sales Season Starts July 1st, ends January 1st.

1971-1972 Season - 20,000 units -- 4% of Market
1972-1973 Season - 25,000 units -- 5% of Market
1973-1974 Season - 40,000 units -- 8% of Market
1974-1975 Season - 60,000 units -- 13% of Market

Annual Snowmobile Sales (SPR) book, which shows the snowmobile industry sales and JD projected sales (courtesy Jack Hoffman).

Cat in Thief River Falls, Minnesota, to manufacture a different design of snowmobile. The Arctic Cat Panther, first produced in 1967, was a front-engine chassis with slide-rail suspension. Arctic Cat and Polaris both grew rapidly using this chassis configuration. Other manufacturers began to market their designs of front-engine chassis snowmobiles targeted for the performance rider. However, this chassis configuration improved the sled performance in nearly all operating conditions. With a low center of gravity, the stability and handling at high speeds on rough trails were improved, and superior performance resulted in every racing venue: lakes, rivers, cross-country, and oval tracks.

The rapid growth of the snowmobile market and the invention of the front-engine chassis were discussed at this meeting. The production volume and financial issues Polaris experienced, which caused them to be acquired by Textron, Inc., were considered in the meeting. In 1969, under new management, Polaris manufactured 40,000 units, which garnered them 13 percent of the market with sales of $22 million. In 1970 Polaris sales were projected to grow to $35 million. While the volume growth of Polaris was commendable, their financial difficulty strengthened the concerns of Deere management about the economic stability of the business. Others believed Deere could outperform Polaris with their strong Deere dealer group.

From 1968 on, other companies experienced sales growth with their designs of front-engine chassis sleds because this type of machine appealed to the high-performance rider. Since 1967 the industry production more than doubled from 150,000 to 350,000, primarily due to the front-engine chassis. Since all manufacturers made similar mid-engine chassis sleds, there was a huge buildup of them in unsold dealer inventory. Some Deere dealers already sold competitive sleds. Ski-Doo was especially strong in Canada, retailing in different outlets including John Deere dealers, while Polaris and Arctic Cat were also sold in numerous retail outlets. During the discussion in the special meeting, some in marketing thought a mid-engine chassis would help Deere replace competitive machines in John Deere dealerships. All agreed that Deere customers wanted a comfortable machine for trail riding that would support two riders, and the market would expect John Deere to make a dependable snowmobile. Some marketing personnel expressed the opinion that the strong Deere dealer organization would give Deere an advantage over competition.

However, the marketing personnel were not all of one mind. "R.J. advocated strongly that performance like the machines in the cross-country races should be the main criteria in the decision," John Orvis said. John raced snowmobiles when he worked at Polaris and advocated that Deere should get involved in racing, as it would have a big influence on the market and aid product development. Others voiced concerns about the risk for Deere from racing snowmobiles. By 1970 the front-engine slide-suspension chassis sleds started to dominate cross-country racing. Experienced riders readily understood how much the front-engine chassis improved performance. In 1970, the extent to which this configuration would be accepted in the consumer market was not clear to the meeting's participants. Deere's conservative financial history weighed heavily in support of the final decision.

The Horicon Works manufacturing managers also supported the mid-engine design. They believed it lowered the risk for the factory with the new materials and purchased components. Most other snowmobile OEMs purchased the major power system components like engines, transmissions, belts and track, so this minimized the Horicon factory's capital investment for Deere. The proposed Deere sled tunnel frame was to be made from aluminum, which was new to the Horicon Works manufacturing experience. Manufacturing engineering planned a large investment in new tooling for the snowmobile chassis, due to the expected high volumes.

Competitors in the industry witnessed Arctic Cat's production of the new front-engine chassis snowmobile. "They sold tons of them," according to Dick Teal. Dick then worked for Fox in Janesville, Wisconsin and discussed this with Bob Trapp in a phone call in 1969. Ski-Doo produced front-engine Blizzards designed for racing in 1971. With those developments, the three major industry market leaders were already in the market with high-performance consumer machines made on a front-engine chassis. It was obvious the high-performance riders preferred the front-engine design. With it and a slide-rail suspension, they were superior in cross-country racing, where better stability was needed.

Martin Berk offered Dick Teal a job at the Horicon Works in 1972. He declined the job at that time but accepted a design position with Horicon in 1974. Dick discussed front-engine vs. mid-engine sleds with Bob Trapp, who was in charge of the design of the Deere snowmobile in 1969. "I was working for the Fox Corporation designing the 1970 Fox Spoiler model with a mid-engine and slide rail suspension when Bob Trapp called me and asked to borrow a prototype engine. I suggested strongly to Bob that Deere choose the front-engine design for their entry into the snowmobile market. Many times after I started working for Deere I wondered what could have been if Deere had chosen the front-engine design at the start versus the mid-engine design," Dick said.

The Special PRM on February 23, 1970, gave Horicon the formal approval to proceed with the mid-engine chassis design. Marketing, manufacturing, and accounting supported this decision. Small manufacturers were dropping out of the market. Polaris and Arctic Cat front-engine sleds were being marketed as high-performance consumer machines. Both companies used racing to improve durability and performance of their products. The slide-rail suspension performed better in nearly all types of snow conditions. It improved the stability of the entire machine, as the track suspension was designed to provide vertical travel that helped cushion the jolts experienced when the sled was traveling on rough terrain. The mid-engine chassis became obsolete a few short years after Deere entered the business. Unfortunately, it took until the 1976 models before Deere followed the direction in which the industry was headed.

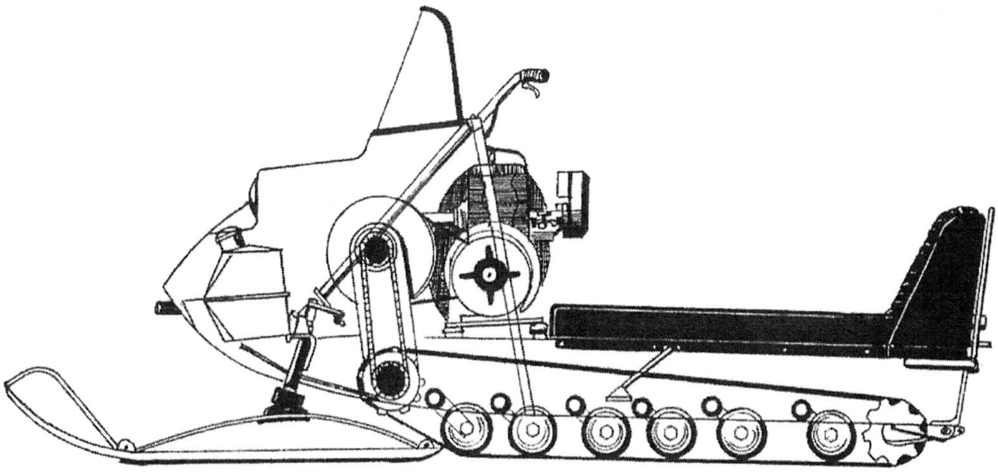

Mid-engine from Product Review Book (courtesy Jack Hoffman).

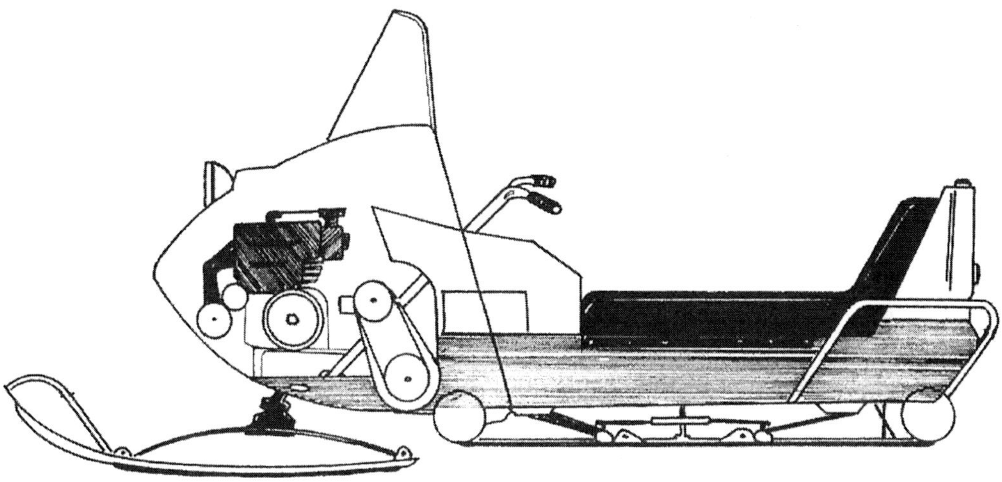

Front-engine from Product Review Book (courtesy Jack Hoffman).

Who Would Supply Snowmobile Engines?

Deere planned to start a separate business unit for agricultural and industrial engines at the time Horicon Works prepared for snowmobile production. Since 1918, when Deere brought the Waterloo Boy Tractor Company, engines were manufactured at the tractor factory at Waterloo, Iowa, and supplied to other Deere units that manufactured self-propelled machines. After President Wiman started the Dubuque plant in 1945, the smaller tractors and their engines were manufactured there. By 1965 Deere also manufactured diesel engines in Orleans, France, that were shipped to the Mannheim

Works for tractors. Some Deere engine production was done at the Deere Rosario plant in Argentina and in Monterrey, Mexico.

For several years senior managers in Moline had debated the merits of starting a Deere component division in the company. Senior Vice-President Delano Brown advocated Deere create a separate component business for engines, hydraulics, transmissions and axles. The component division would have its engineering personnel reporting to each component factory. At Waterloo the PEC engine engineering staff was assigned to the engine factory, separate from the Waterloo Tractor Works. Broehl's book describes in detail how this was done. The selection of the engine manufacturer for snowmobiles brought Horicon Works squarely into the middle of this debate. At the time of the Special Snowmobile PRM in 1970, Horicon Works purchased small (less than 20 hp) 4-cycle engines for garden tractors, walk-behind snow blowers and garden tillers. They were well satisfied with the power, performance and quality of the engines then available to the garden tractor market. Horicon's major engine suppliers were Kohler and Tecumseh. Rather than power, Horicon differentiated its garden tractors from competitors with overall quality, the variable-speed ground drive and the outstanding performance of the mower decks on the riding mowers and tractors. The HDA styling definitely enhanced the market appeal of the Deere garden tractors. As expected, they were very reliable and easy to maintain.

What should Deere do about the snowmobile engine? Since the company had no in-house small engine manufacturing, Horicon planned to purchase engines for snowmobiles. Their choices for snowmobile engines were Kohler, Wisconsin Motors (Hirth) and JLO, as presented in the Special PRM information, with Kohler as the leading candidate. Engine engineering and dynamometer facilities for testing engines were located at the PEC in Waterloo, Iowa. During the Special PRM it was decided that Horicon should seek the help of PEC engine engineering to select the engine manufacturer for snowmobiles. PEC began durability testing snowmobile engines from several companies and ultimately made the recommendation for the snowmobile engine supplier.

The scope of the snowmobile work assigned to PEC Engine Engineering expanded beyond the recommendation on which supplier to use in the first year's machines. With high volumes planned at Horicon Works, the engine business saw this as an incredible opportunity for Deere to manufacture their own design of small engines. The vision for design and manufacture of small engines included all Horicon Works products that required 2- and 4-cycle engines. With snowmobiles and garden tractors, the annual engine production volume could easily be 120,000. Acquisitions were contemplated as a possible way to enter the business. After all, Hewitt wanted Deere to grow, so why not engines for consumer products as well? There were some skeptics of this at the Horicon Works since there was little design or application experience with small engines at the PEC. The average annual use of Horicon garden tractors was about 30 to 50 hours a year compared to 500 hours or more for tractors and even more hours for industrial products. There was a large industry of small engine manufacturers who were very competitive in the U.S., Europe and Japan. Gerry Buelow recalls the engine discussion at the Special PRM: "The engine supplier was raised and R.J. suggested going to PEC at Waterloo for help. After this meeting Gordon Millar was contacted regarding the snowmobile engine. As I remember, Gordon was definitely interested due to his past experience at Scott-Atwater with 2-cycle engines before he began to work for Deere."

Gordon began his Deere career in 1963 as the director of the newly configured Deere Technical Center located in Moline. Deere employees there were a multidisciplinary group whose primary assignment was research related to Deere business unit needs. By 1969 Gordon was directly involved from his new positions as director of PEC and assistant general manager of the Waterloo Tractor Works. Gordon strongly supported the proposed Components Division within Deere. Glen Kahle, an engineering manager in the PEC organization who was responsible for advanced engine work, was assigned responsibility for the snowmobile engine selection. Within a short time several tractor engine engineers were involved. The engine components group seized the snowmobile engine referral as a way to gain knowledge of small engine manufacturers and their engineering capability. Laboratory testing at PEC produced a strong recommendation to work with CCW/Kioritz because their engine's performance was better than Kohler. Meanwhile Horicon engineering proceeded to design the next generation of test machines with the Kohler engine. The selection of the snowmobile engine supplier had become a roulette wheel. Where and when it would stop was not clear at the Horicon Works.

By 1970 Deere was marketing products manufactured by others through the John Deere Merchandise Division (JDM) in Moline, which were brand-labeled John Deere. These included small homeowner engine-powered products like weed trimmers and blowers that were made by Kioritz in Japan. Kioritz had a good reputation in Japan's market for small-displacement 2-cycle engine-powered products. Kioritz typically made 20 to 30cc displacement engines, about 1/10th the size and power of a 340 or 440cc snowmobile engine. To gain access to the U.S. market, they signed a distribution agreement with Canadian Curtis Wright Company (CCW). Under that agreement Kioritz could not sell directly to any original equipment manufacturer (OEM). Kioritz began to manufacture and CCW marketed small volumes of larger (340–400cc) displacement engines to OEMs. The final decision on which engine to use was made by PEC after Horicon engineering built the last test machines in the fall of 1970.

Roger DeWitt, a test engineer in the engine lab at PEC, describes the engine activity:

> As we know, Kohler and Kioritz were tested. Prototype engines were received from Kioritz and some were disassembled to see what they looked like inside, some were performance tested, and some were put on a mini-durability test in the PEC lab. I remember meetings with Kioritz people about the engine performance package, especially ignition system, plugs, and carburetion. There was lots of plug fouling in the early days of the industry and some scoring problems too. I am not sure what pushed the final decision to go with Kioritz over Kohler. It may have been cost, performance, willingness to tailor the engines, or all the above.

I recall some Kohler crankshaft weakness and Kioritz had more beef where it mattered. Kioritz had engineering support at PEC to ensure that they could make any of the changes Deere requested.

Gerry Buelow wrote about some of the work with different engine suppliers:

Going back to the pre-production days, we were having problems with CCW/Kioritz and began working with JLO. The initial testing showed that JLO performed better than CCW and did not have as much of a piston-seizing problem. We considered an 11th-hour decision to switch to JLO. We met with factory manager Jack Moore to discuss the engine selection. I remember his analogy: You know a lot about your wife since you have been with her for a period of time, thus her good points and the bad. Then you see this young lady in a slinky dress and you immediately think that would be wonderful. However, you don't know her bad points. That is where I think you are with the JLO engine. As testing continued, the JLO engine did not perform as well as we initially experienced.

This somewhat humorous anecdote is one example of the fluid process of selecting component suppliers for snowmobiles. The factory personnel lacked experience with suppliers of powerful 2-cycle engines. As with any rapidly growing business, new suppliers were competing for business with the OEMs. Some of them lacked knowledge of, and experience with, the demanding snowmobile use conditions.

While the engine carburetor calibration and air intake and exhaust design was being done at PEC Waterloo, Horicon and PEC engineers traveled back and forth to coordinate the design changes needed for the hood, the console, and the rest of the chassis. One significant performance component in a 2-cycle engine is the expansion chamber exhaust pipe. The pipe must be tuned to the exhaust airflow pulses from each engine and include a muffler to reduce the noise. Roger DeWitt described how this was done at PEC:

One of my major challenges was to take the performance we were able to achieve with the straight expansion chamber which we had developed for that model copying motorcycle race machines, etc., and fit it under the hood without losing performance. There was no space allowed for such a contrivance. Remember the long straight expansion chambers used in the lab? We did not have computer-aided design and simulation as we do today although we did have some early stages of both. The dynamic pulse created a shock wave that had to expand uniformly in the expansion chamber. The pipe had to wrap around in a path never planned for such use. I had a draftsman lay out the thing in 2-inch flat segments of sheet metal that when rolled into a ring, twisted just so, and welded together, produced the prototype. You may remember that it got called all kinds of names, mostly derogatory comparisons to pieces of living anatomy. But it worked when subsequently tooled and with the Cowl muffler on the bottom, became the essence of the exhaust performance package.

When the PEC engine analysis and laboratory testing was finished, CCW/Kioritz was selected as the supplier of engines for the snowmobiles. The photograph of the CCW/Kioritz engine illustrates the compact packaging required to achieve the sleek design projected in the HDA styling sketches. The exhaust pipe expansion chamber in black is attached to the engine exhaust manifold on the front of the engine. It is directed up over the ski steering mechanism, then back down to the muffler outlet below the

CCW/Kioritz engine installation (courtesy Joe Wanie).

machine footrest. Each engine manufacturer required different components: carburetors, air intake box to absorb sound and screen out snow, and a unique shape of exhaust expansion chamber and muffler.

The change from the Kohler to the Kioritz engine in September of 1970 required extensive involvement of Horicon factory personnel, especially purchasing, in addition to the PED. Late in 1970 Horicon engineering reworked their last build of field test sleds to replace the Kohler engines with Kioritz. The specific factors that led to this decision are not well documented. "One significant fact was the yen/dollar exchange rate was about 220. This made the Japanese manufactured engines lower in cost than the U.S. suppliers," Jack Hoffman said.

Designing the Snowmobile for Production

The product engineering staff relied on the information gained from test and evaluation of the first concept prototypes to guide them in the design and build of new prototypes for test and evaluation in the engineering shop. The majority of the Horicon engineering staff worked on snowmobiles in order to meet the production date in April 1971. Fourteen months until production was a very aggressive schedule that required the other factory departments to work closely with engineering. The tooling for new plastic parts that included the hood had to be ordered by January 1971 to meet the production schedule.

Kohler engines powered the first test sleds. Other drive train components were ordered from new suppliers. The rubber track was a major long lead-time part. Gates Rubber Company was developing a new track that was molded with stronger cords embedded in the rubber to minimize stretch that was expected to improve the performance of the bogie wheel suspension in deep snow. Extensive testing in different snow conditions was the normal method used in the industry to verify a design for performance and durability. Since the test work was often done in remote locations, a Horicon Works trailer served as the mobile shop for the mechanics and engineers.

Laboratory testing was done by operating a component for a set number of hours subjected to a typical field load. Horicon engineering needed more space to perform laboratory testing of components for snowmobiles. Two small metal buildings, J5 and

Horicon field test trailer (courtesy Ed Kruel).

J6, were constructed near the Horicon Marsh where some of the foundry buildings had been sited. Entire vehicle testing in a test laboratory was many years in the future. At Horicon, test engineers John Meylink and Vilho Mutka designed test fixtures for the clutch and belt and built a snowmobile chassis dynamometer. These were used extensively during the next several years to accelerate development of component performance and durability. John Orvis was hired from Polaris to head testing the snowmobiles. After the first prototype sleds were completed in March 1970, John took them to Houghton Hancock for evaluation. Competition outperformed them in most respects. John recalls that he rode up a hill among trees where the competitive sleds could operate. Only one JD experimental sled made the climb. Tree limbs knocked off the tractor headlights mounted on the side of the hood. "They were a disaster," John said.

During the period from July 1970 until production started in April 1971, nearly the entire engineering staff at Horicon was needed to complete the second build of test machines prior to release of the complete design to production. Jack Hoffman, the PED Division Engineer for garden tractors and riding mowers and their attachments, wrote in his October 1970 monthly report that he was supervising the design of the hood, console, gas filler cover and headlight mount for the snowmobile. In November 1970, Jack attended an industry product show where Martin Berk asked him to supervise the design of the snowmobiles, as Bob Trapp was no longer with the company. The second-build machines were tested in the winter of 1970–71 while the parts were being released for production. Another important but time-consuming work was the engineering Decision document that was used to communicate the specifications and drawings within the factory. Any revision to the original design required extra work for the manufacturing engineering, purchasing and marketing departments. Accuracy of the specifications in the Decision document was absolutely essential. Late Decisions required considerable time for product engineers to work with other departments in the factory to accomplish the intended result.

The torque converter, another of the major drive system components in the snowmobile, was commonly referred to as the clutch or belt drive. It operated through a speed (RPM) range of about four-to-one. Simply varying the throttle position on the handlebar changed the travel speed. As the engine speed increases, the drive clutch diameter increases, while the secondary gets smaller. When the load on the track increases, the spring-positioned secondary increases in size so the engine doesn't bog down under the load. Salsbury was selected as the supplier. The primary clutch is fastened to the engine crankshaft; therefore it operated from about 1000 RPM at idle to 7000 RPM at full throttle. It functioned as an automatic torque converter due to the centrifugal weights in the primary and the spring load in the secondary. Throughout the first two years in the business, Horicon machines were plagued with continuing failure of belts and torque converters. One huge load variable was the different riding styles. These varied from a family trail ride at modest speeds to wide-open throttle (WOT) in the roughest possible terrain during cross-country racing.

The decision on the engine location and the type of suspension for the first snowmobile design would have lasting influence on the snowmobile venture during the next several years. Horicon marketing and engineering had supported the decision to use the mid-chassis engine and the bogie wheel suspension in the meetings with Moline management. Suppliers had manufactured components for this type of machine design for many years; yet Horicon Works soon learned that several of these components were not durable enough for the Deere snowmobile. Extensive field tests were required to calibrate the engine performance of the air intake, carburetor, and exhaust system with the variable belt drive clutch and secondary pulley. This work was done in different snow conditions at different altitudes and in a wide range of operating temperatures that a rider could experience. Horicon PED placed a great deal of emphasis on rider comfort, safety and durability of the machine. Field-testing was done with several competitive machines to make machine performance comparisons. The production design of the machine powered by CCW/Kioritz engines was verified during the 1970–71 winter prior to start of production in April 1971. PED personnel were excited and satisfied with the results of their extraordinary efforts to meet the production schedule.

Manufacturing

Before snowmobile production, the Horicon Works made lawn and garden tractors and attachments, numerous low-annual-volume agricultural products, and grain drills and field cultivators. The factory launched an aggressive program for the manufacture of snowmobiles. Grain drills and field cultivators were transferred to the Des Moines

Horicon grain drill, circa late 1960s (courtesy Bob Strassmann).

Works, and other low-volume agricultural machines were transferred to different Deere agricultural factories. Before the transfers were completed, sales branch and Horicon marketing estimated volumes of these machines for the next two years. Horicon Works then manufactured enough products to supply the market for two years, while the Des Moines Works and other factories prepared to make the products transferred from Horicon.

Lawn and garden tractor production continued at Horicon while the factory prepared to manufacture the new product. Snowmobile assembly was to begin in April 1971 and finish by the end of October. Changes were required in the factory assembly building and in the warehouse for the planned high snowmobile volumes. The factory needed more space for production of primary parts, so a new building was included in the capital equipment budget and was completed in 1975. Before it began operation, Horicon sourced primary parts from suppliers that were later made in the new primary building. It was sited outside of the city of Horicon, as there was no buildable area on which to expand in the old factory site alongside the Rock River.

The production scheduling system was a monthly batch process based upon annual requirements. Both Horicon-manufactured and purchased parts were stockpiled in the warehouse before the monthly assembly. This procedure often accumulated large work in process (WIP) inventory. Production schedule changes were costly to both Horicon and its suppliers. Many of the engines and molded parts required long lead times. The purchasing function at Horicon changed dramatically for snowmobile production with the new materials and suppliers required. Purchasing personnel required new and different technical skills for the molded fuel tank, rubber tracks, drive belt and clutch components.

During the years that Horicon manufactured snowmobiles, Duane Dummer worked in the manufacturing methods lab, where the assembly procedure was developed for the snowmobiles. This work involved disassembly and reassembly of the engineering-made prototypes to establish the assembly procedure. The lab designed an assembly fixture for snowmobiles that fit on the roller conveyors used in the factory to assemble garden tractors; the employees installed parts from both sides. The snowmobile was pushed manually to the next station. With the anticipated high production of snowmobiles, two additional assembly lines were required. Along with industrial engineers, the methods lab established the assembly rates for the incentive workers in production.

Horicon Works manufacturing acquired new process equipment for the aluminum tunnel and other parts made from aluminum. Duane recalls that an outside firm designed a large spot welding fixture for the tunnel. New large presses and dies were needed, as the unit volumes for the snowmobiles were projected to be very high. Additional manufacturing personnel were hired to support the increased workload for both primary and assembly work. Duane helped build an engine runoff in the assembly building to test each engine before sending it to the assembly line. This investment was made to ensure the dealers would have minimum engine problems. Those two test

Snowmobile assembly line (courtesy Bob Strassmann).

fixtures ran 24 hours a day. Since snowmobile assembly was counterseasonal with garden tractors, it helped to level shop employment. In 1958, when Duane first started at Horicon, the factory employed about one thousand people. When Horicon closed their foundry and transferred the grain drills to Des Moines Works, employment fell to several hundred. "Snowmobiles were good for the company and good for the employees. I was thankful to have a job during that time," Duane said,

Ron Wheeler was the manager of the Production Control Department in Horicon from 1972 until he transferred to Waterloo Works in 1976. This department prepared the production schedule for the factory. Ron began work at Horicon in 1963, the first year of garden tractor production. Before the production control job, his assignments in manufacturing engineering, factory supervision and product engineering provided him with a broad understanding of the factory operations. He worked in product engineering during the prototype snowmobile builds. "The effect snowmobiles had on the factory was they created a lot of interest and excitement, brought additional volume to fill the summer employment void and some new process technology," Ron said. Horicon used the same approach to schedule manufacture of snowmobiles that was used for all of its other products. "The employment ratio of incentive wage, non-incentive wage and salary employees changed very little due to snowmobiles. This made it very difficult to accomplish much cost reduction from the additional volume," Ron said. "The biggest changes were in engineering and purchasing."

The Deere factory organizations had evolved over the years and served well during the post–World War II manufacturing operations. Horicon's factory departments were organized similar to the other Deere factories—recall the tentacles of an octopus all connected to the main body at Moline. A works manager was responsible for the factory operations and had responsibility for staff departments that included manufacturing engineering, scheduling, purchasing and materials. A production superintendent managed the shop operation, organized into primary and assembly divisions. Strong staff departments of functional disciplines like quality control (inspection), industrial engineering (IE), purchasing, accounting and industrial relations supported the manufacturing operations. Detailed accounting records were recorded for each manufacturing department, with those data consolidated into a financial exhibit for the factory.

This organization required a lot of time to implement new product designs, as it was a linear batch process. The design release schedule normally allocated months for the factory to process new designs. Before a final Decision document could be issued, the PED needed to build the prototypes that were used by manufacturing engineering and marketing to complete preparation for production. Any redesign required for machine performance and durability or for manufacturing reasons caused the iterative process to be repeated. When final agreement was reached on the design, it could require a year for all of the factory departments to complete their work. The short time schedules from design to production with snowmobiles pointed to the need for new work processes within the factory.

Factory Marketing

In October of 1970, Ray Gregg, Jr., transferred from the Syracuse branch to Horicon as the factory marketing manager. Ray recalls that R.J. Carlson came to Syracuse, New York, to interview him for the job. Specifically he was to prepare the factory, along with the Moline departments, to market the new snowmobiles. "By March 1971 selected dealers were in Horicon for preliminary exposure to the new products. Fortunately the Rock River and Horicon Marsh were still frozen in March so they could operate the snowmobiles. Feedback from these dealers was very encouraging," Ray said. In addition to managing new product introductions for dealers, the factory furnished product performance data to the Deere Advertising Department in Moline about Deere and competition sleds. Machine photographs showing them in snow were normally coordinated with an engineering test program. Additional prototypes for those photos were made in the product engineering shop.

The factory marketing department service personnel wrote the owner-operators' manuals and product service manuals that were published by Deere in Moline. The factory service department designed and purchased any special tools that dealers would need for snowmobiles. The Horicon marketing department also prepared the sales volume estimates for all production. This information was formally approved or modified at the quarterly schedule meeting in Moline. At one of these meetings the first year production schedule of 13,000 Model 400 and 500 snowmobiles was authorized. Following that decision, the Horicon factory production control department was authorized to release this schedule to manufacturing.

Ready for Production

The final plans for manufacturing and marketing snowmobiles were discussed at a special meeting called by R.J. Carlson held at the factory in April 1971. PED Monthly Reports and personal recollections provide a clear picture of the event. The meeting covered the scope of Horicon Works, JDM and sales branch plans for snowmobiles. Horicon attendees recall that the tone of the meeting was optimistic. The mood was strengthened by the feedback from the selected group of dealers who had ridden them on the frozen Rock River in March and spread the news to other dealers in their locality. Product engineering tests of the last build machines with the Kioritz engine were satisfactory. The first year production was only two models, JD 400 and JD 500, not the four models that were proposed in the Special Meeting to launch snowmobiles in February 1970, fourteen months earlier. Models 3 and 4 on this chart became the John Deere 400 and 500.

John Orvis recalls attending that meeting, during which the chassis design configuration was discussed again. The advocates of the mid-engine location repeated their conviction that it reduced the risk for manufacturing and engineering. The prevailing rationale advanced by marketing was this design would be more familiar to JD dealers who were already selling competitive machines. This would assist the sales branches to displace the competitive machines sold at JD dealerships. Others in this meeting voiced strong support for Horicon Works to design a front-engine chassis.

There were no plans for a factory race team. John along with others advocated that Deere must have a race team in order to attract customers and acquire design information for the consumer snowmobiles. John stated the case for racing this way: "Even during trail riding, when a group stops at a tavern or restaurant, the first rider to arrive has the bragging rights." Jack Moore concluded the discussion by announcing that the factory would field a race team for the upcoming cross-country race season in the winter of 1971–72. After this meeting, Horicon Works did establish its first factory race team. Their assignment was to prepare to race that coming winter, especially in the Winnipeg to Saint Paul International 500 mile (WSP I-500) cross-country race. The race teams are described in detail in Chapter 8. Since the factory race team was to focus on development of technology, they could pursue the front engine design. The JDM division presented the snowmobile clothing and other products like oil and trailers that were needed for snowmobiles. In addition to Horicon-manufactured consumer products, R.J. worked tirelessly to develop a broad line of John Deere merchandise to support dealer sales.

David Apple worked in Moline in the Product Planning Department from 1965

5.2 John Deere Snowmobile Specifications

	MODELS			
	I	II	III	IV
PROPOSED LIST PRICE	$ 875.00	$ 950.00	$1,150.00	$1,275.00
ENGINES				
Displacement in cc	295	340	340	440
Number of cylinders	1	2	2	2
H.P. (Per Mfg.)	18	24	24	33-35
Electric Start	Field Installed - Optional			
Exhaust System	Power Tuned			
FUEL SYSTEM				
Capacity	5.75 gallons			
Tank Material	Terne Plate Steel			
Location	Front of Engine Compartment			
Fuel Filter	Self Cleaning, Inside Fuel Tank			
Primer	Injects Raw Fuel Into Engine			
DRIVE TRAIN				
Transmission				
Make	Salsbury			
Model	780	780	780	910
Ratio Low Range	3.76:1	3.76:1	3.76:1	3.14:1
Ratio High Range	.87:1	.87:1	.87:1	.78:1
Final Drive				
Type	Enclosed Double Strand Chain			
Chain Size	ASA 35-2			
Ratio (Stock)	2.60:1	2.30:1	2.30:1	2.06:1
Optional Ratios	To be available for field installation			
Brake	9 in. diameter disk, caliper			
Track				
Width	15.5 in.	15.5 in.	18.0 in.	18.0 in.
Type	Molded reinforced polyurethane			
Drive Sprockets	Molded polyethylene			
Suspension (Standard)	Trailing arm bogie			
(Field Kit)	Slide bar			
Dimensions				
Overall Length	102.8 in.			
Overall Width	35.3 in.			
Height with Windshield	42.8 in.			
Weight	335#	350#	380#	380#
CHASSIS AND TRIM				
Chassis Material	Aluminum Tunnel & Pan			
Hood Material	Fiberglass			
Windshield	Clear Polycarbonate (shatter-proof)			
Lighting				
Headlamps	Twin 35 Watt Sealed Beams			
Tail Lamps	Twin Wrap Around (for side visibility)			
Bumpers				
Front	Wrap Around Extruded Aluminum			
Rear	Chrome Plated Steel Tubes			
Seat	Energy Absorbing Type			
MAXIMUM SOUND LEVEL	80 (Db(a) or less at 50 feet			

John Deere snowmobile specifications (courtesy Jack Hoffman).

John Deere color-coordinated helmets are designed to exceed the American Standard Institute's specification for safety. In addition, the deluxe interior provides thick padding and exceptional warmth. Tab at back of helmet helps prevent goggles from becoming lost.

John Deere face shields protect your eyes in various sunlight conditions and your face from wind and cold. Choose either Vari-Shield, pictured, or full-flip.

Premium Sorel boots for men, left, and nylon-top boots for men and women, provide hours of comfort and warmth at cold temperatures during long trail rides. An attractive "leaping deer" patch is sewn on the nylon-top boots to "personalize" them.

Super-See-R goggles have interchangeable clear, amber, and smoke lenses for night, overcast and sunny conditions.

There's nothing like a full face mask to protect you on those really cold days. John Deere face masks are available in a variety of colors all coordinated to match John Deere suits.

Stocking caps are an old-time favorite among men, women, and children in snow country. And John Deere stocking caps match the colors of your John Deere Snowmobile Suit.

JD snowmobile clothing, circa 1972 (courtesy Bob Strassmann).

to 1970. "I was assigned to evaluate the market potential of many different products for the Deere consumer market: machines like estate tractors, boats, jet skis, motorcycles and bicycles. The excitement about the future growth of Deere in new markets was contagious," David said. A new advertising theme "Nothing Runs Like a Deere" was created to support the snowmobile introduction. It was used with new Deere snowmobile advertising literature and for dealer promotional materials like caps, belt buckles and clothing. The Deere leaping deer logo was frequently shown alongside, "Nothing Runs Like a Deere" to emphasize the idea that Deere had expanded its market beyond the agricultural base to include consumer products. Also, it conveyed the image the customer could expect to receive a dependable machine that performed well if made by John Deere.

"Nothing Runs Like a Deere" cap (Ron Leonard collection).

"Nothing Runs Like a Deere" belt buckle (Ron Leonard collection).

Nothing Runs Like a Deere Belt Buckle (Ron Leonard collection).

Future Model Plans

As production of the models JD 400 and 500 was underway, the annual Horicon Works 1971 PRM was held in June 1971 to update Moline management on 1972 and 1973 model plans for all Horicon products that now included snowmobiles. For 1972 production, the June 1970 PRM book had shown the specifications of four models—not two. Only two models could be completed in time for 1971 production, as there weren't enough resources to design and test four models before production began. For 1972 production of 1973 models, the plan was changed again, with higher power levels and other improvements needed for 1972 production. The model lineup was to expand from two to four with higher power levels along with many other specifications changes. A new topic of considerable concern was the requirement to certify that sound levels for all snowmobiles manufactured in 1972 be lowered to 82 dBa. This work required major tests and analysis that would cause significant redesign of the JD 400 and 500 as well as for the two new models. This was a new business, in a different industry, with demanding government regulations. How to position the Horicon Works to be capable to respond to meet all market needs was a major discussion topic in that meeting.

1971 Product Review Meeting book (courtesy Jack Hoffman).

The proposed model lineup for 1972 production as 1973 models, shown in the PRM, added two new models and continued production of the JD 400 and JD 500 with improvements. The four models were to be the JD 300 with a 295cc engine at 21 hp; JD 400 with a 340cc engine at 30 hp; JD 500 with a 440cc engine at 40 hp; and JD 600 with a 440 cc engine at 40 hp and a wider 18-inch track. All models were to be made on the mid-engine chassis. To obtain the increased engine power, Kioritz and PEC engine engineering were working to revise the engine design in Japan for production of 1973 models only ten months in the future. This meeting ended with the Horicon Works directed to utilize resources from other Deere units and to hire additional staff to accelerate the work in order to build the new

SPECIFICATIONS

	MODELS			
	300	400	500	600
PROPOSED LIST PRICE	$995	$1195	$1325	$1450
ENGINES				
Displacement in cc	295	340	440	440
Number of cylinders	1	2	2	2
H.P. (Per Mfg.)	21	30	40	40
Electric Start		Accessory Dealer Installed		
Exhaust System dB(A)	82	82	82	80

Specifications (courtesy Jack Hoffman).

higher-power sleds ten months later. The Horicon personnel left that meeting determined to overcome the obstacles. Some were skeptical, as Horicon lacked the technical skills for sound engineering work and, based on the first year's experience with Kioritz, there was a high level of anxiety about the work to develop higher-power engines and complete the machine winter test and evaluation to ensure proper calibration of all systems with the new components. The unknown effect of the sound reduction work was especially challenging, as most of the sound sources were from the engine and drive system.

Snowmobiles provided the launching pad for Deere to modify their sales branch organization to completely implement the Hewitt growth vision in consumer product markets by providing enough products to support another dealer group within the Agricultural Sales Branch marketing organization in North America. With his vigorous support of snowmobiles, it seemed R.J. Carlson alone carried the Hewitt banner for the new marketing and manufacturing business within Deere. In 1971 an important management change occurred when R.J. was named the senior vice-president for North American Agricultural Manufacturing and Marketing. This was the first time that the manufacturing and marketing leadership for the North American agricultural (NA Ag) business was consolidated under one senior manager at Moline. A similar organization structure was in place for the Industrial Division and the International Operations. Since NA Ag was the most profitable and highest sales volume division of the company, it was clear that consumer products would have strong support and leadership in Moline. In the years R.J. championed snowmobiles, his goal was to create a strong independent consumer product dealer organization supported by a full line of JD products at each dealership.

4

Expanding the John Deere Snowmobile Line

The dealer product introduction of the JD 400 and 500 snowmobile was held in August 1971 at the Waterloo, Iowa, airport. Dealers and sales branch marketing personnel rode the machines in the gravel road ditch, running on grass, and listened to the sales promotion in an outdoor grandstand. Excitement generated at the dealer introduction in Waterloo continued when dealers returned home. They soon received shipments of snowmobiles and made their first sales. The trial production in April 1971 was increased so when dealers returned from the August product introduction in Waterloo, Iowa, they could order snowmobiles. The first year's production of 12,664 machines was completed in November 1971. It had been a busy and hectic two years since the first snowmobile design began in 1969. JD was in the snowmobile business. Ron Leonard's first ride on a green snowmobile was in August 1971 during the dealer introduction that was attended by all Ag factory managers and some of their staff. His motivation to work for Deere came from growing up on a farm, driving a 1937 John Deere Model A tractor. Working on snowmobiles or garden tractors, often called toys by employees at other units, was far removed from his roots. Perhaps this was why there were many in Deere who were uneasy about a recreational type of product.

Many customers were able to ride their shiny green snowmobiles after early snow in late October and November. Feedback from dealers and customers was generally positive. Sales branches had made good progress in setting up new consumer products dealers. The early success of the 1972 Model 400 and 500 snowmobiles set the stage for feverish activity in sales branches and the Horicon factory for the next year. The factory personnel had worked hard to meet customer expectations, and they accomplished that.

Territory Manager Bill Lee attended the dealer introduction of the 1972 Model 400 and 500 and described his dealers' reaction: "They were excited about Deere getting into the business. Some of them said it was about time. Since the machines were painted green many were concerned they would weigh too much as the JD green paint meant the machines were heavy and strong. Others thought the machine should have an aluminum tunnel like competition. I assured them the tunnel was aluminum — only painted green." As part of the flexibility in dealer selection, Bill and other territory managers could place the John Deere snowmobiles with existing competitive dealers or with full-line John Deere dealers. Competitive dealers thought the bogie suspension was heavy and old, as newer machines from companies like Arctic Cat and Polaris were lighter and had front-mounted engines and slide rail suspensions.

Concern melted within Deere about the market acceptance of snowmobiles and was replaced by unbridled optimism about the future. For the company this meant that the long wait for a separate consumer products dealer organization in Deere was over. However, there were some John Deere 400 and 500 failures and performance complaints that had to be corrected. Customers experienced failures of the Salsbury clutch and drive belt, and others complained engines were hard to start. Many of these complaints were considered normal, as some customers were not familiar with snowmobiles; however, all were serious issues and required improvement to meet Deere standards. The factory personnel worked to correct significant failures before the start of production of the 1973 models that was to begin in May 1972, just a few short months away.

Randy Preston, the service manager for consumer products in the Minneapolis branch, recalls that the reaction to the 1972 models with the consumer product dealers was generally good. Most of them understood the business and had service support at their dealerships. The reaction varied with the agricultural dealers: "Ag dealers like Junior Pederson at Hatton, North Dakota, or Enns Brothers in Manitoba, Canada, who sold competitive snowmobiles, had few complaints," Randy said. Dealers who sold a few machines needed parts or technical support more often than higher-volume dealers. Frequently it took too long to resolve some of their customer complaints. Customer expectations for a Deere machine were high. "When a track, belt or engine fails on the weekend the customer's recreation is lost for that entire weekend, especially if the correction required parts were not stocked at the dealership. As Deere was able to improve its parts support in later years to reach the 24 hour goal for dealers to receive parts from the Parts Depot in Moline, this greatly reduced the complaints," Randy said.

Horicon factory Service Manager Wayne McClellan recalls the dealers' reaction to snowmobiles: they accepted them as a job to be done. Some were not familiar with the market and had never ridden one. Many dealers thought of themselves as farm equipment dealers, and it took time to make adjustments in their marketing plans to include a focus on consumer products. The transition to independent dealers for consumer products took several years. Each sales branch continued to seek new locations and establish dealers in facilities that would support the growth of the business. Some of the new dealers were unsuccessful and had to be replaced. Personnel changes in the sales branches for the Consumer Products organization were still underway as the Horicon Works prepared for the 1973 models. In the first years of the business, the transition to independent dealers limited sales.

In general, customers and dealers liked the 1972 John Deere 400 and 500 snowmobiles. They made an excellent family trail-riding sled, which was the major market in most of the branch sales territories. This enthusiasm carried over in dealer sales estimates for 1973 models. They asked for more models with higher power and a slide-rail suspension. While the bogie wheel suspension provided for a comfortable trail ride, the slide rail outperformed it in deep snow and in climbing hills.

Lower Sound Levels

The challenge to reduce sound levels of snowmobiles had to be addressed. The International Snowmobile Industry Association (ISIA) represented the high-volume snowmobile producers. With support from Deere and other manufacturers, the ISIA had proposed the industry would lower drive-by sound levels measured at 50 feet, to 80 dBa for 1972 production of the 1973 models in an effort to head off preemptive legislation and governmental regulation. Each company was to self-certify compliance. Since several companies found that 80 dBa was very difficult to achieve in the limited time, the ISIA negotiated a variance delay to 82 dBa for one year. The drive-by sound level, set at 82 dBa for bystanders at a distance of 50 feet from the machine, was a steep reduction for the industry, as some machines measured over 90 dBa. Most manufacturers planned to increase engine power to respond to customer requests to improve machine performance, and this exacerbated the challenge. Horicon had no sound-level engineering expertise or instrumentation to measure sound levels. Preliminary analysis and measurements demonstrated that many components would need to be modified to reach the lower levels.

Changing the Plan for 1973 Models

In late 1971 the Horicon factory was at work to prepare for production of the 1973 models. New products planned were to complete the JD 300 and JD 600 that were delayed the first year, along with improvements to the first year's production JD 400 and JD 500. The 600 featured a wider 18-inch tunnel and track. This plan for the 1973 models was approved during the 1971 PRM at Horicon on June 8, 1971.

SPECIFICATIONS

	MODELS			
	300	400	500	600
PROPOSED LIST PRICE	$995	$1195	$1325	$1450
ENGINES				
Displacement in cc	295	340	440	440
Number of cylinders	1	2	2	2
H.P. (Per Mfg.)	21	30	40	40
Electric Start		Accessory Dealer Installed		
Exhaust System dB(A)	82	82	82	80

1973 model specifications (June 8, 1971) (courtesy Jack Hoffman).

The engineering design and prototype builds for 1973 models began during the summer of 1971 while production of the 1972 models was underway. Additional personnel were needed to strengthen the snowmobile design group and provide staff for lawn and garden tractors. Jack Hoffman recalls attending a meeting in R.J.'s office in Moline with factory manager Jack Moore in mid-summer of 1971 when Horicon Works was asked to produce a huge increase in 1972 production to 36,000 from the first-year production of 12,660. In addition, R.J. began to discuss with Horicon management the possibility of producing the JDX performance machines as 1973 models that were originally planned as 1974 models. These machines were to have more powerful engines and improved suspensions. R.J. wanted the new performance machines to leverage the successful first year with a stronger model lineup and higher production during the second year, as this would accelerate growth of the consumer products division. At subsequent visits to Horicon during September and October 1971, R.J. continued to discuss these possibilities with Horicon Works' management. Jack Hoffman also remembers that the JDX line took a big leap forward during a lunch at Rock River Hills golf course in Horicon. "R.J. was quite enthused about the higher performance machines and possibly suggested JDX for their name," Jack said.

To introduce the JDX machines a year early required the factory to compress two years' work into one. The JDX performance models not then designed would need to advance one year while Horicon engineering continued work for improvements in durability and performance for the first year JD 400 and 500 machines. Still to be considered was the requirement to reduce the sound levels. Machine design changes to lower the sound levels were complex. The sound levels were measured on the dBa sound scale. To accomplish 3 dBa reduction required the sound power to be cut in half. So the task was to complete a rigorous analysis of the sound sources and then make the needed modifications to all models to accomplish the huge reduction from 87 or 88 dBa to 82. Horicon Works lacked the engineering resources to do that amount of work with just six months before start of the next year's production.

Another meeting was held with Moline management at the Horicon Works in November 1971 to address the issues to be overcome with this new model plan, and for the increase of factory production to 36,000. Our research did not produce a document similar to the PRM for that meeting. However, the PED monthly reports in this period clearly state that little work had been completed on the JDX line. Horicon Works relied heavily on the PEC for engine and power system design and development work for the engines and accessories like exhaust, air intake and carburetor. Since power levels for the JDX line were higher than the green machines, this meant new engine systems—yet to be designed—were required for the new, more powerful 1973 models. Marketing planned to position the JDX line as sport machines and continue the green machines as the family trail-riding sled. The conclusion reached in the November 1971 meeting was to implement the 1973 revised model plan that included the JDX line as well as the exponential increase of three times the production. The JDX machines were to be made with slide-rail suspensions and more powerful engines. The "green machines" were to have higher engine power along with an improved bogie track and suspension. All models required prototypes to confirm the performance and durability after the changes were completed to lower the sound levels.

Engineers for design, shop build and testing were needed immediately. The PEC in Waterloo, Iowa, was assigned the responsibility to accelerate the power system development of the higher horsepower engines for the JDX models. This meeting authorized Horicon to expedite hiring additional resources for manufacturing and the purchasing department to work concurrently with the engineers before the PED could design and build test machines. It is difficult to describe this plan without concluding it was likely to fail. Perhaps the enthusiasm for achieving rapid growth of the consumer products business created the propensity of some to think that any obstacles could be overcome which blocked out the voices of concern that undoubtedly were raised during that meeting. Hiring new technical personnel doesn't ensure immediate, high quality productivity. At times businesses underestimate the ability of technical resources to accelerate their work when proven processes are modified to save time — without allowing for the increased risk this creates.

To obtain additional resources, the Horicon Works, especially manufacturing and product engineering, began an aggressive hiring program in late 1971 and continued it throughout 1972. As new personnel were hired, they were assigned to the areas where their expertise could best be utilized. Steve Braun was assigned to product engineering and recalls that he was part of a group of fourteen personnel who were hired from Giddings and Louis, a machine tool company located in nearby Fond du Lac. They were assigned throughout the factory to strengthen existing staff in product engineering, manufacturing and purchasing. PEC continued their work with engine design and power system component engineering. Steve Scholten transferred from the Plow Planter Works in Moline in December 1971. His assignment was to do the chassis design and suspension for the JDX line.

Vigorous efforts were made by Horicon Works PED to obtain the technical resources for sound reduction from within the company. Finding new engineers took months, as engineering resources in sound technology were in high demand by many industries. Rudi Peterson, one of the Horicon engineers and a test technician, attended a short course at the University of Wisconsin in the summer of 1971 to become qualified to make sound measurements, and Horicon Works purchased instrumentation to measure sound levels. PEC provided some sound engineering technical support to Horicon and did part of the development work for engine components to lower the sound levels. In July of 1972, Bill Mitchell transferred from PEC to Horicon with responsibility to continue the sound reduction work that was being done at PEC. "Reduction of sound levels was the major driving force in evaluation of design/development changes to the 1972 production snowmobiles," Bill said.

PED Monthly Reports and Memos Describe the Dilemma

Statements from the PED monthly reports help to explain the dilemma that was discussed in the meeting with Moline management in November. Tom Lohr, project engineer, wrote in his December 1971 MR: "It is quite evident there is an immediate need for styling and engine decisions. The entire snowmobile program has reached the critical point, as all of the above listed items (not shown) have long lead tooling time. At this point in time, it is doubtful that the handgrips can be completed for the coming model year. In addition to the above design work, field test for reliability, vapor lock, cooling and silencing must be completed. Clutch work must be done on all models after the engine selection is made. Eight hours per week overtime has been scheduled until the project is on schedule." The vehicle design group was virtually powerless to complete their work until the engines and accessories were developed to meet the power goals and to reduce the sound.

Jack Hoffman's December 1971 MR featured a lengthy analysis of the engine dilemma: "From the engineering standpoint, the pros and cons being considered of three engine possibilities are as follows." Jack then details the comparison of CCW/Kioritz, JLO and Kohler as potential suppliers. Higher power levels for CCW/Kioritz engines had been scheduled as 1974 models. There was very little development work completed on them at Kioritz. JLO had a new design of engine that reduced the sound from the engine that was very appealing due to the mandatory lower sound levels and produced the power desired. Kohler as always was still knocking on Horicon's door with engines that were already in production for snowmobiles.

Jack Hoffman's January 1972 MR: "The major area not completed yet is related to the engine and components; such as, intake, exhaust systems and silencing. Final CCW production engines with the latest transfer ports won't be available until approximately 1 June. These internal engine changes are required to achieve the higher power level. This date is too late for May production, and therefore, the CCW engines must be last year's models with revised porting (different pistons and lower power output). So far the 340 cc engine has produced about 27 hp with silencing (sound reduction) and the 440 cc engine 34.5 hp with silencing." Both were well below the desired power level of 30 and 40 respectively. His report continues, "A major effort has been put on the slide suspension this past month and one very discouraging thing has been confirmed. That being, even with the addition of bogie wheels to the slide rails, the polyurethane track and steel slide arrangement is dependent on fairly generous amounts of snow for lubrication. Although we continue to try to make the combination of the poly track and steel slide work, it appears that the only satisfactory option to the slide problem will be to use a track with the steel clips running on a replaceable plastic rail."

It is easy to speculate that Hoffman's January report triggered an immediate meeting held on February 1 with Moline Director of Manufacturing Dick Blow and the Horicon Works factory management. Jack describes this meeting's results in a memo dated February 2, 1972: "...it was Dick's feeling that the JDX machine program would have to be postponed for one year until a satisfactory system was developed which gave the desired track and component (engine) life. He wanted to discuss this aspect with Mr. Bob Carlson later in the week." The memo describes in detail the quandary with the engine and track. Jack Moore, factory manager; Ray Gregg, marketing manager; Ray Allsbury, purchasing manager; Jon Fleming, works manager; and Tom Lohr from PED participated with Jack in the meeting with Dick Blow. Jack recalls almost immediately Ray Allsbury and Glen Kahle from PEC went to Japan to visit Kioritz. Allsbury returned with a prototype engine made from a sand cast mold for the JD X8. A sand-cast prototype is made from temporary low volume tooling that may be different in shape and wall thickness from those made with a production die. After the design is final a production die is ordered. Normal procedure was to build new engines from the production die to confirm the configuration was correct before production startup. There simply wasn't enough time to complete this work cycle.

The Kioritz 440cc production engine was unable to achieve 40 hp. It was redesigned to use a new reed valve air intake system that differed sharply from the piston ported design that Kioritz had used in the first year model JD 400 and 500. The JD 300 was delayed again and the Kohler engine was used in the JDX4. The PEC was to focus on the new, more powerful Kioritz engines and their components, especially the new Kioritz 40 hp 440cc reed valve engine for the JDX8. With the increased power levels and reduced sound level requirement, all components of the engine system had to be redesigned. The race was on to build 36,000 machines. The five models produced as the 1973 model lineup were:

JD 400–340cc piston ported CCW~32 Hp	7348
JD 500–440cc piston ported CCW~36 Hp	4792
JD 600–440cc piston ported CCW~36 Hp	3600
JDX4–295cc piston ported Kohler~25 Hp	10,353
JDX8–440cc reed valve CCW~40 Hp	10,897
Total	36,990

In hindsight, one can only conclude this was a very risky plan. The sanguine voices turned into hushed whispers of concern. It was like an 18-wheeler going down a mountain without brakes that was certain to wreck but you didn't know when. Conflicts were inevitable. Suppliers had two engineering departments to contact within Deere. Horicon purchasing and manufacturing engineering departments were flooded with late decisions as the engineers completed segments of the work. Early design releases for long lead components were changed as progress was made to achieve the performance goals on each of the different models. These changes caused excess costs in engineering and manufacturing and delayed production schedules. Modifications to reach the sound levels often took a long time to complete. Both the engine power system and torque converter were under continuous development as the plans for first production were underway. Increased power and lower sound levels were interdependent until

Specifications

(Specifications and design subject to change without notice.)

	JDX8	JDX4	400	500	600
Engine make	2-cylinder, 2-cycle Canadian Curtiss-Wright	2-cylinder, 2-cycle Kohler	2-cylinder, 2-cycle Canadian Curtiss-Wright	2-cylinder, 2-cycle Canadian Curtiss-Wright	2-cylinder, 2-cycle Canadian Curtiss-Wright
Displacement (cubic cm)	438	292	339	436	436
Horsepower (mfr's rating)	40	25	28	36	36
Exhaust System	Power-tuned muffler systems				
Fuel system					
Capacity	5.5 U.S. gallons				
Tank material	Terne-plate steel				
Gauge	Standard	Optional	Standard	Standard	Standard
Fuel pump	Diaphragm-type carburetor has fuel-recirculating feature to minimize vapor lock. Built-in air-intake silencer.				
Carburetor make	Walbro	Walbro	Walbro	Walbro	Walbro
Transmission type	Two-sheave, variable-speed, torque-sensitive				
Clutch make	Salisbury 850	Salisbury 780	Salisbury 780	Salisbury 850	Salisbury 850
Suspension and track					
Track	Endless, reinforced polyurethane				
Track width	15 in.	15 in.	15 in.	15 in.	18 in.
Suspension	Trailing-arm bogie wheel suspension				
Dimensions					
Length with skis	102.8 in.	102.8 in.	102.8 in.	102.8 in.	102.8 in.
Length less skis	86.8 in.	86.8 in.	86.6 in.	86.8 in.	86.8 in.
Width	37.9 in.	37.9 in.	37.9 in.	37.9 in.	37.9 in.
Height less windshield	34.5 in.	34.5 in.	34.5 in.	34.5 in.	34.5 in.
Height with windshield	40 in.	40 in.	44 in.	44 in.	44 in.
Weight (net)	386 lb.	396 lb.	382 lb.	386 lb.	410 lb.
Controls					
Throttle	Right-hand actuated, built-in emergency-stop switch				
Brake	Left-hand actuated, built-in high-low beam switch				
Electrical system					
Capacity	120 watts	100 watts	120 watts	120 watts	120 watts
Headlight	Automotive-type high-low, adjustable sealed beam				
Tail/brake light	Single-lamp taillight incorporates brake light				

1973 model specifications (November 1971) (courtesy Jack Hoffman).

both performance and sound level goals were met. Throughout this period the factory personnel were forced to short-cut work procedures in order to make parts in April to supply the assembly that was to start in May. Another organization change was made in February 1972 as the Horicon Works worked feverishly to prepare to manufacture the 1973 models. Jack Moore, factory manager, transferred to Moline and Ray Gregg was appointed as the Horicon Works general manager. Mike Heitman transferred from Waterloo Works to the Horicon Works as marketing manager.

Horicon held their annual PRM in June 1972 while production of the 1973 models was underway. The 1971 PRM booklet shown earlier in this chapter described the plan that was altered in late 1971. The 1972 PRM included the revised plan and specifications for the expanded line of 1973 models. The PRM manual stated the justification for advancing the JDX performance snowmobiles to be manufactured as 1973 models.

Product Review 1972 (courtesy Jack Hoffman).

As scheduled, production began in May of 1972. Two additional assembly lines and more factory labor were required for the higher production. Bill Mitchell recalls that problems with production machines became evident during quality audit testing by the PED. These same problems were confirmed again on later sound level audits. Bill's JDX4 quality audit report makes clear that the customer machines were destined to give trouble. The report stated: "JDX-4 starting problems became evident during quality audit testing and confirmed during operation on sound level audits." This problem was caused by an error in calibration of the carburetor with the air intake silencer required for sound level reduction. A correction had to be found and JDX4 factory inventory would need to be reworked before shipment to dealers. George Bovis at PEC launched a program to recalibrate the carburetion. The Horicon design/development engineers found a correction for the intake silencer. Bill continued, "While Rudi Peterson worked to confirm that the machines met the sound levels with these corrections, George and I traveled to Colorado to test the modifications and the re-calibrated carburetors at altitude. Testing a snowmobile in the sand and sagebrush of the Rockies in August was especially vivid in my memory because it was the first time I had ridden a snowmobile. Altitude performance was acceptable for all proposals but the re-calibrated carburetors did not totally alleviate the starting/flooding problems."

"The sound level work required a continual round of changes to the engine

RECREATIONAL PRODUCTS DIVISION

Since last years Product Review meeting the Recreational Products Division has become deeply involved in an entirely new area...that is, bicycles. This is in addition to the full scale program on introduction of the 1973 snowmobile line. In between these two major projects we have continued our investigation and search for a suitable source of trail bikes.

At the last Product Review meeting we discussed a sports line of snowmobiles to be introduced in 1974. However, as the season progressed we reviewed our needs for additional models with the marketing group, and it was felt necessary to speed up the introduction of the sports machine to our line. As a result, we introduced the JDX4 and JDX8 snowmobiles as a part of the 1973 snowmobile line. The JDX4 was substituted for the 300 and the JDX8 was added as a new model. In addition to these two machines the 18-inch wide track Model 600 was introduced as planned. The complexity and effort required to achieve 82 dB(A) with the entire snowmobile line was much greater than expected and a considerable part of the snowmobile development work done during the late winter and early spring of 1972, was devoted to reaching the required sound level.

During my discussion of the 1975 model snowmobiles there will be additional information on our future sound reduction program. However, from the complexity and effort required to reach 82 dB(A) it is apparent that as future requirements force the machine sound level to become lower and lower, the time and effort required to accomplish this will greatly expand. It appears that the true challenge in achieving the lower sound levels will be to retain a desirable snowmobile that has light weight, good performance, and a cost that the customer is willing to accept.

The bicycle program picked up interest and momentum in the first part of 1972. An investigation was made of various potential sources both in the Far East and Europe by Horicon and Deere & Company personnel. The out growth of this investigation was the announcement of six models of bicycles for our expanding recreational line.

The trail bike investigation has not progressed as rapidly and a status report on this will be given as a part of the general presentation.

Justification for changing the 1973 model line (courtesy Jack Hoffman).

performance components in the 1973 Models," Bill said. "The cooling baffles in the hood had to be screened so they didn't transmit sound outward. In addition, all of the engine calibration components emitted sound, so this required changes to either reduce the sound or direct it away from the drive by test microphone. The JDX8 engines, with the reed valve air intake system, horsepower and torque curves, were different from the 440cc engines used in the 1972 models. This along with a different carburetor and exhaust meant the calibration work was not completed before the start of the JDX8 production."

Jack Hoffman recalls that JDX8 production was assembled and crated for shipment without the engines. After the Horicon High School had closed in May, the factory hired a number of the teachers as temporary employees. In a separate area of the factory they installed the Kioritz reed valve engines in the JDX8 machines along with the required components as the engines were received from Japan. He also recalls that Kioritz chartered a 747 to fly engines to the U.S. so Horicon Works could meet shipping deadlines to dealers. We did not verify this as factual, but the situation was so bizarre this could have occurred as Jack recalled. Hoffman's July monthly report describes more quality concerns: "Paragraph A: the major snowmobile (assembly) line problem during July has been trying to obtain consistent quality. PED audited a number of machines and discrepancies were found that vary from machine to machine. In an effort to improve the quality, a new check list for inspection was provided to Works Manager Jon Fleming that covered the areas that we have recently found incorrectly assembled."

Market Acceptance and Reaction to the 1973 Models

With early snow again in the winter of 1972, many customers were able to operate their sleds in November and December. Bill Lee, the territory manager in southern Wisconsin, had this to say about them: "The 1973 models were ... a friggin' disaster." Before dealers in his territory could sell the first machines, they had to rework every one of them to install a modification on the Salsbury clutch in the X8. Then, in the early running, the machines were being returned to the dealers covered with oily fuel. Customers strapped extra fuel containers onto the machine due to the high fuel consumption.

Bill Mitchell summarized the results of work done at Horicon to better define the customer machine problems:

> "Early snow in the Horicon area prior to Christmas resulted in a lot of customer machine problems for the 1973 Model sleds. Many performance complaints, mostly with JDX-8's, resulted in engineering inviting many Horicon locals to bring in their sleds for performance evaluation over the Christmas vacation break. Several issues that were reported by customers were confirmed: Sparkplug fouling (causes flooding and hard restarting), Stripped sparkplug threads (many changes + short reach plugs contributed), improper heat range plugs as well as improper gap (incorrect calibration), Carburetor miss-adjustment and Cowl muffler scroll failure. The problems with the 1972 production proved the widely quoted Murphy's Law: If it can happen it will.

Dealers called the sales branches for help, who in turn called Horicon for help. There was little information on how to correct the problems. Bill recalls that his area service manager, Jim Salmon, came up with a solution for part of the JDX8 carburetor problem. "He disassembled a Walbro carburetor and concluded that the fuel-metering hole was too large. To correct this he simply took a ball peen hammer and pounded the hole on an anvil to make it smaller. After reinstalling it, this machine ran fine." Since the factory had no solution at that time, Bill called all of his dealers to the dealership in Green Bay, where they demonstrated the fix. A bench test was used to demonstrate the lower fuel flow through the smaller hole which made this problem go away.

A mixture of durability and performance complaints from customers flooded Horicon marketing and service department personnel in the winter of 1973. The factory and sales branches worked feverishly to correct the problems that resulted from performance complaints: hard starting, failed belts, torque converters and tracks. Work continued through the rest of the winter of 1972–73 to correct these problems. There was no shortage of naysayers about the 1973 models. Machine failures and customer performance complaints occurred on all models. The biggest disappointment was the flagship JDX8 sled. Faulty carburetor calibration caused plug fouling, hard starting or poor performance, especially with the X8. Increasing the power on this chassis exacerbated the performance and durability complaints, especially failure of the Salsbury clutch and belts. Lowering the sound levels without time to verify the sled performance affected all models. For some customers the mid-engine chassis sled was not satisfactory compared to front engine machines.

The dealers and sales branch personnel had to cope with customer complaints with limited information until Horicon could provide solutions. Many customers and dealers lost confidence in the JD snowmobiles, and two years of costly field modification programs were required to regain it. Performance and durability problems are a double-edged sword. Sometimes machine performance deteriorates due to wear and structural failures. The cause of other performance problems can be more elusive. In those years the state of the art of engineering required operating the complete design of the machine in a wide range of expected conditions to confirm the correct calibration of the power systems before production. Horicon had managed to do that for the production of the 1972 model JD 400 and 500 machines even with the uncertainty of which engine (Kioritz) would be used. Scheduling the JDX line as 1973 models limited the time available to do the necessary test and verification work, even if the new engine design and power system development had been completed before the November meeting. Building 37,000 machines added to the mixture of uncertainty as production quality problems contributed to the mess. The market expectation for durable Deere machines compelled Horicon to develop corrections for the customers' snowmobiles. Over the next two years, the factory issued numerous mandatory customer product improvement programs (PIPS) to modify all customer, dealer and branch inventory. Branch service personnel worked with dealers to install the PIPS and administer warranty claim allowances to regain customer confidence in their JD snowmobiles. These additional costs were charged to the factory.

Wayne McClellan tells an interesting story about the new seats that illustrated how just about anything that could go wrong did for the 1973 models. The engineers and the factory had worked hard to design and build the best seat in the industry. It featured a patented three-layer foam construction that reduced the shock loads on the rider's back that were a major safety concern. After the first machines were sold to customers, seat warranty claims flooded the factory. The problem was dogs were chewing up the seats. Why was this happening? After failing to come to any conclusion, Wayne phoned the seat supplier to schedule a meeting in Davenport, Iowa. Chuck, his warranty processor, prepared a long list of seat replacements. The supplier could not shed any light on the reason for the dogs' eating the seats.

During the meeting, Wayne happened to remember a license-plate incident that caught his attention in 1946. Due to the shortage of steel caused by the war, the State of Illinois decided to make license plates from plastic. Wayne had one of those plates, Ill 1946 #38222. Farmers soon discovered that when a truck or car was parked in the farm lot, the hogs would eat the license plates. This caused considerable consternation and public outrage. It was discovered that the plastic used in the license plate was derived from soybean meal. Apparently the pig's sharp sense of smell could detect the possibility of a free meal by eating the plate. No more license plates were made that way. Wayne asked the Sears seat company personnel if there was any possibility that a soya material was in the plastic used to make the foam for the snowmobile seat. After some investigation the answer was yes! And so it was, the hogs ate the plates and the dogs ate the seats. Problem solved. Wayne obtained Horicon's first warranty expense sharing agreement with a supplier as a small reward for the agony this caused customers, dealers and the factory.

Although not the topic of this book, bicycles and trail bikes also consumed resources at Horicon during 1972 and 1973. Deere planned to introduce the bicycles to all Ag and consumer products dealers in the fall of 1972. George Otterson from the Horicon purchasing department was selected as the program manager for those products. He traveled to Europe and Asia to find a supplier. By then the design group for snowmobiles was renamed recreational products. The obvious intent of this name conveyed the idea that there would be more such products in the future for dealers to sell. Jack Hoffman's May 1972 monthly report describes the status of bicycles:

> "George Otterson returned from his trip to Austria to investigate sources for bicycles. At a meeting with the factory product review group, George reported long lead times were required for European suppliers so an early entry into the bicycle market will have to be with bicycles from Taiwan. George is currently pursuing the bicycle program to establish specifications and terms of a contract. There have been no promising sources found for the trail bike so this appears to be a longer-range program. The next meeting on these products is scheduled for the 5th of June at Deere to present the Horicon and HDA proposal for one size of trail bike."

After this meeting, a Taiwan manufacturer was selected to make the JD bicycles. With no viable manufacturer, feasibility work was continued for the trail bikes.

The 1972 model JD 400 and 500 snowmobiles equaled the performance of mid-engine chassis competition. The Horicon focus on durability at times became a tradeoff with added weight that contributed to poorer machine response and handling. Deere machines acquired a reputation in the market of being too heavy. The paradox is when you focus on performance first, durability often comes easier and sooner. To focus on durability at the expense of performance is like going in the back door of the market.

Overall the 1972 model 400 and 500 machines were judged to be successful. They fulfilled the Deere objective to market a comfortable trail-riding snowmobile.

With assistance from other Deere units the Horicon Works personnel tried to design and manufacture good machines in the time allocated before production of the 1973 models. Attempting to make the bogie machine chassis into JDX high-performance machines in the 1973 model program without time to do the design and verification testing in cold weather and snow conditions was a mistake that nearly wrecked the business. Customers who purchased the JDX sleds thought they had bought a Ferrari but instead found they had a Land Rover. A quote from Shakespeare seems appropriate: "The fault, dear Brutus, is not in the stars but in ourselves." This was the nadir of Deere in the snowmobile business, and the next two years were tough for Deere to hold the independent consumer products business together in the northern sales branches.

5

Implementing Changes

Ron Leonard Learns About the Job at Horicon Works

In January 1973, Ron Leonard was appointed as the manager of product engineering at Horicon Works. At the Des Moines Works his engineering experience was in design and test of self-propelled cotton pickers, cotton strippers and high clearance crop sprayers. The job interview with Horicon Works General Manager Ray Gregg was held in Moline after the 1972 production run of nearly 37,000 snowmobiles was finished. Enthusiasm was high at Deere, as this was before most of the 1973 machines were in customers' hands. The job was communicated in the interview with Ray Gregg as an opportunity to grow with the business. Horicon needed to expand the engineering department by hiring more resources, not only for snowmobiles, but also the other Deere products planned to increase sales in the new consumer products dealer organization.

Although Ron planned to spend Christmas week in west Texas to finish the test season with the JDDMW cotton strippers in order to be with his family for the holidays, they rented a motor home and drove to Horicon, Wisconsin, to see where they would be living. While there they met Martin Berk, who took them to the Hackbarth farm south of Horicon to ride John Deere snowmobiles on the hilly farm fields. They discussed the situation that was developing with the 1973 model snowmobiles. While this was shocking news, it was only the start of a long and strenuous winter working in a different factory with different products, while looking for a home for his family.

The initial assignment was to become familiar with the personnel and the current products, then make recommendations on the engineering staff and facilities needed to grow the business with newly designed products. The first day at the Horicon factory provided a graphic overview of the challenges ahead. The new engineering building at the Des Moines Works contrasted sharply with the Horicon facility located on Vine Street near the north end of the factory. The office was on the street level with a shop one story below. Access to the experimental shop was provided by two stairways on the side of the design room. The factory buildings extended north from Lake Street between the Rock River and Vine Street, which served as a border between the factory and the residential section of town. The factory assembly building was alongside the engineering shop, separated by an alley where a trailer provided temporary office facilities for some of the newly hired engineering staff. Test facilities were in the two metal buildings, J5 and J6, that were sited near the Rock River; this is where the snowmobile belt test fixtures and the chassis dynamometer were operating.

The Horicon engineering staff was about half the number at Des Moines Works. Design work at both locations was done manually with layouts on drafting boards. The appearance of the office area was straight out of the green eyeshade era of the 1930s with varnished oak wood panels and glass on the top half of the walls. When standing up and looking through the glass, you could see the engineers and draftsmen bent over their drafting boards. A narrow passageway from the engineering office entrance led past the managers' offices to the open area where the design boards were located. The department secretary, Maureen Wallin, was located close to the entrance alongside the engineering manager's office. Martin, in the newly created position of advanced products manager, moved across the hallway. Midway in the design room one stairway led down to the PED experimental shop and test area. Some of the new employees were located in the trailer in the alley between PED and the factory assembly building.

From the first day it became obvious that snowmobile problems were omnipresent, especially with the JDX8. It may be unfair to characterize the environment as chaotic, but that was Ron's impression as marketing and service personnel made frequent visits to discuss progress on solutions for the snowmobile problems. Nearly everyone in the department was working on snowmobile projects either for corrections required for the 1973 models or the necessary work on the new machine 1974 models. An endless round of meetings with marketing, service and purchasing department personnel consumed the first weeks on the job. Ron recalls one meeting with Purchasing Manager Ray Allsbury about an upcoming trip to Japan to advise Kioritz that Horicon was going to cancel half the engines forecast for the 1974 models. By that time in the use season, Horicon Works recognized that there would be a huge carryover of the 1973 models in branch and dealer inventory. The production forecast of 60,000 snowmobiles that was approved in the Special PRM as 1974 models would be drastically reduced.

Marketing Manager Mike Heitman and Service Manager Wayne McClellan frequently visited the engineering department to assist and hasten development of solutions to the 1973 model performance and durability problems. Since Mike had transferred to Horicon in March 1972, he was well aware of the turbulent months of production of the 36,990 machines. Although Mike worked in marketing at the Waterloo tractor factory before this assignment, he had no prior experience with snowmobiles. With the avalanche of dealer and customer complaints that began in November, solutions were needed to advise sales branch personnel on how to satisfy customer complaints. All factory departments were involved in finding solutions.

The fuel/oil mix ratio for the engines in the 1974 models was the subject of another significant meeting. Marketing, purchasing and engineering were invited to attend. The purpose of the meeting was to resolve the debate over which fuel/oil mix to use in snowmobile engines. This was Ron's first meeting with the PEC engine engineers who traveled to Horicon to meet with Kioritz and the Horicon personnel. The PEC and Kioritz engineers advocated the 50:1 ratio—as it contained less oil and would reduce the likelihood of plug fouling which caused hard starting of engines. PEC and Kioritz engineers recommended this ratio to be changed to the 50:1 that was being used by others in outboard motors, motorcycles and snowmobiles. The Kioritz interpreter introduced Dr. Tanaka, head of Kioritz engineering, to make their case for the change. His credentials were reinforced when it was mentioned that he was the chief engineer at one of the Zero fighter plane factories in Japan during World War II. On the blackboard he began to write numbers and sketch pistons and cylinders. Then he showed equations that ended with the 50:1 ratio. Even to an audience that couldn't understand Japanese, written or spoken, it was clear that he recommended the 50:1 ratio.

The meeting concluded with the Horicon Works personnel agreeing to change the factory recommendation to the 50:1 mix for all the machines. Even though the technical aspects of how and why this recommendation would work were difficult to comprehend, the meeting left a lasting impression. This was a different business, and more importantly, the Horicon Works snowmobile business was in an ever-changing technical environment. An anomaly in the room that day was the presence of both Wayne McClellan, who held a Distinguished Flying Cross medal for his service in World War II flying bombing missions in B-29s over Japan, and Dr. Tanaka, who redesigned the 2-cycle engine that powered the Japanese Zero fighter plane used to counter the B-29 raids. Technical knowledge about engineering and manufacturing was easily transported around the world. Technology was the bridge that connected Kioritz and the Horicon Works across the decades since World War II ended.

By the end of January the WSP I-500 race was over and the factory race team returned to their regular work assignments. Engineering work for the next season's race sled was assigned to the Advanced Products Division in the PE department directed by Martin Berk. This separated the advanced project work from the current product engineering work that continued under Division Engineer Jack Hoffman. John Orvis and three others were assigned to Martin to design the race sled that was to be available by November for the next season. This was Ron's first exposure to what would become frequent racing discussions. Gerry Buelow, the engineering test manager, was expected to return to his position after serving as the 1972 race team director. That changed when the factory decided he was needed for his organization skills and engineering experience in the production department. Harold Schofield soon transferred from Moline to assume the job as engineering test manager.

Although Horicon hired additional engineers during 1972, the factory needed more staff for the backlog of grounds-care projects. The problems with the design and test for 1973 model snowmobile production consumed most of the newly hired staff. Competition from domestic garden tractor manufacturers along with the entry of Japanese companies in the U.S. market made it imperative that Deere design new and more powerful garden tractors with larger attachments for the changing market. Deere was no longer increasing its garden tractor market share in a rapidly growing market. U.S. engine suppliers Kohler, Onan and Tecumseh, among others, were designing more powerful engines needed for wider mowers. Sales branches were asking for new walk-behind mowers, snow blowers and garden tillers. Product engineering required more space for the additional personnel as well as for modern test facilities. Recommendations for changes to improve the engineering productivity at Horicon, increase the technical staff, and build modern test laboratories were discussed in meetings with Ray Gregg.

Similar to the ISIA for snowmobiles, the Outdoor Power Equipment Industry (OPEI) trade association represented most of the homeowner grounds maintenance equipment manufacturers. Cook County, Illinois, which included the Chicago area, passed an ordinance that limited the maximum sound levels of all homeowner maintenance equipment. Congress had created the Consumer Product Safety Commission (CPSC) with regulatory power over the industry. New sound regulations required for all of the 1975 consumer products presented a serious challenge to the limited technical staff that was available to lower the snowmobile sound levels. Horicon PED needed to do sound engineering work for all grounds-care products similar to that required for snowmobiles. As Yogi Berra famously lamented, "It was déjà vu all over again."

In the summer of 1972 Deere introduced eight models of bicycles to their growing Ag and consumer products dealer organization, but they were still not available for shipment to dealers. Plans for marketing a trail bike floundered when Deere was unable to find a suitable product and manufacturer. High dealer expectations for more new products were on hold until the problems with the 1973 snowmobiles were corrected.

As described in the previous chapter, a mixture of durability and performance complaints about snowmobiles flooded Horicon in the winter of 1973. The factory and sales branches worked feverishly to correct the problems that resulted from performance complaints: hard starting, failed belts, torque converters and tracks. The immediate priority was to correct those problems and obtain additional staff for all projects. The question that kept Ron awake at nights was how to improve the productivity of Horicon engineering, not just the capacity. Yes, a number of new engineers were hired who were functioning well under the work direction of experienced Horicon staff, but what would increase their productivity? Gradually the fog began to lift on what was needed. Ron recalled his early career experiences at the Des Moines Works and compared those to Horicon. After returning from Michigan State University to the JDDMW in October 1958, his first engineering job was design work on cotton strippers under the work direction of a senior engineer. That was followed with the opportunity to work at the remote cotton picker and stripper test sites. "Blackie" and Wally Hubbard supervised the cotton machine test programs. Both Blackie and Wally began working for Deere in Moline and transferred to the Des Moines Works in 1947, where Deere planned to start production of their first self-propelled cotton picker.

Every year the Des Moines Works tested their cotton machines in the southern cotton-growing states on customer farms and ranches. By starting to work in south Texas in August and moving north and west, they could complete up to four months of fieldwork in several different customer locations. Each location exposed the machines to different growing seasons in various types of soil and weather. The operating agreement at each customer's farm was that JDDMW would provide a certain number of machines to harvest the cotton with no cost to the farm owner. The farmer would furnish the machine operators, provide fuel, and haul his picked cotton crop to the gin. When the Des Moines Works machines were not available, the owner could operate his own machines in order to finish the harvest as soon as possible. These conditions were the essence of all good business agreements, which is mutual advantage.

On the first test trip, mechanic Jerry Hefflefinger and Ron drove an El Camino from the Des Moines Works to the cotton stripper test site at Mathis, Texas. This was the most valuable experience any young engineer could have to learn firsthand what farmers in different areas expected from the machines and what was changing in their farm practices. The weather and crop conditions were never the same from one season to the next. An engineer learned as much as possible in the conditions that season. Production machines had to function in all different crop conditions for the next ten years or more. By operating test machines in real farm operations, the engineers learned how well they satisfied the needs of the farmer. This was long before the advertising slogans of Nothing Runs Like a Deere™ or Meeting Customer Needs. Although one objective of field test was to get durability hours, even more important was the function of the machines. Did they do the job as well as or better than competitive machines? If not, why not, and what could be done to improve them? These test experiences demonstrated the importance of the machine function to successful engineering program management.

This kind of snowmobile performance understanding in a broad range of weather and terrain conditions was insufficient at Horicon. Improving the productivity of snowmobile engineering was vital to successfully increase the productivity of the factory. Horicon had talented engineers, but few of them had deep experience with snowmobiles. Every successful engineering project must be guided by a clear understanding of what to end up with. With that in mind, the design and test verification work can be focused on how to best accomplish that. The snowmobile race program became more important as a means to develop understanding of high-performance snowmobiles within Horicon engineering.

But it was even more complex than that, as there was a technology gap as well. To perform in a wide range of snow, terrain and weather conditions, it was imperative to understand how the 2-cycle engine with the centrifugal flyweight clutch and the belt drive functioned to design a snowmobile that met or exceeded expectations. There was general understanding of what the system did, but not enough understanding of how important those elements were to successful machine performance. There was a wide range of snow and weather conditions in the snow regions. Just as in cotton harvesting, weather and terrain made a huge difference in performance of the machines. Deere snowmobiles needed to perform well in all conditions of weather and terrain not just on trail rides.

Horicon Works' product engineering needed an aggressive program to obtain measured field loads in a wide range of conditions along with the load cycle frequency. These data could then be used in new test laboratories planned for the Horicon Works. Modern-day engineering is done with modeling and digital analysis integrated with the geometry. However one constant that has remained is that the engineer needs to understand the load data and customer use, regardless of the design tools available. There is no substitute for accurate definition of the boundary limits of the project before you start to design. A prototype is an operating model of the proposed production machine. Verification can be done in different ways: mathematical analysis, accelerated laboratory testing in simulated conditions, and operation in customer use conditions.

With help from PEC and the Technical Center, Horicon had done a satisfactory job of performance calibration of the 1972 model 400 and 500 machines, even with the uncertainty of which engine (Kioritz) would be used. Deere promoted and marketed them as comfortable, family trail-riding sleds. That was the target market defined in the original plan discussed several times in the PRMs in 1970 and 1971. Advancing the JDX sleds as 1973 models did not provide adequate time for calibration of performance and durability testing. This theme was repeated over and over by people who had tried their best to design and manufacture good machines in the time allocated for the 1973 models.

Numerous failures and customer performance complaints occurred on all 1973 models, but the most disappointment was with the flagship JDX8 sled. For those customers the mid-engine chassis was not the desirable machine configuration. The guts of the performance and durability issues were related to engines and torque converters. Faulty carburetor calibration caused problems like plug fouling, hard starting or poor performance. Early wear of the torque converter components caused performance deterioration and premature belt failures. Increasing the power on this chassis just exacerbated the performance and durability complaints. Reducing the sound levels without time to integrate these changes with the engine performance affected all models. Many customers and dealers lost confidence in the JD snowmobiles. The immediate task was to continue the work to define the causes of each machine problem and verify the design solutions for the problems. It required two years of costly field modification programs before the customer confidence in JD snowmobiles was restored. The critical issues for the Horicon PED became clear —how to obtain the right mix of technical resources, and how to plan schedules to design in less time and manufacture high quality products.

The dealer product introduction of 1974 models was held at Land O' Lakes Resort in northern Wisconsin in March 1973. At this meeting the factory described the 1973 model problems and solutions. Horicon would supply parts as modification programs to correct these problems. The dealers were required to install factory modifications on customer machines. This effort continued throughout the year. The parts were furnished at no cost to the customer and the dealers were paid labor expenses to install the modifications. There were no new consumer snowmobile models introduced to dealers at that meeting. During the dealer meeting at Land O' Lakes, Ron rode all of the competing machines provided for comparison against Deere sleds. One morning after a freeze, the trail ride was on an Arctic Cat sled with a grouser bar (steel cleats) slide suspension. On the crisp early spring morning the thrill and excitement of the experience ended abruptly on a sharp curve when the sled skidded sideways and hit a rut. Ron ended up with a broken collarbone, bruised ribs, severe muscle strain and a bruised ego. The steel grouser bars were like riding on ice skates when the machine slid sideways. This was a wakeup call that riding a snowmobile was not only fun but could also be dangerous. This experience demonstrated the truth of the thought that competition is a gift. It gives you the opportunity to do your best, but you have to learn from it and correctly apply that knowledge.

Formatting for the Future

When the snowmobile test season was over in April 1973, Ron Leonard developed recommendations to improve the effectiveness of the Horicon engineering effort. At all Deere factories, the Product Engineering Department is responsible ultimately to ensure the integrity of the design of the product. Although there can be quality errors in manufacturing, the PED is the court of last resort. It has to verify the machine design before releasing the parts for production. Even though the accelerated schedule and large increase in volume for the 1973 models was thrust upon Horicon, in the end the problems created were left to the factory and sales branches to correct, hoping to regain the customer's confidence. There were three critical needs: First, to secure engineers with knowledge and skills of machine performance, 2–cycle engines, and belt drive torque converters; Second, assign the program management for the total machine to Horicon; Third, set and adhere to realistic schedules for new model design, verification, and preparation for production for all Horicon products. To accomplish these took some time and difficult work within Deere.

Operating with these recommendations not only would give Horicon control of all resources required for the design of their new products, but also would increase the productivity of engineering. The factory manager could then be made fully aware of significant issues and concerns that are inevitable with new product design and development. With the urgency to respond to the rapidly changing market, there was no time for slow communications and awkward handoffs among the technical community. Each machine must be capable of performing its function in the expected operating conditions and satisfy the customer who buys it. These results were the hallmark of the culture started by the founder, John Deere. The flood of customer complaints with the 1973 models severely damaged the credibility of engineering and the factory. It was imperative that the issues in performance, durability and quality be corrected. The factory needed to move forward to resolve the heavy baggage of old problems while facing the strong headwinds of new challenges.

Design and development schedules needed to provide the time for the factory to prepare for quality manufacture of the design. This was essential to deliver a high quality product to the customer. Horicon Works lacked the facilities to do the major vehicle and component testing that would enable them to shorten the design and verification time for all new products. Test laboratories were needed for an anechoic sound room to eliminate the costly and variable outdoor measurement of machine sound output, vehicle cold and hot rooms with capability to operate the drive system at varying speeds, and dynamometer cells for engines and drive train components. Test engineering personnel needed more expertise and instrumentation to collect performance data of machines during field operation to provide load and cycle data for accelerated laboratory testing. More expertise in design analysis was needed. The field test of complete vehicles could then focus on calibration of the machines in different operating conditions.

Recommendations that addressed these issues were discussed with Ray Gregg in several meetings and received his full support. Horicon Works had to overcome some significant resistance at Deere and Company in Moline to obtain the engine and drive train expertise. The arrangement for PEC to do the engine system engineering and durability testing required costly travel time between Horicon and Waterloo. Coordination with Horicon purchasing and manufacturing was more difficult with two engineering groups changing the design. The high cost of personnel and test facility operations at PEC was billed to the Horicon factory. Although the engine group at Waterloo was very talented, their focus was on high-horsepower heavy-duty diesel engines for tractors and industrial machines. Horicon Works simply required the resources and facilities to do the work correctly with every new product. The consumer products required much lower-power engines in smaller and lighter weight machines than the larger agricultural tractors and industrial machines. Thus Horicon Works test laboratories needed to be scaled for the size and power levels in snowmobiles and garden tractors. Many factors beyond the control of the factory had influenced the outcome of the 1973 model snowmobiles. Dale Reece, one of the project engineers at John Deere Des Moines Works, was fond of repeating the aphorism, "If you don't have time to do it right the first time, you will always have time to do it over."

Every industry is faced with challenges. The Deere agricultural culture was implanted deeply in the Horicon personnel in all factory departments. While the employees' former experiences with agricultural products was useful, they were now in a different business, and some misjudged the magnitude of changes in traditional work processes that were required to compete effectively in the consumer products business. The product and services that the company delivers is what the customer experiences. In a competitive market one must focus on the market needs and design, manufacture, and market products that meet those expectations. Stated simply, Horicon had to reinvent itself to compete successfully in this market.

Ray Gregg communicated the engineering recommendations to the director of manufacturing at Deere. Dick Blow was an experienced factory manager at the Deere Plow Works in Moline before this assignment. These recommendations were made known to R.J. Carlson, who supported them. Horicon PED was authorized to hire additional staff for all new product programs. A high priority was to staff the grounds-care design division with sufficient personnel to design the 1975 model new garden tractors and riding mowers concurrent with the snowmobile work. These garden tractor products involved the same requirements as snowmobiles: higher engine power, improved function and lower sound levels. Construction of new engineering test facilities with the capacity to support all the new product work was essential and would reduce the total engineering expenses simply by reducing the time from start of design to first production, with all of that work being done more efficiently. New model tractors were to be restyled to distinguish them from previous models. The new styling could be done in conjunction with the sound reduction. Horicon hired Frank Smith from a nearby manufacturer of transmissions and axles for garden tractors. Frank made a substantial contribution to the design of the 1975 and later models of garden tractors in this assignment as project engineer, of garden tractor engineering.

It took months to lay the groundwork within Deere for Horicon to be authorized to add staff for engine and drive train engineering. There were many stakeholders in Moline and Waterloo who had concerns or supported a different approach from what Horicon Works advocated. Purchasing drive train components from suppliers had made it clear that Horicon needed drive train expertise to control the component design for both snowmobiles and garden tractor products. Planning for the expanded office and test facility was initiated with the plant engineering department in Moline. The year 1973 was a time of planning changes in the Horicon Works engineering department. The PED building expansion was completed in stages in late 1975 and finished in 1976, providing additional office space for both engineering and purchasing offices as well as the test facilities described earlier. Communication was significantly improved between purchasing and engineering by locating the purchasing department in the new PED facility.

Engines for Consumer Products

Engines have fascinated mankind since the birth of mobile power. In the nineteenth century steam engines propelled paddleboats, locomotives and later farm tractors. The Otto cycle internal combustion engine began in the middle of the nineteenth

Ground breaking for PED building expansion (Ron Leonard collection).

century, and Rudolf Diesel's first diesel engine was invented in 1876. By the early years of the next century, diesel engines were used in numerous commercial products. Internal combustion engines have undergone continuous development and improvement throughout their history. The basic engine concept of a reciprocating piston driving the crankshaft in both 2-cycle and 4-cycle operation has been adapted for specific machines in diverse markets in a wide range of engine sizes and configurations.

In the early twentieth century the lighter weight 2-cycle engines were developed for small power applications in products like chain saws and outboard motors. The power-to-weight ratio was much higher than the four-cycle engines used in most transportation vehicles. They were a natural fit for snowmobiles. By 1971 the U.S. manufacturers had huge production capacity for 2-cycle engines for outboard boat motors, walk-behind mowers, chain saws, and small hand-held weed cutters. Most of these markets were well served with the high power-to-weight ratio 2-cycle engines. With the emergence of a market for snowmobiles, several Japanese companies like Fuji, Kawasaki and Suzuki began to supply U.S. snowmobile companies with 2-cycle engines adapted to the operating conditions in a snowmobile. Thus they were in competition with the U.S. engine manufacturers for the market. After World War II ended, Japanese manufacturers continued to apply their knowledge of 2-cycle engines to small agricultural and industrial machines used in Japan. Honda got its start by adapting a small 2-cycle engine to a bicycle — of course, this led to motorcycles. Other companies expanded into outboard motors and small hand-powered equipment. The first two years in the snowmobile market demonstrated that Deere snowmobiles needed engines with more power to improve sled performance. With the complaints about the 1973 model snowmobiles fresh in everyone's mind, the Horicon management made plans to focus the direct responsibility for small engine engineering needed for consumer products at Horicon. To hire an engine engineer at Horicon Works was controversial within Deere.

A company Blue Bulletin signed by Bill Hewitt years earlier had directed that all engine work in Deere be done at the PEC. We were heading into "rough sledding" conditions. The concern was how to configure the organization to house the expertise and control at Horicon and still honor the intent of the Blue Bulletin. The 2-cycle engine is not just one block of material. Extensive collaboration with the snowmobile chassis engineers was required to optimize the vehicle and engine design. The air intake and the exhaust system, attached to the engine, required lots of space under the hood. The engine and its related components significantly affected the styling of the machine. Airflow through the engine compartment under the hood is essential to successfully control the engine intake air temperature. Likewise the expansion chamber for the exhaust gas is critical to sustain power output of the engine. Therefore coordination of the design of the 2-cycle engine and its components with the chassis was essential in project management of the snowmobile design work.

During the summer and fall of 1973, Horicon management discussed the snowmobile engine responsibility with stakeholders in Moline. At times this effort seemed like Horicon Works was digging a hole in concrete with an icepick. The engine design responsibility issue was finally resolved at a meeting held at Waterloo in late November with Waterloo Works and PEC managers. Before the meeting at Waterloo with the Horicon Works, many people were asked for recommendations for the engine design responsibility at Horicon. Lee Hardesty was the unanimous choice. At that time Lee was working at PEC with Kioritz and traveling to Japan to design a more powerful 295/S engine to race the next season in the winter of 1973–74.

On a Friday evening in November 1973, Ray and Ron flew in the company plane to meet Bob Giertz, the Waterloo factory manager, PEC Director Mike Mack, and Sid Olsen, chief engineer for engines, at a restaurant in Waterloo. The memo of this meeting describes the agreement reached, and the conditions of the agreement. Lee Hardesty came to Horicon in December 1973 to interview and accepted the offer to transfer to the Horicon Works. This agreement was contingent on Moline's management approval for Horicon to expand the engineering office and test facilities that were completed in two years. Three engine dynamometer test cells, a sound room, a hot and cold room, total machine test cells and a styling room for HDA were included in the plans for the engineering facility.

Small 2-cycle engine technology was improving rapidly for engines that were in high volume production in other markets. This new technology migrated to the snowmobile industry from the outboard motor and motorcycle industries. Horicon understood that they did not have engine expertise when they started the snowmobile project.

During the first years with snowmobiles, Horicon relied on their suppliers and ultimately the PEC for engine expertise. Upon arrival at Horicon on the first of January 1974, Lee Hardesty was the go-to guy for resolution of engine design and application issues. Lee became very influential in working with engine suppliers Kioritz and Kawasaki in Japan and U.S. engine manufacturers Kohler, Briggs and Stratton, and Oman. He continued his work with Kioritz to develop new race machine engines after the first 295cc engine that was used in the 1974 295/S race machine. The engine technical staff at Horicon was kept small in number. Their focus was on definition of engine specifications and application of purchased engines in Horicon products.

During the years Horicon made snowmobiles, Lee's engine design expertise supported work with the vehicle product design groups to design for efficient manufacture and for the marketplace. Not only did he improve the Deere snowmobile engines with

295/S race engine (Richard Teal collection).

Kioritz, Kohler and Kawasaki, he was later responsible for the installation of small diesel engines from Yanmar in the grounds-care machines. With KHI, Lee designed a new single-cylinder vertical-shaft engine for lawn tractors and riding mowers. The two-cylinder FB460V engine made by KHI was designed by Lee for more powerful garden tractors and later used on front mowers and Gators. This engine fueled the growth of the higher horsepower mowing vehicles with wider mowing decks. After they were introduced to the market in the 1980s, the products with the V2 engine became the most successful sales and profitable products at Horicon. Jack Hoffman commented about Lee's work, "The lawn and garden engines were somewhat the result of our ending the SM program. Lee was not successful in convincing the U.S. engine suppliers to upgrade their engines for our future programs. These included overhead valves, full pressure lubrication, and a full flow oil filter. Kawasaki had engineering people and facilities available after the snowmobile work was not going to be continued and they were current in the technology used in motorcycles. For the single cylinder engines (for garden tractors) from Kawasaki, a balancing system was incorporated that was simpler than the system that Kohler had been using on their larger single cylinder engines."

Drive Train

The other component skill Horicon Works needed was an experienced engineer for the snowmobile drive system. The system included the variable-speed clutch and belt-driven secondary sheave as well as the chain case that reduced the speed to the track drive. The Salsbury primary clutch was designed years earlier for lower-power engines. As the industry increased engine power, this clutch failed and Salsbury worked to improve it. The Horicon Works engineers needed to verify correct engine and drive train components before the sleds went into production. This could best be accomplished by having both the engine and drive train engineers working at Horicon with the chassis engineers.

To find a skilled engineer for the drive train was as challenging as it had been for the engine. Some of the snowmobile competitors designed their own drive system. Others purchased the clutch and secondary that were designed and manufactured by suppliers like Saint Lawrence, Comet and Salsbury. Several companies made belts. Drive train engineering candidates were offered to Horicon from the PEC with experience in design of tractor transmissions and axles. None of the Deere agricultural products used a variable-speed clutch with a torque-sensing secondary as the snowmobiles did. None of the snowmobile drive train engineers from competitors were available. After recommendations were sought from Horicon's engineering, service and purchasing departments, one name surfaced—Dick Teal. Ron had never met either Lee or Dick before they came for interviews. Bill Mitchell, while conducting sound tests in the winter of 1974 for Horicon experimental snowmobiles at Eagle River, Wisconsin, stopped at the Salsbury trailer in Ironwood, Michigan, to tell Dick that Horicon was interested in talking to him about a job. Bill gave him the phone number to call to set up an appointment to come to Horicon for an interview, and he accepted the job offer.

Dick's experiences in design and manufacturing at Parker Pen and FoxTrac in Janesville well served him in his work at Deere. Fox manufactured go-carts and snowmobiles, and while at Fox he raced both kinds of machines. Dick won the world's championship for snowmobiles in the open class at Eagle River, Wisconsin, in 1965, riding a sled he designed while working at Fox. This work prepared him for his next experience as an application engineer for Salsbury, whose business included supplying torque converters for snowmobiles and other industries. Dick recalls that he had a client contact list for 105 Salsbury customers who manufactured snowmobiles. He had worked with Deere to calibrate the drive system with the engine and the track on the first year of production of the JD 400 and 500 snowmobiles while working at Salsbury.

Excellent design and manufacture of the complete snowmobile power system from engine to the track coordinated with the chassis engineers was required to be successful. With these resources at hand in Horicon, both supplied valuable direction to the continuous efforts underway with suppliers to develop new engines, torque converters and belts for the JD snowmobiles. Above all else, Horicon Works needed a better performing and more durable clutch and belt drive system. Both Lee and Dick were excellent communicators with engineers and test drivers and were extremely effective in support of the race teams. Horicon now had a capable engineering staff to do the complete machine design, including engines, drive train and chassis.

Dick had innate understanding and broad experience with engines and drive train systems for recreational vehicles. At Salsbury he acquired invaluable experience with the competitors' performance expectations of snowmobiles that prepared him to successfully calibrate the drive system to the torque curve of every engine. He understood what performance was from sitting on the seat and operating a snowmobile. With the exception of John Orvis, this kind of experience was limited in the Horicon engineering staff. Lee had knowledge of engine power systems and experience at PEC that improved engine performance. By applying their knowledge and skills, Lee and Dick accelerated the pace of snowmobile development at Deere. The PED at Horicon then had the expertise needed to design and develop better products in less time and would have had a difficult time achieving later success without them on the staff. Yet improving the organization must be a continuous process; it is not a one-time event. Beneficial change occurs when you have the required skills to perform the task, and individuals work to improve those skills. Team members can improve the value of their skills to an organization when they learn how to work effectively within a group, and both Lee and Dick were solid contributors to the total product engineering design and development tasks.

How to set realistic new product schedules was a glaring issue that still confronted the factory. Synchronizing all of the factory interaction required with engineering was virtually impossible without that. Manufacturing experienced great losses of efficiency at Horicon in the first years of snowmobile production due to the short time schedule imposed by premature production of the JDX models at the same time as the huge increase in production from 12,664 to 36,990. Horicon was in a business in which improvement in organization effectiveness was imperative to respond quickly to the changing markets. With full implementation of all factory changes, the Horicon PED would be able to increase productivity and improve the quality of the new designs. How to establish a realistic schedule for design and development of the new series of JD snowmobiles was a challenge. How this was accomplished for snowmobiles is described in the next chapter.

In June 1973, Ray Gregg and Ron participated in an experience that provided them with their first look at modern manufacturing of industrial products in Japan. Deere and Company planned the trip to Japan for several key Deere executives, factory managers, and their engineering managers who were responsible for engine-powered products. The purpose of the trip was to see factories that made quality products and components. These included construction machines, transportation vehicles and the Yanmar Diesel Company's engine and tractor factories.

As an extension of this trip, they accompanied R.J. Carlson and Dick Blow to Taiwan to observe production of the new bicycles and to understand why they were not being shipped. The purchasing buyer from Horicon who oversaw the production of the bicycles took them to the seat supplier in Taipei, the capital of Taiwan. There it was determined that the seats were being held at the shipping dock and efforts to get them released for shipment were unsuccessful. The reason was Deere had to pay a bribe to get the parts loaded on a ship to deliver them to the assembly plant. The moral dilemma of the buyer was clear. Deere did not approve of doing business that way. Soon after this trip, a solution was found by contracting services provided by a third party.

At the assembly plant in Kaohsiung in southern Taiwan, they had a surprise welcoming experience the first morning upon arriving at the factory. The two cabs stopped in front of a lengthy stone stairway that led up to the factory entrance. The company hosts were lined up on the top steps to greet the visitors. As the lead cab door opened, they lit firecrackers strung over the doorway. This traditional Chinese welcome produced loud snapping and banging as the string of firecrackers continued to explode. Ron looked back to see where his cab partner was. Lying on the floor of the cab, Dick asked, "Are they shooting at us?" Before coming to any conclusion, you, gentle reader, must understand he had combat experience in World War II. The bicycle assembly factory was a trip back in time. The tubes for the lug frame had been sourced from a quality supplier in Japan and were stacked in piles around solder pots in the ground under a long, open-side bamboo pole building. Each worker squatted beside the solder pot, then reached back for the rusty tube. With a knife he scraped off the rust before soldering the lug frame.

All too often assembly processes are underestimated when new ventures are planned. The prevailing conventional accounting procedures didn't assign much "value" to product assembly processes. What was never explained is why assembly could lose so much value but not add much! Ray asked for a report on our visit to the bicycle factory when we returned to Horicon. It required a weekend to decide how to describe what we had seen. The summary in the report was, "We have two problems. They are quality and quantity. In my opinion we will never resolve either of them." Unfortunately this assessment came true when Deere quit the business after two years. However, Deere later sourced parts and components from Taiwan suppliers that were very satisfactory. And today Taiwan, along with many other Asian countries, is building world-class products that are very competitive in price.

The experiences in Japan were 180 degrees opposite of that. We saw modern machining and assembly of construction machines, tractors and engines. Japanese manufacturers of capital goods were investing heavily in machining technology to increase productivity and produce high-quality parts. The Japanese enterprises were serious competitive threats to many capital goods producers in the U.S. They were exporting successfully high-quality products like motorcycles, outboard motors and small agricultural tractors to the U.S. market. The great Honda-Yamaha (HY) motorcycle war was not yet underway. Yamaha was already manufacturing a small volume of snowmobiles and selling them in the U.S. and Canadian markets. Honda was becoming well established in the U.S. consumer products market with quality walk-behind mowers and lawn tractors. The Japanese manufacturers were simply designing and producing products that the U.S. market liked. Some John Deere dealers were marketing them alongside the Deere products in their dealerships.

Other key learning experiences in 1973 were traveling with Horicon management to visit several Deere sales branches. These always included visits to dealers and customers who gave us firsthand knowledge about the task at Horicon Works to supply quality products to grow the consumer products business. It was an exciting and challenging time to be at the Horicon factory.

6

Improving 1974 and 1975 Models and JD 340/S

Horicon Works' production of 26,016 of the 1974 models was finished in October 1973. The factory had continued to correct most of the major issues that occurred with the 1972 production sleds. This work benefited from the additional technical staff hired for design, testing and sound reduction work. After three years the shipments to dealers totaled over 75,000 machines. While this could be acceptable performance for a new business, unfortunately there was a huge inventory of unsold sleds in dealer and sales branch inventory. Deere did experience success in selling the green machines in the Midwest, the Eastern States, and the Canadian provinces for the family trail market. Customers still had performance limits in deep, heavy snow; however, the complaints were much fewer compared to the 1973 models, as most corrections were supplied to owners of 1972–73 models by the PIP processes. Although PIPS were very costly, they restored customer and dealer confidence that Deere snowmobiles would demonstrate the quality they expected from John Deere.

Although intended for the high-performance market, the JDX line fell short of meeting expectations compared to competition. A huge positive was customers who bought the 1974 models were able to operate with fewer failures and were better satisfied with their snowmobiles. As additional newly designed parts were available to sales branches and dealers, service parts inventories increased, which helped to reduce customer machine down time when a failure occurred. Improvements for engines, drive clutches and belts addressed both performance and durability complaints.

The factory race team from the first year was reassembled to race the model JD 295/S. The advanced products engineers designed this race sled using the latest design of improved drive system parts. Other modifications were made to the JD 400 chassis before the factory produced 1000 JD295/S machines for the 1973–74 race season. Lee Hardesty worked with Kioritz to improve the 340cc production sled engine and made a smaller bore 295cc engine from it that met the race association rules. While at Salsbury, Dick Teal worked with the Horicon engineers to calibrate the torque converter with the new engine. An optional slide-rail suspension improved the race sled performance and handling. With it the JD race team was competitive in several races. Even more encouraging, the independent drivers also had success racing the JD 295/S against

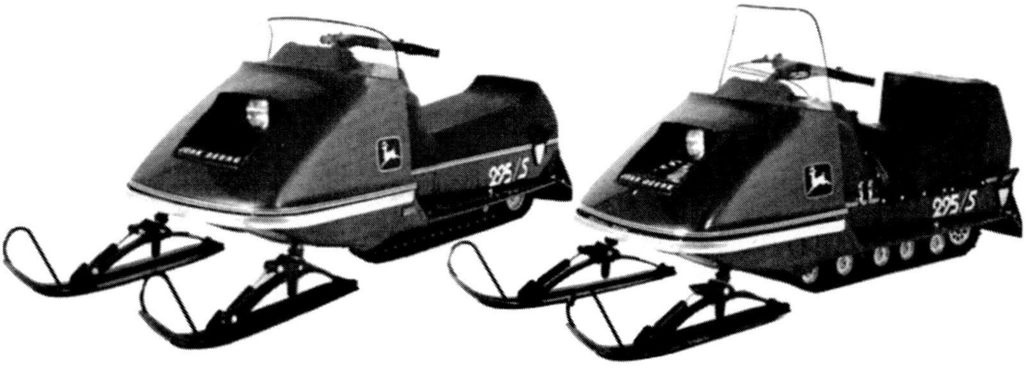

295/S With Slide Rail Suspension System

295/S Winnipeg With Bogie Rail Suspension System

One thousand, JDS 295/S snowmobile are being built as John Deere's first entry into the "high-performance" snowmobile field. The JDS sled is powered by a Kioritz KEC 295-RS/2 engine which produces approximately 39-horsepower [29 KW] at 8100 rpm.

The JDS 295/S Snowmobile has been tuned to operate as a high performance race machine within the limits of our current chassis configuration. It was also developed to work as a cross-country race machine or high-performance trail machine. The JDS 295/S Snowmobile is available with a choice of suspension systems:

1. Slide rail suspension system, same as used on the current "X" machines.

2. Bogie suspension system, same as on current "green" machines.

3. Bogie-rail suspension system. The bogie-rail is a hybrid in which bogie wheels are attached to the slide rails. This system gives the ride characteristics of the slide rail with the marginal snow

295/S snowmobile description (courtesy Jack Hoffman).

competition. The improvement in durability helped in cross-country racing, as you don't win unless you cross the finish line.

With 9th and 10th place in the January 1974 Winnipeg Saint Paul International 500 mile race (WSP I-500), Deere was in the market with a good, durable machine. Although these results were encouraging, the mid-engine chassis was doomed for future racing. It was clear that Deere now had to build a front-engine chassis for the market

1975 MODEL PROGRAM

1975 Models

STYLING - Sharp, new appearance is provided on the existing chassis with the new hood and bumper. By raising the bumper 1.5" and lowering the side "highlight" line on the hood sides, a lower machine appearance is achieved.

To provide additional operator comfort but retain the sportier lines of the "X" machines, a new windshield has been designed. The full width now deflects the wind past the operators hands and the large recurve on the top provides a blunt, safe edge should the driver hit this edge.

A full coverage handlebar pad now conceals the cables and wires on the bottom side of the handlebar.

The green line of sleds will be painted with the new metallic green as used on the JD295/S. The "X" series will retain the current "Blitz black" color.

SAFETY AND RELIABILITY - A strong emphasis has been placed on both safety and reliability for the '75 models. Critical control and steering components have been improved. These include forged ski spindles, tie rod assemblies, ski springs, brake cable and mount, throttle cable, brake lining and fuel tank vent.

The greater safety factor obtained with many of the parts will also improve machine reliability. In particular, the ski springs which have shown an improved cycle life of 4 to 18 times that of the current production parts.

as competition would make even better and more powerful front-engine chassis sleds for the next race season.

Two key decisions for the future design of snowmobiles were made following the January 1974 WSP I-500 race. The *first* was to manufacture the 1974 model consumer machines again as 1975 models with small but important changes, not a major new model change. One exception was the JD 500, which was discontinued and replaced

New metallic green for 1975 models (courtesy Jack Hoffman).

SAFETY AND RELIABILITY - A strong emphasis has been placed on both safety and reliability for the '75 models. Critical control and steering components have been improved. These include forged ski spindles, tie rod assemblies, ski springs, brake cable and mount, throttle cable, brake lining and fuel tank vent.

The greater safety factor obtained with many of the parts will also improve machine reliability. In particular, the ski springs which have shown an improved cycle life of 4 to 18 times that of the current production parts.

Safety and reliability notification (courtesy Jack Hoffman).

***Opposite*:** 1975 snowmobile models (courtesy Jack Hoffman).

with the wide-track JD 800, powered with the improved Kioritz 440cc reed valve engine. Improvements were made on all machines in styling, performance and durability. The 1974 production of 1975 models dropped to 18,433 machines due to the unsold inventory at sales branches and dealers.

The plan to manufacture the 1974 models as improved 1975 models provided Horicon with the time for a full winter to test the new design of 1976 model front-engine prototypes before production. Horicon had begun the design of a front engine machine in the summer of 1974. Dick Teal and Lee Hardesty had new designs for torque converters and engines for the 1976 models, and the chassis engineers were designing the all-new front-engine snowmobile with a slide-rail suspension. Safe operation of the snowmobile was always a major design consideration. The paragraph in the 1975 model specifications addressed most of the safety concerns that were designed for the new machines.

Marketing a mid-engine chassis sled was increasingly difficult, as the industry was aggressively introducing new model front engine chassis machines with slide rail suspensions. Manufacturers continued to exit the market. A display in the Harley-Davidson museum shows their snowmobile was typical of the style and construction of mid-engine chassis that Deere used for its sleds. Both companies' snowmobiles were typical of the conventional wisdom among many manufacturers at that time. Harley's market experience was summed up in the words "family snowmobiling" and "cracking the market was difficult," hence they got out of the business.

Deere advertising prepared an aggressive marketing plan for the 1975 models and promoted the Deere sled line as Big John. This theme was used in advertising and dealer promotion with a record album to support dealer marketing of the Deere machines. The Big John theme on the cover of the album was continued on the record with a song named "Big John." Radio advertising played this theme song in the fall and winter in most of the major snowmobile markets. Other accessory items like belt buckles and suit patches displayed the Big John name.

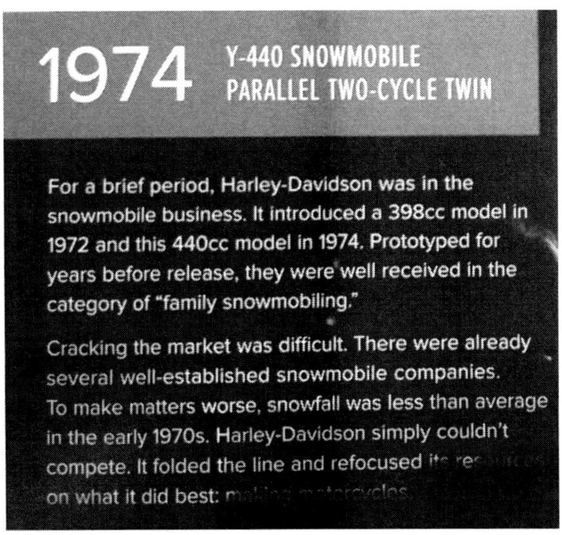

Harley-Davidson snowmobile history (courtesy Diane Gundrum).

In March 1975 the dealer product introduction was held at Cadillac, Michigan. While there, the dealers rode the 1974 models that were soon to be manufactured at Horicon with the upgraded torque converter, improved engine calibration, and revised suspensions. They performed well in the demonstrations, but only received polite acknowledgment, as the dealers wanted to know about the plans for a race sled. The Horicon marketing people could only tell the dealers that Deere planned to have a race sled for the coming race season and they would be advised later when it would be available.

Big John promotional record album sleeve (Ron Leonard collection).

How to Get a Race Sled?

The *second* important decision was to build a new front-engine race sled in 1974 without interfering with the design of the 1976 consumer models. For the 1974–75-race season, the rules set by the cross-country race association allowed a more powerful 340cc engine that would increase the sled's top speed and acceleration. To qualify to be raced in stock classes in the next winter, the WSP I-500 race association ruled the sleds had to be stock-built factory machines with a minimum quantity of 1200 manufactured before October 31, 1974. At Horicon many interpreted this as a deliberate attempt to squeeze Deere out of cross-county racing, since Deere didn't have a front-engine chassis. With more powerful engines and prior sales of front-engine chassis machines, competition would have superior race sleds to anything that Deere could produce in that short time.

This conundrum was resolved in the following way. The race sled chassis was assigned to the Advanced Products Group under the direction of Martin Berk. With limited resources they took a new approach to define the specifications for the sled. John Orvis recommended that Horicon hire race driver Dale Cormican, who twice won the WSP I-500 riding an Arctic Cat, to help Horicon engineering develop the race machine specifications. This was the first major design project for which Horicon contracted professional racers to provide consulting services for the design. Input was obtained as well from all members of the 1974 factory race team. The performance specifications were defined carefully before the detailed design was created. Design engineer Carl Firehammer in the Advanced Products Division was highly motivated by Deere's being in the snowmobile business. After the 1974 WSP I-500, he and Chuck Phelps designed a rough prototype with the engine in front supported by extensions from the tunnel. They theorized that moving the ski spindles as far forward as possible from the track contact point would reduce or eliminate the "hop" that typically occurred

John Orvis working on the front engine prototype (courtesy Ed Kruel).

with the bogie machines when they landed after jumping over obstacles. John Orvis also provided input to this design that did function better in the rough terrain but was still not equal or better than the leading competition.

Successful race drivers Dale Cormican and Roger Jansen were finished with racing that season and came to Horicon to provide recommendations on how to make the prior season's JD 295/S into a front-engine design. Carl and Chuck Phelps designed the prototype front-engine sled that was sent to Hatton, North Dakota, for testing in conditions similar to a cross-country race. They also provided Dale and Roger with Deere components to make a prototype at Dale Cormican's shop in Crookston, Minnesota.

Steve Scholten describes how the first prototype was made at Horicon: "I was the senior engineer and Carl Firehammer and Chuck Phelps were the other full-time engineers on the concept build. Drawing board layouts of different arrangements had been made when Martin gave us the 'challenge' to have a running sled ready to be hauled to Hatton, North Dakota, in six days. We just had to decide what we thought was the best thing to do and get it done quickly. Bud Kenning and Ken Koerner were our two shop build mechanics that made it happen." The prototype 340/S race sled was completed on Saturday in time to be loaded onto the trailer that departed Sunday for field test evaluation at Hatton. The research for this book revealed there were two prototype 340/S sleds tested at Hatton. Dale and Roger made a mockup of what they thought the geometry of the chassis should be. The evaluation took place in snirt — slang for a mixture of dirt and snow that was common in the area where cross-country races were held — and was completed in late March. The field test focused on performance of the sled in cross-country race conditions. After this field evaluation, Roger and Dale brought the machines to Horicon and assisted the engineers to develop the final specifications for the new race snowmobile.

Agreement was reached on the specifications and geometry from the evaluation of the mockup prototypes. Ideas were used from both of the prototypes. EO 777, the 340/S Race Sled, was published on April 26, 1974. The engineering personnel assigned to the project are listed in the EO. The upgraded 340cc Kioritz fan-cooled engine was used to power the JD 340/S. The critical geometry set for the machine included a wider ski stance that enabled the engine to be mounted lower between the skis. New structural parts were designed so the factory could produce them without expensive tooling. The welded assemblies to support the engine and skis were attached to the tunnel that was made from high-volume production tooling. A low-cost tooling approach was chosen for the hood and pan.

The JD 340/S engine featured the fan-cooled 340cc Kioritz prototype that was planned for the 1976 model consumer machines. Lee Hardesty was at Kioritz to develop new fan- and liquid-cooled engines with higher power levels for the 1976 models, as well as the engine for the JD 340/S. It was operated at the highest power level to date for a Deere 340cc displacement fan-cooled engine. Both Lee Hardesty and Dick Teal were involved deeply in developing performance of the JD 340/S.

The redesign and prototype build by PED were completed quickly. The engineers wanted to operate the machine in snow even though the winter was over in most of the traditional areas. Some snow was still available in the Colorado Rockies, so a test trip was planned there. Eddie Kruel and Bobby Hoffman soon left for Colorado with the test sleds on a trailer pulled by the Horicon Works pickup. During an overnight stop at a motel in Colorado, they hung up their jackets in the restaurant near the motel. When they left the restaurant the pickup and trailer with the snowmobiles were gone. Someone had stolen the truck keys from their coat pocket and driven away. Immediately Horicon Works made telephone calls to several legal authorities, and within two days the pickup and trailer with the machines were recovered. The Colorado State Police called to advise Horicon Works where to pick them up so the test program continued. Ed Kruel recalls that their toolboxes were not returned. Unfortunately, Eddie couldn't continue, as he suffered a kidney stone attack and was hospitalized. Another test mechanic flew to Colorado to replace him, so the test program was completed as planned.

With little test time in snow, Horicon engineering then relied heavily on stress and laboratory testing to develop the durability and performance during the summer. Many shortcuts in test procedures were used to accelerate test of the components, and

JOHN DEERE HORICON WORKS

O N F I D E N T I A L   PRODUCT ENGINEERING DEPARTMENT   C O N F I D E N T I A L

ENGINEERING ORDER

): ADVANCED PRODUCTS Division (2)

cc: General Manager
~~Works Manager~~ Mgr, Process & Tool
Manager, Product Engineering
Manager, Factory Marketing
Manager, Reliability
Manager, Product Testing (2)
Manager, Advanced Products
Manager, Product Engineering Services
Book File
Jack Adams

Engineering Order No. 777
Issue Date 26 April 1974
Account No. 57777-77
Project Personnel S. Scholten
J. Orvis
C. Phelps
C. Firehammer
R. Tesch

Approved:
Division Engineer [signature]
Mgr. Engineering [signature]

ritten by: S. C. Scholten Proposed by: Product Engineering Department

roject Title 1975 MODEL RACE SNOWMOBILE (PRODUCTION & WINNIPEG RACE)
xperimental Model No. X777V Drawing Series: X777V-0000
dopted for Production ______ Decision No. ______ Project Closed ______

MAN WEEKS	ESTIMATE	ACTUAL
Engineer(s)	30	
Designer(s)	40	
Draftsmen	10	
Safety (Design)		
Engineering Shop	50	
Stress Analysis	5	
Field Tests	10	

COSTS (Includes Overhead)		@
Salaries & Wages		
Shop Labor *		
Shop Labor, Safety		
Material Cost		
Outside Labor		
TOTAL COSTS		

*Includes Eng. Shop Stress Analysis & Field Test

Project Initiated ______
Scheduled Completion ______
Scheduled Review ______
Completed ______
Dropped ______
(Authorized by: ______)

Previous Review Date	Costs to Date

@Actual Cost provided by Accounting Department

stimate Yearly Sales: 1st 1974 1,000 2nd ______ 3rd ______ 4th ______ 5th ______
roject Dropped because: ______

BJECTIVE: To design, test, and report for production a snowmobile with stock features necessary to qualify for the 1975 Winnipeg to St. Paul race and per USSA & other racing associations.

ROGRAM: This snowmobile will use a modified production tunnel to reduce tooling requirements. Pan and hood will be made from low cost temporary tooling. This machine will have a front mounted engine and wide ski stance for superior handling

.E.D. Form #28
Sept. 1973

340/S product engineering order (courtesy Martin Berk).

the complete machine was operated in dirt at the Horicon test farm. The styling of the 340/S resembled the low profile envisioned by the first HDA concept sketches used in the 1969 Hewitt meeting with R.J. and Jon Carlson that gave approval to enter the business. It was a beautiful snowmobile.

This race sled project enabled the Horicon Works to establish a reasonable schedule for the design, verification and tooling for production of the new front-engine consumer chassis scheduled for production in the summer of 1975. The risk of a shortcut development schedule for the JD 340/S justified the year gained to complete the verification and calibration work for the 1976 models. That design work was ongoing in parallel with the JD 340/S work. Every future product program for Horicon Works benefited from this approach to scheduling.

Production of 1200 of the JD 340/S sleds was completed by the race association deadline of October 31, 1974. The factory build of 1210 machines was the highest annual volume of race machines built at Horicon. The production design was done with some critical assumptions. There was very little money for expensive tooling, as the production assembly was scheduled for October in the EO approved in April 1974. That schedule required all primary parts to be made by the end of September. The Horicon Works had done nothing of this magnitude before in that short amount of time. All of the factory departments were involved with PED to prepare the JD 340/S for the production assembly in October that satisfied the rules of the WSP I-500 race association. The results from racing the JD 340/S are in Chapter 8.

Snowmobile Clutch and Belt Changes

After Dick Teal arrived at Deere in April of 1974, he was assigned the responsibility to design a new torque converter drive system that included both the primary and secondary clutch and the drive belt. Prior to working for Deere, he acquired broad experience doing calibration of the Salsbury torque converter with nearly all the snowmobile manufacturers' drive systems for snowmobiles and other recreation vehicles. The focus of his work was to make each sled perform up to its potential with the Salsbury clutch system matched to the different engines. John Orvis's JD 295/S Winnipeg Saint Paul I-500 race sled was calibrated on the Salsbury chassis dynamometer before Dick began working at Horicon.

John Deere used Salsbury torque converters on the first year 1972 production sleds, and all machines since then. Because of the power growth of engines in the industry, Salsbury upgraded their clutch in 1973 that had good performance, but was not durable in heavily loaded applications. When Dick arrived at Horicon in 1974, Deere had modified all of the prior production sleds with the new Salsbury clutches to upgrade customers' machines so they performed better.

Dick's first assignment at Deere was to correct the failures Deere sleds experienced with the torque converter belt drive system. He became familiar with the tests that Horicon had completed to verify that the new Salsbury clutch system was more durable than the first year's production. His work assignment also included the design of the complete drive system for the 1976 model sleds. His work at Salsbury obviously gave him a keen understanding of the problems; however, he was not constrained to use Salsbury and elected to compare them with the Comet torque converters. Comet was interested in working cooperatively with Deere, as the owner, Steve Huff, had confidence in the capability of Deere design and test engineers. Although the initial need was to correct the issues with the Salsbury clutch, the focus shifted to design an all-new Deere clutch and secondary.

There was little time between model years to develop new components. Dick worked with the test department to build a fixture that replicated field use in the lab. The new test stand had the drive system built into it, which included the engine and torque converter that drove a dynamometer to vary the load. After satisfactory operation was demonstrated on this test stand, the PED made additional fixtures and developed a load curve that replicated field failures of production drive belts and torque converters. These test fixtures ran 24 hours a day until the components were durable enough for production. This work was done jointly with the Horicon design and test engineers. The accelerated testing that correlated with field failures was a major advancement for the development of new drive system components.

Drive system test fixture (courtesy Lee Hardesty).

The drive belt was the first major component that needed to be corrected, as it caused the most customer complaints. Since most machines were still under warranty, the belt failures were the highest-cost service part in the history of the factory. Deere engineers at the Technical Center in Moline had determined that the drive belt would not survive if loaded with more than 50 horsepower. The Kioritz 340cc engine, at 50 hp, and higher-power 440cc engines required the belt to be stronger to transmit the higher power. After close work with the different belt suppliers for many months, the Gates Rubber Company was chosen to supply belts for the Horicon Works snowmobiles. Stronger Kevlar cords replaced the nylon cords that were then used by the industry. In the first belt test samples, the Kevlar cord would not adhere to the rubber, as it just separated from the belt. Gates experimented with various cord bonding agents that were tested at Horicon until one worked. Years later, Gates had to stop using this chemical to treat the cord, so Horicon helped them develop a new solution. The location of the cord in relation to the top of the drive belt was the other key to longer belt life. Gates made test sample belts with the cords in different locations until the optimum place was determined. The drive belt improvements that Dick directed working with the major belt suppliers represented a major advancement in the industry state of the art for belts used to transmit more power at high speeds. It was a successful demonstration of Deere as the OEM, and Gates as the component supplier, working jointly to develop the production belt.

Drive pulley improvements were tested in parallel with the development of the new drive belts. Improvements were needed to control bushing wear of the centrifugal arm, roller-bushing wear, and bushing wear under the movable pulley half and cover bushings. Premature wear of these parts caused machine operation to deteriorate, resulting in belt failures and loss of engine power. At a visit to the Rexnord Company in Milwaukee, Wisconsin, Dick discovered a material they used for low speed/high pressure bearings in jet engines and military applications. After learning about this material, Dick worked with Salsbury and Comet to use it in their torque converters, and Horicon verified the improvement in life of the bushings on the Horicon test fixtures. All of the bushings in the Comet clutch were later changed to Rexnord's PTFE material. Another major cause of wear in the clutch was the high internal temperatures. "Sometimes the obvious solution eludes the designer; Steve Huff, the owner of Comet, pointed out the cause by suggesting removal of the 'tin can' cover. The clutch towers then became fan blades and everything cooled down," Dick Teal said.

The material that supported the movable sheave towers also wore out too quickly. They discovered this was caused by glass-filled nylon fibers wearing the aluminum towers. Duralon was selected to replace nylon; it withstood the high loads without being glass-filled. The result of joint development work with Comet was Comet's model 102C torque converter that is still being used today. The Comet secondary pulley was also improved by changing to better material used for bearings and bushings, but it still wasn't durable enough for a JD machine.

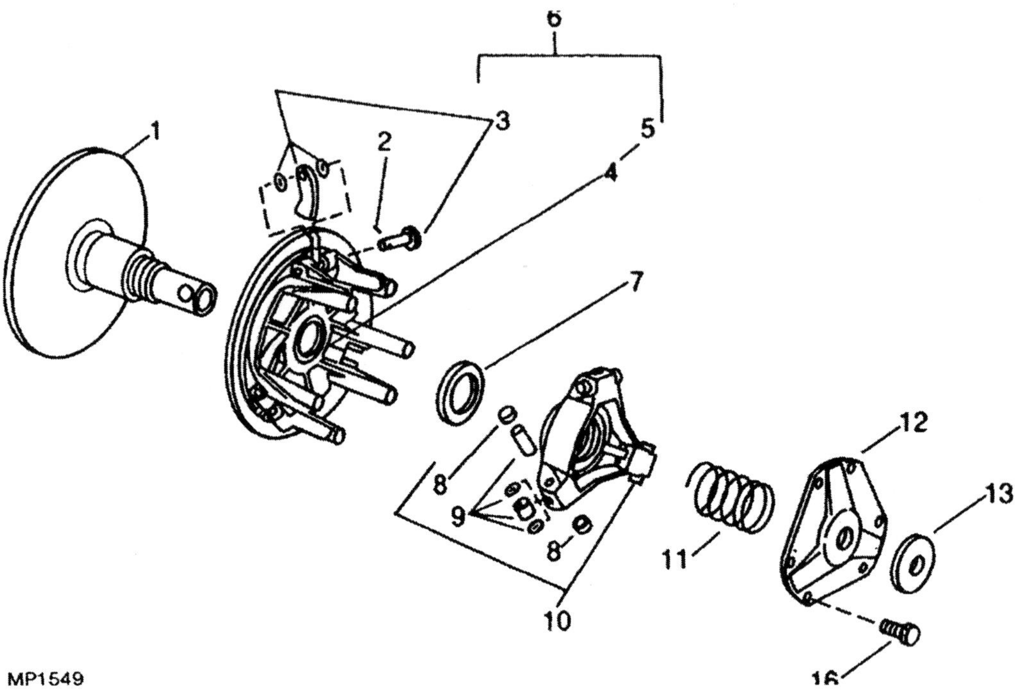

Comet 102C torque converter (courtesy Roger Tesch).

While testing the revised Comet drive system, Dick designed a new Deere secondary pulley and chain case for the 1976 models. Dick recalls that the design for the secondary came to him one night while sleeping and he sketched it the next morning. This isn't unusual, as the mind works on a difficult problem until it is solved. Deere patented the design that was used on all Deere sleds until production ended with the 1984 models. The design was called a reverse secondary pulley because the torque-sensing cam was positioned on the opposite side of the driven pulley. The benefit to the snowmobile was a lower center of gravity and reduced bearing loads on the secondary pulley.

Once the clutch design was approved, the chassis designers changed the location of most engine components to take advantage of these benefits. The 1976 model chassis was committed to use the reverse secondary before the first prototype was made. Horicon Works had no prior experience manufacturing torque converters, so this was a new process for them and it required a significant investment for tooling. The sheaves were designed using 80,000 psi yield strength steel, which is a very strong material and difficult to form with close tolerances. Dynamic balancing was also required for the secondary sheave assembly. The development schedules for snowmobiles were always under time pressure, but this design, testing, and tooling for production of the Deere

***Opposite*: Snowmobile Torque Converter Program (courtesy Jack Hoffman).**

SNOWMOBILE TORQUE CONVERTER PROGRAM

Increased power levels of John Deere snowmobile engines have resulted in a need for torque converter improvements. A general problem with snowmobiles has been performance deterioration with use caused by poor durability of torque converter systems. To solve this problem, the the following design changes and testing systems were made.

Significant improvements have been made to the JD/Comet primary drive sheave. They are:

1. Moveable sheave and cover bearing material changes for improved life.

2. Improved cover bearing mounting

3. Increased spring working length to eliminate spring set

4. Bearings added to rollers for improved roller life

A completely new secondary sheave was designed for the 1976 model year. In addition to improved sheave reliability from the unique double bearing design, the following additional benefits were realized:

1. Increased secondary shaft and secondary shaft bearing life due to positioning the load closer to the bearing

2. Increased secondary shaft bearing life due to the use of larger diameter sheaves which reduces shaft speed

3. Reduced engine mounting height (lower center of gravity) allowable due to offset construction.

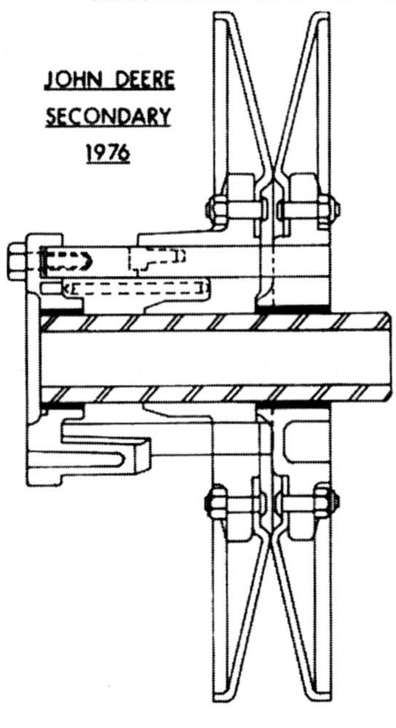

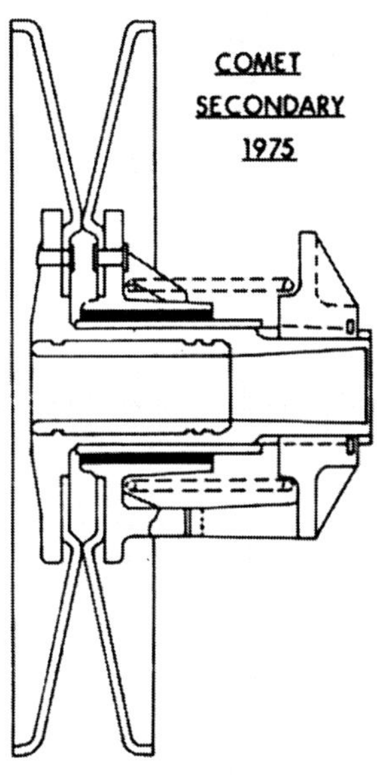

A Horicon Works designed power absorber test system has been a very important tool in torque converter development. Engine power is transfereed through the converter system to an eddy current dynamometer. Engine throttle position and load is programmed to cycle engine speed and the converter ratio. This has been very effective in accelerated testing.

A chassis dynamometer system is used to calibrate the primary and secondary drives to match the characteristics of the engine. This enables duplication of all snow conditions by load variation. Repeatability of testing and the ability to calibrate when snow is not available make this system particularly valuable.

A program just getting underway is the use of a stationary dynamometer to investigate drive efficiencies. This will result in development of force curves for different ratios and torques. The end result will be optimization of efficiency which will result in improved belt and converter life.

FUTURE TORQUE CONVERTER PROGRAMS

A new John Deere primary is being developed to further increase performance and durability. Bearing areas in the roller and arm have been increased over the space limited JD/Comet design. The mass of the arm and cam contour have been separated which gives the ability to calibrate the unit through computer modeling, an approach that is not possible with the present design.

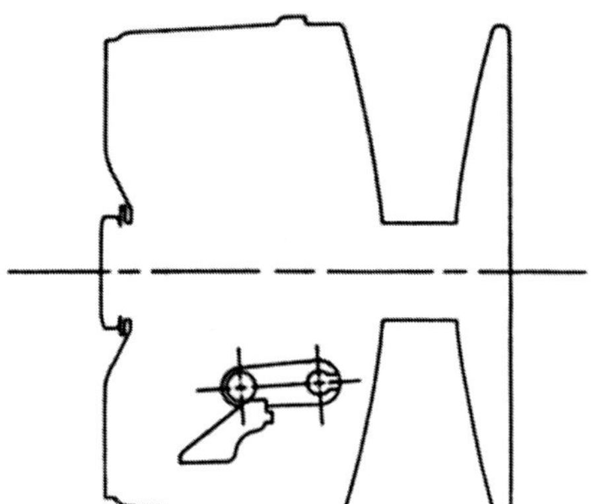

Snowmobile Torque Converter Program (courtesy Jack Hoffman).

torque converter was done in a little more than one year. Focused cooperative work with the right blend of technical skills produced great results in a short period of time.

A new chain case was designed to take advantage of the secondary drive pulley. The final design was in a simple die-cast aluminum case and cover. The cover closed over the case seal that was made from an extruded rubber part. The seal was cut to length on the production line and then was glued together with Super Glue to ensure correct location during assembly. A new link-belt chain that was compatible with powdered metal gears was used in this application. Testing the chain case and the other components for shock loads was accomplished by operating a sled on grass at Horicon when the prototype components became available. The test sleds were jumped over a ramp at high speed, and while airborne the brake was applied. When the sled hit the ground, the resulting shock load tested all of the components for maximum loads.

Another of Dick's projects was to design a new drive pulley to replace the Comet primary clutch. A few drive pulleys of the first design were prototyped but not put into production because the 102C Comet provided suitable life and durability at these power levels. Ken Prasad later redesigned the primary clutch and put it in production for higher horsepower snowmobile models. Horicon Works stopped development of drive systems for JD snowmobiles in late 1976 except for the new drive pulley on a later model Liquifire. Dick was assigned to the mid-priced snowmobile development project that became the 1979 Trailfire. The Comet improvements, with the Deere secondary pulley and chain case assembly, stayed in production until Horicon Works stopped snowmobile production in 1983.

"The enjoyable part of my job was calibrating the torque converters for each model of snowmobile," Dick said. The calibration was done at different elevations because the air density is progressively lower in higher altitudes. With state-of-the-art fixed jet carburetors, the air/fuel ratio needed to be corrected with less fuel at higher altitudes to obtain the proper performance. The calibration work also involved changing the primary clutch centrifugal weights and the secondary spring load to match the available engine power on each model. This required considerable time and repeated runs to optimize the snowmobile performance in the different conditions because the torque available changed continuously as the engine speed increased. Horicon Works PED tested sleds wherever there was snow. Trips included Flin Flon, Manitoba, in Canada; Cantwell, Alaska; West Yellowstone, Montana; Hurley, Wisconsin; the Rocky Mountains; and other locations with race teams as they prepared for races.

The magnitude of the improvements Dick directed and designed quickly may be difficult for readers to appreciate today. Customers who rode snowmobiles in extreme weather conditions or in high-performance situations regularly carried spark plugs, belts, and duct tape along with a tool kit in the glove box on the machine. Riding across a wide frozen lake or on a long country road at night was common. It was not unusual for belts to disintegrate during a high-speed run. OEM companies like Deere often had to help some of their suppliers improve their components, as Dick experienced with belts and torque converters. The test fixtures built by Deere test engineers reduced the development time for belts and clutches. The load cycle data obtained in prior test programs in snow was essential to correlate the laboratory test fixtures with customer usage in all critical operating conditions.

Deere's decision to invest in tooling for the secondary drive sheave was contrary to the initial assumption that the company could buy suitable drive train components from suppliers to reduce investment costs. Nobody had forecasted the rate of power growth of snowmobile engines when Deere entered the business. None of the suppliers were interested in manufacturing the unique Horicon design, as most of them maintained that the other manufacturers were not having these problems. Yet there were companies like Gates Rubber Company and Comet Industries who welcomed the work with Deere to develop improved components. Deere marketed this clutch by advertising it as an exclusive component in John Deere snowmobiles. The newly designed secondary was used on the entire line of 1976 model Cyclone, Liquifire and Liquidator sleds, and on every front-engine snowmobile made after that at Horicon. Marketable Deere snowmobiles needed to live up to the durability reputation expected for all Deere machines. Certainly they needed to perform their intended function for all major segments of the market. With significant improvements in belt life and more durable primary and secondary clutch, along with improved engine design, the Horicon Works was in a leadership position with snowmobile drive system components in the industry. However, it took the JD 340/S race sled and the 1976 consumer models to provide a front-engine chassis that was long overdue for the high-performance segment of the market.

In the early years of snowmobiles, much of Lee Hardesty's work was done in engineering test labs in Japan. His first project was the 295cc engine for the JD 295/S race machine. The quest in each new race engine was for the most power and performance in a given displacement. People have always learned from what others have done and devised new ways to perform the same operation or task better. That sounds too simple. To accomplish that, the person must be capable of understanding why things work as they do and apply reason and intuition to visualize how to improve that which has been demonstrated by others. Likewise the engineer must understand the operating environment where the machine will be used. Lee quickly made the transition from high-horsepower diesel tractor engines to light-weight, small-displacement 2-cycle engines in snowmobiles. These skills were later applied to all the engine-powered products made at Horicon. During the summer of 1974 Lee worked in Japan with Kioritz to develop the performance of the 340 and 440cc liquid-cooled engines for the 1976 models. After the 1975 WSP I-500 race, the decision was made to convert some of the JD 340/S race sleds to prototype liquid-cooled engines that were being developed for the next year's race sled. Some of the race team ran those engines in the modified stock classes the rest of the year. The development of the new liquid-cooled engines was accelerated with race team drivers operating them in extremely high load conditions. The success of the JD 340/S, combined with positive results from testing the new

340/S prototype liquid-cooled engine (Richard Teal collection).

front-engine experimental machines, helped rekindle enthusiasm for the forthcoming 1976 models.

The Horicon Works Loses Money

For the first time in its history, the Horicon Works lost money in fiscal 1974. (Deere fiscal year was from November 1 until October 31.) The increased costs at the factory were higher than budgeted due to engineering costs accrued at PEC and the Horicon

1976 liquid-cooled 340/440 Kioritz engine (courtesy Lee Hardesty).

Works. Investments for tooling, new buildings, and more employees contributed to the higher factory costs. In 1974 the profit margins disappeared entirely with the high cost of all PIP modifications billed to the factory. Lower sales than forecast reduced production schedules, and that lowered the income available to cover the higher costs. Part of the higher costs in engineering and the factory were for the investments for both the new model snowmobiles and the 1975 new model lawn and garden tractors. The garden tractors were redesigned to relocate the fuel tank from under the tractor hood to the back of the tractor to eliminate a potential fire hazard. The tractors were restyled as part of the effort to meet lower sound levels. Just as with snowmobiles, the lower sound levels increased the cost for some of the new parts and consumed engineering time for design and development.

Another burden for the Horicon Works was the excess cost to relocate the primary parts manufacturing into a new facility about one mile west of town. It was expected that investment costs for the new building would be recovered with future cost reduction as the factory operations became more efficient. The new building was equipped with larger presses and other new manufacturing equipment. However, until the higher volume production occurred, the period overhead cost had to be absorbed by the current production. The operating loss at Horicon increased the criticism by some Deere executives about the snowmobile business, and Horicon Works' operations were audited frequently. Several management changes were made in the factory manager's staff, and the PED was challenged to operate with fewer resources to further reduce the total cost to operate the Horicon factory. It was easy to engage in finger-pointing and blame snowmobiles for the financial plight. Although this criticism might have deterred others, R.J.'s support didn't waver. He was determined to build the independent consumer products marketing and manufacturing division for Deere. He had confidence in the direction the Horicon factory was heading with the 1976 model snowmobiles and new garden tractors. The JD 340/S success in 1974–75 racing, along with the planned 1976 models of front-engine chassis machines, reinforced his confidence in the future Deere consumer products business. The new dealers were more productive and had acquired considerable experience with the way Deere did business in reaching back to modify the first two years of customer sleds.

Expenses for product development and factory investments for new products always occur before sales. Due to the front-end expenses, the ROI calculation for new products usually shows a negative return on investment in the first years of sales. It takes time to get a positive return on the investment. Also it is expected that a factory will have extraordinary expenses the first year of new model production. However, the higher startup costs should be offset in later years as the schedule increases and the factory learns how to produce more efficiently. With snowmobiles there was never a next year. The models and designs kept changing too often for the factory to become more efficient. Sales never reached the planned volumes that were established in the initial meeting that authorized the factory to manufacture snowmobiles. The 1976 model program needed to be successful to validate the new approach to design and tool new products in a disciplined time schedule. To remain in the business, Deere had to have a competitive front engine snowmobile.

During this period the Deere agricultural business was booming. In North America, farm sizes were increasing, and Deere was building higher hp tractors and other machines that were profitable. In 1974 the Fortune 500 data show the Deere & Co. sales topped $2 billion for the first time. Sales continued to set new records with $2.495 billion in 1975 and $2.955 billion in 1976, a sales increase of nearly 50 percent in three years. The company also set new record profits. It was not a good time for Horicon to lose money when the other agricultural units were setting record sales and profits. It seemed like the future of Horicon Works was wedged in a financial vise. To secure Moline management approval for investment capital for new products required approval by a senior management committee in Moline. The Horicon Authority for Expenditure (AFE) for the 1976 model snowmobiles was approved in late 1974, even though the factory had lost money that year. The 1975 fiscal year (November 1, 1974, to October 31 1975) forecast was for marginal profitability at Horicon Works. By mid-year 1974, due to high dealer inventory of unsold snowmobiles and lower dealer estimates for new models, the snowmobile production was reduced to 18,433 machines as improved 1975 models. It was clear that the factory would lose money again in 1975 operations. This was like a lightning strike that set off a firestorm of criticism for approving more investment capital for Horicon. All Horicon factory departments were required to reduce staff and cut expenditures to return to profitability in 1976. The PED could finish the testing and release the new 1976 snowmobile models for production, but was required to reduce staff and cut development costs.

This was not a negative for the engineering department. It was important that PED contribute to the effort for the factory to become profitable. By this time the factory was breaking down some of the past heritage of rigid departmental lines by doing design and manufacturing work concurrently. One of the immediate benefits of the new engineering facility was that the purchasing department staff was located in the same building. With the high purchased-part content, it was much easier to involve the Horicon buyers and suppliers in the design at the earliest possible time. Recall that in those years business was done by mail, phone, fax and personal visits; only accounting was supported with a mainframe computer.

1976 JD Liquidator race sled (courtesy Roger Tesch).

1976 Cyclone, Liquifire and Liquidator

Horicon continued with its plan to manufacture and market the new 1976 consumer snowmobiles. The consumer sled chassis for the new front-engine machines was designed to accept both the fan- and liquid-cooled engines. Another key decision for 1976, as in the prior year with the JD 340/S, was how to provide a race machine. Due to strict orders to reduce capital expenditures for snowmobiles, it was decided to make the next season's race machine, later named the Liquidator, on the 1976 model consumer sled chassis. By doing this, the factory cost was less than the cost to redesign and tool a revised JD 340/S chassis for the liquid-cooled engine. However, the Liquidator did require changes from the planned consumer sleds because to be competitive it required a more powerful engine.

The 1976 consumer machines were two models each of three families of snowmobiles: Green Machines JD 300 and 400; two Cyclone models with 340 and 440cc fan-cooled engines, and two Liquifire models with 340 and 440cc liquid-cooled engines. The new snowmobiles featured all-new drive systems with a new front-engine chassis, and a new slide-rail suspension.

After four years the factory had produced 94,103 snowmobiles. Many competitors were dropping out of the business. At Horicon, hopes were high that the new line of front-engine 1976 models would put Deere in a stronger position in the market. The new models had features the market demanded for snowmobiles. These machines, along with the new and more powerful Liquidator for racing, provided Deere with a snowmobile product for all market segments, from the bogie machine to the high-performance market. A new race team, named Enduro Team Deere, was formed during the summer of 1975. Chapter 8 covers all JD race teams and results with their race sleds. The 1976 consumer sled production of a mixture of mid-engine chassis and new front-engine snowmobiles and the market reaction to them continues in Chapter 7.

7

Front-Engine Chassis Snowmobiles

In March 1975, as Horicon Works prepared to manufacture the all-new Cyclone and Liquifire snowmobiles, the dealer introduction was held in West Yellowstone. A full dress ride and drive was staged at the park headquarters located at the west gate of Yellowstone National Park. The lodge atmosphere was appropriate for the product introduction with the surrounding snow-covered mountains and a wide street in town that led directly into the park that was buried under several feet of snow. Deere & Co. marketing realized that their dealers had weathered some tough market conditions that deserved more than the normal gathering somewhere in the Midwest, as had been done for the first four years in the business. The dealers attended in smaller groups to accommodate the limited space for lodging, indoor meetings, and fifty sleds to ride. The feature event was the ride and drive that gave the dealers firsthand experience with the new, more powerful front-engine chassis sleds. Horicon Works had manufactured a small quantity of pilot-built sleds to verify that the production processes were correct before high volume production. While the dealer meetings were ongoing, back at Horicon the factory modified production processes to produce quality parts before assembly of the production sleds scheduled in May.

The success of the JD 340/S race sled accelerated dealer expectations for the next selling season. The long wait for new snowmobiles was over after a tough winter selling the current line of mid-engine chassis sleds in most of the markets. The power and performance of the new Cyclone and Liquifire snowmobiles were demonstrated as dealers rode them in different snow conditions during the meeting. The Cyclones were powered with the redesigned Kioritz fan-cooled 340 and 440cc engines, and the Liquifire demonstrated superior acceleration and top speed with the all-new liquid-cooled engines. The Green Machine line of bogie sleds was reconfigured with two models: the 295cc Kohler piston-ported engine in the JD 300, and a 340cc Kioritz engine powered JD 400. All 1976 front-engine model sleds featured the new Deere-manufactured torque converter. The front-engine chassis Cyclone and Liquifire had more power than previous models and the best drive train in the industry. The wider ski spacing of 32 inches, combined with the lower center of gravity, improved the stability. All of the new drive system components passed rigorous laboratory and field tests with flying colors.

Dealer enthusiasm was high after this meeting, and their orders poured into the

snow goer test report

Everything's perfect but the price.

John Deere Liquifire 440

John Deere's liquid-cooled Liquifire 440 is designed for the dedicated enthusiast who is willing to pay the price. That price is $2295. But, liquid-cooling is only half of the Liquifire story. Advanced engineering, outstanding performance, and solid construction comprise the other half. A precision handling, fast and quiet sled, the Liquifire is a top flight sled that meets every major snowmobiling criteria.

John Deere has always produced a better than average snowmobile, even at the beginning in 1971. The company even had a more than fair performer in its JDX series of mid-engined, slide rail sports sleds. But, this year, watch out. Deere has joined the battle in the high performance snowmobile market. Just to prove it they have taken the best features of their cross country

John Deere 440 Liquifire *Snow Goer* test report (courtesy *Snow Goer* magazine).

racing line have always been fan-cooled machines. Couldn't the sound levels be cut on conventionally cooled engines? The answer is yes, and the Deere Cyclone is a prime example. It corresponds closely to the Liquifire in suspension, looks, and mechanics, except for the engine. The Cyclone uses a fan-cooled Kioritz engine that registered 78.5 decibels at SNOW GOER's sound tests while the Liquifire measured 77.3 db(A). Both sleds meet the 78 db(A) limit set for this season. The difference lies in the future.

A John Deere spokesman stated that because of the downward trend in decibel levels over the past few years, and because the future may hold decibel levels below the 78 db(A) mark, liquid-cooling may well be the only viable option in the future. In the case of two identically powered snowmobile engines—each with the same exhaust, silencing intake and underhood paraphernalia—a liquid-cooled engine would be about 3 decibels quieter than a fan-cooled engine. Noise reduction comes primarily from water jackets insulating the engine's mechanical noise. Other advantages of liquid-cooling are: consistent engine temperatures as opposed to the power drop frequently seen in a free-air or fan-cooled machine; closer engine tolerances; cooler underhood temperatures that means prolonged life of underhood components; and, the fact that liquid-cooled engines do not require the sophisticated air intake systems that the fan-cooled and free-air engines need.

Liquid-cooling is not all pluses. There is the disadvantage of increased weight for the cooling devices. While the John Deere/Kioritz liquid-cooled engine weighs within a pound of the Cyclone's fan-cooled unit, the five quarts of coolant, tunnel mounted heat exchangers and necessary plumbing add up to over 20 pounds difference in the two snowmobiles. SNOW GOER tests showed the Liquifire weighing in at 505-lbs wet, whereas the Cyclone came in at 482-lbs. Then there is the cost factor. A liquid-cooled engine with its attendant heat exchangers, etc., will cost more than a fan-cooled engine. The difference in price between a 440cc Cyclone, $1995, and a Liquifire 440 is around $300.

With three liquid-cooled snowmobiles at the SNOW GOER spring tests it became evident that there was more than one way to cool the engine. Rupp, which has introduced a liquid-cooled Nitro, has chosen a radiator mounted in the console area. Massey's Cyclone, nee Brut, and the Deere Liquifire both use heat exchangers. Massey's are located at the rear on the side of the chassis and the Liquifire's are mounted in the tunnel under the seat.

Deere engineers admit that the radiator concept gives a weight advantage, but stated that they found problems when trying to trail ride. Radiators, said Deere spokesmen, must have a good airflow. If you are trail riding in dense woods at low speeds and with virtually no frontal airflow, the system tends to overheat. With the heat exchangers mounted in the tunnel so that the track can throw up snow and water the heat exchangers can be kept cool under almost all conditions. Presumably, if there is enough snow to lubricate the slide rails, there is enough snow to cool the heat exchangers. Plus, the track draws some air over the exchangers by acting like a giant fan. In marginal conditions like ice or extreme hardpack, cooling and slide lubrication could be a problem.

Deere designers studied the problems and decided that the underseat heat exchangers provided the best solution from a cost/efficiency standpoint. Mounted in the tunnel and protruding beyond the chassis skin, the aluminum heat exchangers have a ¾-inch rippled surface that would protect the coolant carrier should a grouser bar break loose. Even if an exchanger were damaged, replacement is relatively simple. It's a matter of draining the system, removing the seat, cutting out the pop rivet holders and putting in a new exchanger. Deere's engineers don't envision any such problems due to the proven durability of the track and the exchanger material.

Aside from the liquid-cooling, heat exchangers and 5-quarts of 50-50 antifreeze to water mix, the Kioritz-built engine is similar to other John Deere/Kioritz designs. It is a reed valve engine with basically the same crankcase and main bearing capacity as used on past Deere sleds. The upper parts of the unit—cylinders, heads—are new. CD ignition is used for the first time on this consumer sled, but had been first proven on both the 295/S and the 340/S racers. The block is aluminum with a cast iron liner. Internal breathing comes from the five port design of 4 transfers and a simple booster.

Since SNOW GOER tests, Deere engineers have revamped the exhaust system, which was the same as on the Cyclone 440. Retuned to deliver peak power at 7250 rpm, a Deere spokesman stated that the production Liquifires should be about 4-5 mph faster at the same altitude than SNOW GOER's test sled.

While racers familiar with Deere's cross country machines will recognize the similarity between the Liquifire's drive and the JD 340/S, the average consumer won't. The basic configuration looks similar to the racing sleds. The primary drive clutch is a variation of the John Deere/Comet design found in the 340/S, using improvements in bushing materials but with weights and springs calibrated for the Liquifire. The secondary clutch is another story.

Designed, developed and built by Deere, the driven unit has the cam spring and bearing mounted on the outside with the moveable face next to the tunnel. The normal cam/spring arrangement has to be attached to the moveable face. On the Deere second-

Wide stanced Liquifire shows its racing heritage.

Secondary driven pulley pushes in for ease of belt replacement.

Highly styled chaincase contains disc brake mounting.

ary there are three pins that connect the mechanism on the outside to the moveable face. This means that the secondary shaft can be moved down lower in the body for a lower center of gravity. It also means that to change drivebelts, just rotate the face inward and slip the belt off. It takes about five seconds.

Power is transmitted across a jack shaft. Used to gain a low center of gravity, the jackshaft also gives a good bearing spread. With the chaincase on the same side as the clutches, there is a problem achieving good bearing support, especially in the higher horsepower sleds. Deere circumvents the problem by having one bearing located next to the secondary drive and the other placed 18-inches away inside the chaincase.

For the first time John Deere uses a disc brake on its consumer snowmobiles. While the external band brake used on the JDX was above average, the mechanical disc adapts better to the cross shaft concept. The 7½-inch disc is mounted integrally with the new die-cast aluminum chaincase. At high speeds the disc pumps air out of the compartment, like a venting fan.

And it's high speeds that the Liquifire really comes into its own. We did things with the Liquifire that would make a psychiatrist question our mental stability. But, there was never a question about the Deere's mechanical stability. It combines weight, length, and horsepower to form close to the ultimate in high speed handling. Tilt tests showed the Deere Liquifire could reach 44.5 degrees to the left and 40.5 degrees to the right before going all the way over. Believe it. SNOW GOER staffers blasted the Liquifire off steep banks, down sharp grades, up moguled trails, around tree-lined bends, hammered the throttle and white knuckled

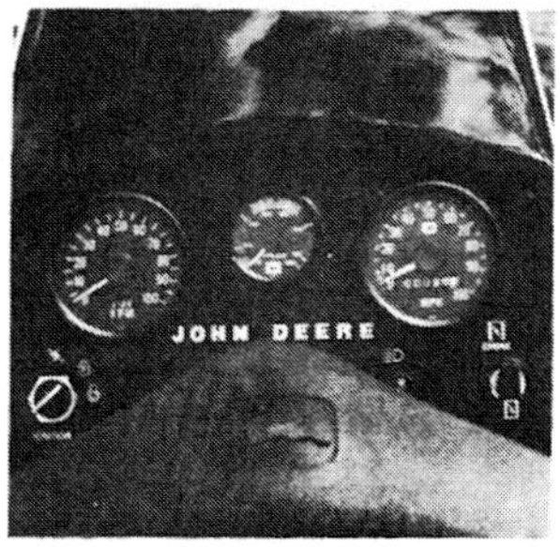

Liquifire's complete set of gauges includes a heat gauge with color coded danger levels.

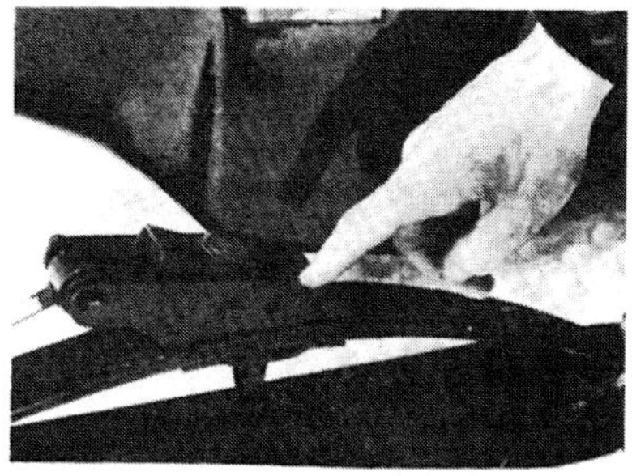

Two ski positions let the rider choose between high speed stability and quick turning radius.

Twin-carbed, liquid-cooled engine sits low and forward in the engine compartment.

the brake until they couldn't take any more. When hammering down the Tiger Run torture trail, where one minor indiscretion would have meant a sudden confrontation with the forests, the Deere never faltered.

It has to be one of the best feelings in testing snowmobiles to know that, like a jockey aboard a thoroughbred, you and the machine are in total harmony. Part of the reason for such confidence comes from the suspension and the firm, positive seat.

The Liquifire follows the 340/S design closely in both chassis geometry and suspension. A modified version of the JDX slide rail suspension, the Liquifire uses different spring rates and valving in the single tube shock. Chassis geometry is the same as the 340/S as far as ski stance (center to center distance of 32-inches), spindle angles, track length and location. One of the changes that resulted from the cross country racing program was the Liquifire's two position ski mounting. In the rear mounting position, the sled turns easily at low to moderate speeds but only supplies average high speed stability. When the shock assisted ski is mounted in the forward most position, the sled steers harder in moderate trailriding, but tends to self-center at the higher speeds. Which means you don't have to fight the skis to straighten out of a turn. Another change is the steering linkage which provides a shorter and smaller turning radius, and also lessens steering effort.

John Deere dealers will be sounding like auto salesmen this year when describing the Liquifire's wheelbase. To give you a slight edge in the dealer's shop you should know that "wheelbase" is the measured distance between the ski spindle and the center of the rear idler. While the term may sound like a salesman's pitch, listen carefully, that extra 7-inches of wheelbase the Liquifire offers over last year's JDX makes quite a difference. The smoother ride that a long chassis Cadillac gives over a shorter import is the difference between the Liquifire ride and the old mid-engined Deere sleds.

When discussing ride you have to consider the effect of the Liquifire's weight. At 505 lbs. loaded with 8 gallons of fuel, the Deere is no lightweight. The past consensus has been that such a sled, any sled, has to be bulky and unmanageable. That used to be our opinion, too. Not any more. SNOW GOER's test sled used its weight to advantage by having it designed between the wheelbase low enough and spread out enough so as to positively influence handling. With drivetrain weight behind the ski centerline and low, the skis carve turns and the tail follows. Sure, you can break the tail out, but the steering is quick enough to catch it and help you around a tricky turn. Over the roughest trails the weight helps keep the sled in contact with the snow. It doesn't jounce your insides outside. To paraphrase an old auto racing adage, a good little snowmobile will beat a bad big sled, but a good big snowmobile will beat a good little sled. The Liquifire is a good big sled.

Mechanically the Liquifire is a liquid-cooled, low slung, slide rail dampened, heavy snowmobile.

Subjectively, the Liquifire is one of the best engineering designs that we've seen in quite a few years. Everything that should be a detriment isn't. On the scale it's heavy. On the trail it's light, responsive and, oh, so steady. It's got all the attributes of a professional football runningback. It's quick off the mark, hits the gap with authority, runs strongly in the open field, can stop quickly and change direction, and, most importantly, can score points against all comers. That's the charm of the Liquifire, it can do it all.

JOHN DEERE LIQUIFIRE 440

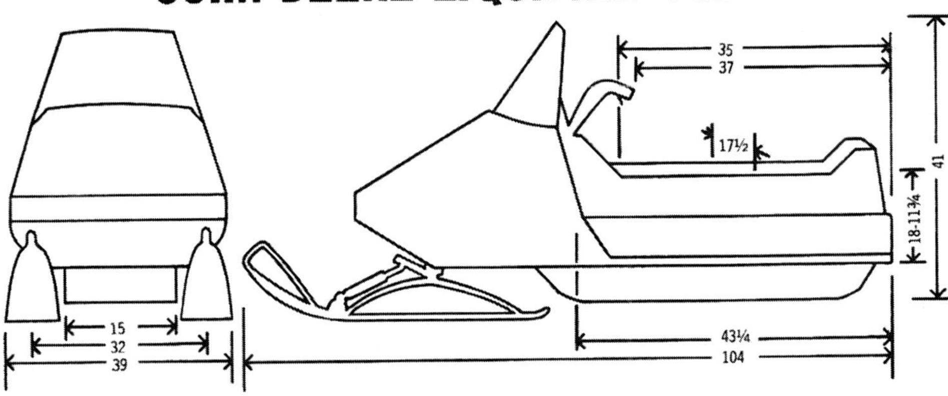

Manufacturer: John Deere, Horicon, Wisconsin.
Suggested Price: $2295.

SPECIFICATIONS

Engine: Liquid-cooled, Kioritz twin, 438cc.
Bore/Stroke: 66mm/60mm.
Compression Ratio: NA
Carburetor: Twin VM34 Mikuni.
Clutch: John Deere/Comet primary; John Deere secondary.
Chassis: Aluminum.
Suspension: John Deere slide rail.
Brake: John Deere 7½-in. mechanical disc.
Dimensions: 104-in. long x 39-in. wide x 41-in. high.
Weight: Wet, 505 lbs. Dry, 454.6 lbs.
Track: Three rubber bands with molded in grousers and rubber cleats. 15-in. wide.
Ignition: CD standard.
Instruments: Speedometer, odometer, tachometer, temperature gauge.
Fuel Tank: 8 gallon, chassis mounted.

PERFORMANCE

Location: Tiger Run, Colorado
Test Conditions: 5 foot base, Spring Snow
Altitude: 10,000 feet.
Top Speed At One-Fourth Mile, mph: 70.
Acceleration ⅛-mile, seconds: 11.2.
Acceleration ¼-mile, seconds: 18.0.
Delivered hp: 20.5 at 32 mph.
Overturn Angle Left, degrees: 44.5.
Overturn Angle Right, degrees: 40.5.
Noise at 50 ft., db(A): 77.3.
Gasoline Economy, mpg: 22.3.

Birth

(Continued)

silver with black trim.

In November, 1974, Deere engineers took the proposed design to company headquarters in Moline, Ill.

While most of the people evaluating the new design agreed that it was attractive, some dissenters felt that it lacked a "certain something."

Unceremoniously, Bill Hewett, chairman of the board, wandered into the meeting room, listened to some of the discussion, and finally remarked casually that he would think that a snowmobile's dominant color should contrast with the snow instead of blending in with it.

Thus, a silver machine with black trim suddenly becomes a black machine with silver trim. The Deere engineers liked it. HDS designers bought it. And Hewett loved it.

The new Liquifire snowmobile for 1976 would have basically the same configuration as the 340S cross country racing machine of 1975 with a dominant color of black and accented by silver trim.

Meanwhile, the components and engineering of the Liquifire were still undergoing rigorous tests throughout the fall and winter.

These tests dictated a number of mechanical changes to improve the machine. The steering required too much effort and would not turn sharply enough according to Deere test riders.

A new steering linkage system was engineered. The test riders also reported on excessive engine movement and vibration. The problem was discovered to be centered in the engine mounting. A Deere computer went to work on this one with the engineers to help redesign the spring located between the primary and secondary drive sheave. Problem solved: very late in the game, too, according to Hoffman.

After ten or twelve meetings between Deere engineers and Dreyfuss designers and more than six months of testing, the 1976 Liquifire was ready to go into production. It was by now, the spring of 1975. Deere officials felt the graphics and shape of the new snowmobile were "sharp without being gaudy," according to Hoffman. And the engineers felt the new snowmobile was sound in its mechanics.

And the machine's color did indeed contrast with the snow.

John Deere 440 Liquifire *Snow Goer* test report (courtesy *Snow Goer* magazine).

factory as assembly began in May 1975 of 34,368 machines, almost equal to the highest production in 1972 of 36,990 1973 models. All departments in Horicon worked diligently to prepare the factory to produce not only a well-engineered and tested sled, but also to reach a new high in the quality of the machine as shipped from the factory. Suppliers also worked closely with Horicon to produce high-quality components. Deere's most aggressive advertising campaign in the key markets in North America supported dealer sales efforts. The advertising slogan "Nothing Runs Like a Deere"™ was continued as part of the advertising campaign. As was customary in the industry, *Snow Goer* magazine reviewed all of the manufacturers' new models prior to the next selling season and was very complementary in their reviews of the Cyclone and Liquifire sleds.

Snow Goer *Test Accident*

Jack Hoffman and Dick Teal experienced an unfortunate life-threatening accident with *Snow Goer* Associate Editor Jerry Basset when they hosted him to ride and drive the new machines for hands-on experience to better prepare him to write coverage for the magazine. This was a familiar assignment for Jerry, as most manufacturers were asked to participate in similar venues to experience riding the new consumer sleds for the upcoming season. Besides riding the new model snowmobiles, this gave *Snow Goer* excellent photos for their magazine articles. The Horicon Works PED provided the new Cyclone and Liquifire machines.

"I was asked to accompany my boss Jack Hoffman on the *Snow Goer* magazine ride and drive of the 1976 Cyclone and Liquifire John Deere snowmobiles. We met Jerry at the Keystone, Colorado, Ski Lodge in the fall of 1975 that was owned by the Ralston Purina Company," Dick Teal said. Keystone is located west of Denver in the Rocky Mountains. Jerry was very interested in the new Liquifire, John Deere's first water-cooled engine, which was getting a lot of publicity. He asked for a ride back into the mountains to see how the new sleds performed. When they left the lodge, Jerry was riding the 440 Liquifire, Dick was on a 440 Cyclone and Jack was riding the 340 Liquifire. They went racing up the mountain trails with Jerry in the lead on the fastest machine. They stopped a few times and discussed the sleds but Jerry wanted to ride further and go WOT (wide open throttle). "There was an open meadow a few miles up the mountain that Jack and I had been to before. After reaching it we were about three quarters across the meadow going WOT when a deep crevasse loomed directly in our path. There was no way to cross it other than going to the left. Unfortunately the crevasse was difficult to see in the white field of snow, especially at the speed we were traveling. We were too far behind Jerry and he wasn't looking back," Dick said. "Jerry's sled went airborne and almost made it across the crevasse. The skis jammed into the far side bank and the sled stopped almost instantly. I still have a vivid vision of Jerry going over the handlebars. As he was being thrown off both of his snowmobile boots went pin-wheeling through the air."

Dick and Jack raced around the end of the crevasse and got to Jerry within a minute or two. He was lying in the snow and was not then awake. When he finally came around he was in severe pain that appeared to be from a broken leg, and he was going into shock. Jack stayed with Jerry and provided whatever comfort he could while Dick went for help. There were no cell phones then so Dick rode as fast as possible, but the trip down the mountain to the lodge required about 25 minutes and there he notified the ski patrol and requested their help. An ambulance was called to meet them at the trail crossing on the road at the bottom of the mountain after they retrieved Jerry. Dick and the ski patrol arrived back at the meadow with a toboggan, an air splint and someone to put the splint on his leg. "I'm not sure about the total time I was gone but it had to be over an hour. We were fortunate that the temperature wasn't below zero. There was no way Jerry was going to move without help," Dick said. After the splint was put on his leg, Jerry was moved to the toboggan and Dick pulled him down the mountain. "The trip down took a long time and Jerry felt every bump. He cussed me out all the way down to the ambulance." Dick recalled a footnote to this harrowing experience: "About 15 or 16 years later I was at West Yellowstone, Montana, with a few John Deere employees on a snowmobile vacation. We were coming back from a trip to the Idaho Mountains and ran into a *Snow Goer* magazine test for the coming year. We talked about the accident and they said that it was a legend in their company." All ended well as Jerry recovered and even wrote about the incident.

The 1976 model machines did live up to the high expectations that had been generated at the dealer introduction. However, Murphy's Law *(continued on page 115)*

New John Deere snowmobiles (courtesy Pat Geddes).

JD snowmobile clothing, circa 1972 (Bob Strassmann).

C2

John Deere 1972 model 400 and 500 snowmobiles (courtesy Roger Tesch).

1973 JDX8 snowmobile (courtesy Roger Tesch).

John Orvis's 1973 I-500 race sled (Richard Teal collection).

1973 JDX8 (courtesy Roger Tesch).

1976 JD consumer snowmobile line (courtesy Bob Strassmann).

1976 John Deere snowmobile models (Richard Teal collection).

Opposite: 1978 Cyclone, Spitfire, and Liquifire (courtesy Roger Tesch).

John Deere 440 Liquifire, as shown in a ***Snow Goer*** test report (courtesy ***Snow Goer*** magazine).

1980 Trailfire (courtesy Roger Tesch).

1980 Trailfire (courtesy Roger Tesch).

1981 Spitfire (courtesy Roger Tesch).

1981 New Breed of Deere models (courtesy Roger Tesch).

1982 Liquifire (courtesy Roger Tesch).

1982 Sprintfire (courtesy Roger Tesch).

was alive and delivered a direct hit to the market. This was another year of sparse snowfall all across the upper Midwest and New England. Gerry Buelow kept track of the average snowfall each season, and this winter it moved 300 miles north. Consequently customers did not buy as many machines, and most dealers were forced to carry over a significant inventory of the new Cyclones and Liquifires to the next season.

In 1975, for the second year in a row, the Horicon factory operations lost money, and most fingers pointed to the snowmobile business as the culprit. Significant restructuring of the industry occurred as smaller companies continued to quit the business and others were in financial difficulty. The Horicon factory was directed to scale back their total costs so that the coming 1976 fiscal year would be profitable. The factory schedule was reduced to 14,661 of the 1977 models, a dramatic reduction from the robust 34,368 the prior year. Dealers had to sell their field inventory carryover that had resulted from the low snowfall.

The same model lineup of Cyclones and Liquifires were produced as 1977 models without a new race sled. The Liquidator was judged to be capable of performing with the best machines in the industry again, and it did, virtually dominating the cross-country races in 1977. The JD 300 was discontinued for the 1977 model year. It was a failed attempt to provide a simple low-cost sled made from the same chassis as the bogie machines with lower specification parts and some components. These changes did not reduce the cost enough to encourage the market to buy it compared to a JD 400 or 500. From this time forward the Horicon PED shifted their focus to design lower-cost machines. Two significant experiences occurred in 1976 that were to have a positive influence on the future direction of snowmobile design at Horicon Works.

Snowbound in Park Rapids Produced a Breakthrough in Design Concept

One Saturday morning in January 1976, Dick Teal, Tom Lohr and Ron Leonard departed the Dodge County, Wisconsin, airport on the Deere Citation business jet for a two-hour flight to Park Rapids, where they expected to see the Liquidator in an ICCSF snowmobile race. It started to snow soon after takeoff, but the flight was uneventful until they were on a long hold over Park Rapids. Larry and Jerry, the pilots, were very experienced flying in the Midwest winter conditions. Ultimately the plane was directed to Fargo, as the weather conditions were better there. However, by the time the plane got to Fargo, the weather there had worsened. The terminal reported the winds were so high that the blowing snow blinded the runway, but the snowfall had stopped. The pilots soon calculated the plane was getting too low on fuel to make the alternate airport at Cheyenne, Wyoming, where the weather was clear. After another hold, Ron had a brief conversation with the pilots on the situation. Jerry stated they would continue to hold and hope for a break in the blizzard before they had to divert to Cheyenne. Until we wrote this book, Dick had never heard the interesting exchange that Ron had when he and the pilots discussed where to land. They asked Ron what he would like to do. He answered that, since the pilots had as big a stake in the decision as the passengers, they should do the right thing. Shortly after that the Fargo terminal advised it was clear above the runway but cautioned that when the descent got to about 50 feet they would lose visibility. One of the pilots looked back to Ron and said, "We're going for it."

Dick recalls that landing:

> I noticed that it was snowing heavily. We kept going down and down for what seemed forever. Prior to working for Deere I had flown multiple times each week so I wasn't a stranger to bad weather landings. This was something else and I was getting uncomfortable. We finally touched down and were on the runway. The plane stopped and I didn't like that we hadn't turned onto a taxiway. It was blowing so hard that I could only catch a few views of the airport buildings and there seemed to be about 8 to 12 inches of snow on the runway. Finally I saw a flashing yellow light in front of the plane. A pickup truck was sent to lead us off the runway to the terminal but the plane got stuck in a snowdrift before we got there. When we got off of the plane I asked one of the pilots why they had landed. He said, "You wanted to go to the races and we got you there."

With the plane stuck in a snowdrift short of the terminal, pilots and the passengers walked through the deep snow to the terminal building. One of the pilots who had grown up in Wyoming never wore socks. He walked to the terminal through the snowdrifts with his low-cut shoes full of snow.

The Horicon engineers rented a car and attempted to drive to Park Rapids. The wind and snow greatly reduced visibility and there was no traffic on the highway. After driving about three or four miles with a window down to see the side of the road, they realized if they got to Park Rapids the race would be over, so they turned back to Fargo and found a Holiday Inn that had rooms. After checking in, someone suggested they go to the movies. The wind was so strong they could hardly stand up and the theater was closed, so they returned to the motel and waited out the storm.

After breakfast the next morning Ron suggested they meet in the dining room to discuss how to reduce costs on snowmobiles. After considering different areas of the snowmobile, Ron asked if the gearbox and jackshaft could be eliminated. Dick made some calculations of engine torque and drive train reduction ratio for the clutch and gearbox and suggested that possibly this could work. This would require an increase in the diameter of the secondary drive pulley and reduction of the number of teeth on the track drive sprockets, which should provide an acceptable gear ratio to start the sled. It also required some engine modification to obtain higher torque at clutch engagement. Dick cautioned this might work if a complete shift (belt movement) could be achieved on the primary drive clutch, and if the track would perform properly with the smaller drive sprockets. Sketches of the chassis developed enthusiasm for the concept, as it would enable the design of a shorter chassis and reduce the weight. Ron suggested that Dale Cormican could make a quick prototype snowmobile to prove the concept. Dale had done similar work for PED on the JD 340/S so he was a natural fit for a rapid build of an operating prototype.

The weather cleared after three days and they returned to the airport, where the pilots had stayed. The Citation jet control cables, that run the length of the plane, were full of "snirt," dirt and snow. Deere aviation sent another plane to return them to Horicon. "It was a pretty expensive flight, but something special happened while we were there that justified our time, as in a few weeks Dale brought an operating mockup direct-drive machine to Horicon. From the ride evaluation on the grass behind the engineering building, it was obvious that we had a working principle that would make a low-cost and lightweight snowmobile," Dick said.

Every year since starting to produce snowmobiles, Horicon marketing had pressed engineering to design lower-cost machines. The name "Little John" on the picture of the prototype Dale made said a lot. It was shorter, lighter and had a lower top speed than any other sled made by Deere but still gave an adult a good ride. All attempts to reduce the cost of larger production machines had been unsuccessful. By reducing the top-end speed, the engine torque curve was modified to increase the engine torque at lower speed so the smaller displacement engines could complete the shift under load. Lee Hardesty and Dick worked together to optimize the calibration of the engine and drive train for the sled.

From this time forward, the Horicon PED shifted their focus in snowmobile design to explore different machine configurations and manufacturing processes. These efforts resulted in lighter, better-performing machines and lower cost of production.

First Spitfire prototype (courtesy Lee Hardesty).

Kawasaki Enters the Picture

Another extremely important event took place that same year on October 19, 1976, at the Kawasaki (KHI) U.S. headquarters in Shakopee, Minnesota. Lee Hardesty and Jim Lamont from PED attended the meeting to respond to an offer by Kawasaki to sell snowmobile engines to Horicon. Prior to coming to work at Horicon, Jim Lamont worked at Polaris, where he became familiar with most of the snowmobile industry suppliers. This opportunity came about because the business relationship between KHI and Arctic Cat was strained by the financial stress at Arctic Cat following the years of light snowfall. Jim and Lee's report from this meeting expressed a strong recommendation that KHI could be a very significant engine supplier to Horicon Works. The specifications of their new design of fan- and liquid-cooled 340 and 440cc engines were very appealing. Other meetings followed from October 26, 1976, through March 4, 1977, at Shakopee with purchasing manager Ray Allsbury and his staff to explore this in detail.

The cost data discussed in the second meeting was as compelling as the performance specifications. Hardesty published an internal memo at Horicon on March 19, 1977, that made the case for the lighter weight of the KHI engine compared to Kioritz. The liquid-cooled KHI engine weighed 15 pounds less than Kioritz, and a 340cc liquid-cooled race engine only gained five pounds more than the consumer version. Unlike the years with Kioritz, Kawasaki had completed the engine development and prepared to tool it for production. On March 4, 1977, Lee and Horicon purchasing personnel Earl Hildebrandt and Michael VandenBrook returned to KHI at Shakopee to initiate the next steps in the relationship. Kawasaki had sufficient technical strength to be attractive to Deere as a long-term supplier of engines. They were the highest volume manufacturer of small gasoline powered engines in Japan for agricultural markets. Although they were not as successful in motorcycles as Honda and Yamaha, they were a significant producer of engines for motorcycles and snowmobiles. These strengths, along with their financial resources in steel and shipbuilding, made them very attractive to Deere. During the first half of 1977, Horicon Works' personnel made visits to the Kawasaki manufacturing facility located west of Kobe in the southwestern part of Honshu Province.

When Horicon Works' intent to change the snowmobile engine supplier was shared with Hiashi Inaga, the executive vice-president of Kioritz Corporation in Tokyo, it was like a great weight was lifted from their shoulders. The pace of annual engine updates for snowmobiles was a severe drain on their personnel and financial resources. Hiroshi Moriki, the managing director of Kioritz Engineering, with whom Lee had direct contact in the development of the Kiroitz race engines, would be free to concentrate on the design of their small-engine-powered products. Kioritz increased their production of small weed string trimmers that the JDM division supplied to Deere dealers. Deere also planned to market the Kioritz Echo chain saw in the U.S. brand labeled JD.

Lee had visited other engine manufacturers during the years that he was in Japan working with Kioritz. Before Deere committed to Kawasaki, Lee and Ron traveled to Japan to evaluate Yamaha, Honda, Kawasaki and Yanmar as future engine suppliers for all Horicon products, not just snowmobiles. Deere expected Yamaha would consider a business relationship even though they were a snowmobile competitor in the U.S. market. Yamaha entered the business about the same time as Deere and was modestly successful with limited dealer representation, primarily by their marine dealers. They were in a fierce battle with Honda in the motorcycle market in the U.S., commonly referred to in the Japanese trade press as the "HY war." This took a lot of time and resources. Likewise, Yamaha was experiencing the same snowmobile market conditions in North America as the rest of the industry.

The discussions with Yamaha were interesting. Lee and Ron were greeted openly and invited to establish further discussions after we completed our talks with the other companies. We were frank about whom we were meeting with on the trip and proposed to them that Deere would make a long-term commitment to whomever they decided to work with. All Japanese companies knew about the relationship of Deere and Kioritz. Japanese companies are fiercely competitive and don't share any information with their own competitors, but exchange information freely with manufacturers in different industries. Yamaha later rejected our query to supply Horicon snowmobile engines. Apparently they wanted to continue marketing their own sleds, and understandably didn't want to sell their engines to Deere.

Our discussion with Honda took place at their Technical Research Center in Hamamatsu, located west of Tokyo on the bullet train track along the coastline. After World War II the Honda Company began to manufacture bicycles that were a primary means of travel for a huge number of their people. Their bike dealers asked Honda to manufacture a small engine to drive the bicycles. Honda secured operating capital from the 18,000 bicycle shop owners across Japan to finance its first motorcycle, the Honda Cub. This was the beginning of Honda Motor Company, which would grow in a short time to be the world's largest manufacturer of motorcycles and gasoline engines. Ever since their founder, Soichiro Honda, who was a self-taught engineer, had started the company, Honda had been heavily involved in racing. They reached the top tier quickly as a manufacturer of motorcycles and cars by focusing on performance in racing. Their aggressive growth in all business segments launched them to become one of the largest car manufacturers in the world. Honda was deeply committed to racing all engine-powered vehicles to accelerate their consumer vehicle development. Their official slogan was "The Power of Dreams."

Their sales engineering personnel welcomed Ron and Lee at Honda with the traditional green tea ceremony in a reception room. Horicon had received very little communication prior to this visit, so we were uncertain of the reception. We were told that a Honda managing director, a member of the Honda board of directors, would join the meeting. This was a welcome surprise, as it was clear that we had their attention. When the director joined the meeting, it continued in the reception lounge, not in a conference room. After greetings were exchanged, he asked for the purpose of our meeting. Lee responded that we would like Honda to sell engines to Deere for snowmobiles and that we would expect Honda to provide their latest engine technology. Since Honda did not produce snowmobiles, this seemed like a reasonable request.

What followed was an object lesson in pursuit of excellence in any business. The director's answer came in the form of questions. He asked about the history of Deere in the garden tractor business. Ron replied that Horicon began to manufacture the JD 110 and 112 garden tractors in 1963. His next question was, after twelve years in the business, what was our market share and volume? Lee turned to me and said, "You answer that question." After my candid answer, he asked why Deere didn't dominate the garden tractor business after being in it for twelve years. The answer must have sounded anemic to Honda. Deere had done well by buying engines from small engine manufacturers in the U.S. and had very high market share in the quality segment of the market. However, there were several high-volume manufacturers who purchased engines for their garden tractors from Briggs and Stratton and others. Most of these products were marketed by mass merchandisers and were smaller and less durable than those Deere made. Deere had no plans to manufacture small gasoline or diesel engines, but did need a quality supplier of small engines for their customers. With the snowmobile business, Deere increased their dealers' numbers that would further increase market share and sales volumes in all products. We agreed with Honda that an excellent engine was essential for greater long-term success in all products.

Obviously Honda wasn't interested in supplying engines to a company that didn't rapidly become number one in the industry. This frank exchange in the Honda meeting provided motivation to both Lee and Ron to consider seriously the issue of how Horicon Works could become as dominant as Honda was in their markets. As we reflected on this meeting, it reinforced the need to align Horicon with a high-quality manufacturer of small engines for all Horicon consumer products. Lacking that, the business would struggle to reach the heights that Honda visualized was necessary for them to sell engines to us. There is no better position to be in than number one in market share in all major markets. Uncertainty and debate about which engine to use in the early years of the snowmobile business created a huge hangover of customer complaints and excess costs and modification programs; unquestionably this had limited the success of Deere's efforts to market snowmobiles.

The next visit was to the Yanmar engine factory, located at Nagahama alongside Lake Biwa in the Honshu Province. The Yanmar Diesel Engine Company started in the 1930s after the founder, Yamaoka, traveled to Germany to study diesel engines at Deutz. Upon returning to Japan he manufactured one-cylinder diesel-powered irrigation pumps for rice paddies. After World War II the factory was rebuilt and continued to grow and expand as the economy recovered, manufacturing modern diesel engines and tractors for rice paddy farms. Later they manufactured a rice paddy harvester. Tadao Yamaoka, the son of the founder, developed a strong relationship with Bill Hewitt.

This led to an agreement with Yanmar to manufacture small diesel engine powered compact utility tractors, brand labeled for Deere to market in the U.S. These tractors were based on the successful Yanmar rice paddy tractor. A joint venture company limited to small agricultural tractors was formed for this collaboration. Horicon was interested in diesel engines for their garden tractors, but the Horicon Works engine business would be separate from the tractor joint venture. Yanmar engine group advised they could make gasoline-powered engines as well. Horicon Works declined this offer, as Yanmar had little experience with the manufacture of gasoline engines. Before this trip to Japan, Yanmar had sent Oishi-san, T. Yamaoka's aide, to Horicon to brief us on their engine business. Yanmar expressed a strong interest in selling us small diesel engines for the larger garden tractors.

Our engine trip culminated at the Kawasaki factory located west of Osaka. This visit reinforced the earlier enthusiasm that Kawasaki had the engineering skills and manufacturing capacity to become a significant supplier of small gasoline-fueled engines for Horicon products. Stated simply, they wanted our business. Kawasaki learned how to collaborate across language and distance barriers between Japan and the U.S. working with Arctic Cat. In the initial discussion with KHI, Horicon expressed concern about the excessive travel time and cost that would be needed for the engineers working in Japan and Horicon to develop the engine and its components. Yamada-san, who had lived in the U.S. when he was president of their U.S. organization, had the solution. Horicon should buy a fax machine and locate it on a secretary's desk in the engineering office. Since Japan is ahead of the U.S. in the time zones, a fax sent to Horicon at the end of the workday in Japan would be at Horicon PED when the engineers arrived to work the next morning. Sketches along with text could be exchanged daily. Since there was only one fax machine in the business office at the Horicon factory, PED purchased a fax and placed it on the desk of Lynne Hedberg, Ron's secretary, so those faxes got top priority every day. This enabled quick exchange of information between the two engineering groups and substantially reduced the frequency of travel. Obviously periodic face-to-face meetings were required to resolve significant concerns or issues. From this association with KHI, Horicon learned significant lessons in how to do joint design and development quickly.

After this trip to Japan, Lee and Ron returned to Horicon with a strong recommendation to select Kawasaki as our engine supplier. Ray Gregg then prepared for a meeting on this recommendation at Horicon with Moline management. This meeting covered the normal range of concerns of a long-term agreement with a distant supplier that could disrupt production. Hank Martens had a ready rebuttal to that concern. It took Kohler, located a short distance from Horicon, six months to turn around an engine change order for garden tractors; KHI could do that in one day, and 21 days later the ship would dock at Seattle, the container would be loaded onto a train, and two days later the truck from Milwaukee could deliver the different mix of engines from Japan. This meeting was a turning point as it brought to an end the corporate concern about small-engine responsibility that had prevailed since the first snowmobile product review meeting at Horicon. There were still naysayers in Deere about that. By that time Horicon factory personnel from engineering, purchasing and manufacturing were familiar with doing business with Japanese companies. We understood and accepted that most major capital goods manufacturers there were more advanced in manufacturing efficiency than the Horicon Works. After this meeting with Deere management, Horicon immediately implemented the decision to use Kawasaki engines in JD snowmobiles.

Kawasaki Supplier Agreement

During that summer of 1977, Ray Gregg, Jr., and Ron traveled to Tokyo, where Ray was to sign a long-term purchasing agreement with Kawasaki to supply their engines for Deere snowmobiles. This produced an interesting experience in doing business with Japanese companies. The concept of a legal contract was not much appreciated by them, as the Japanese business culture was based on negotiations. When conditions changed, this required new negotiations to determine how to respond to the new environment. Deere & Co. in Moline had insisted that Horicon must have a contract with KHI that spelled out the terms and conditions of the agreement to buy engines from KHI for snowmobiles.

Months went by with the two companies exchanging information by mail and fax. Horicon Materials Manager Hank Martens informed KHI that the deadline to get the agreement signed was now. Since negotiations were at an impasse, Hank arranged a trip to Tokyo for Ray and Ron to sign the agreement, as this would bring the matter to a head. As we arrived in the lobby of the KHI headquarters building in downtown Tokyo, we were met by a very nervous Yamada-san, who cautioned us to not raise any questions. We were puzzled at what this meant. He answered their chairman didn't understand why the document was needed but would sign it since Ray was there. This was the contract that Deere legal had prepared, and the face-to-face meeting was the key to getting it signed. The view from the window in the large conference room high up in the KHI headquarters building in downtown Tokyo was a fitting place for the signing ceremony.

This was another lesson in how to conduct business with Japanese companies. The Asian business culture is built on negotiations. Contracts are not needed when both parties thoroughly understand what the business is all about. They include their technical people along with purchasing and management in all discussions with customers so that all parties have the same understanding; hence no contract was needed. The Japanese companies are shrewd negotiators that require time before trust and mutual understanding are developed. After that, the business can be done quickly. This was the beginning of a long and mutually beneficial business relationship between KHI and

Horicon Works that continues to the present day. Years later, new Deere consumer product factories sourced engines from KHI for their products. A small acorn indeed can produce a huge oak tree.

Other Macro Factors Were Changing Snowmobile Customer-Buying Patterns

With the dramatic decline in industry production that occurred from the peak in 1971 of 495,000 machines to 195,000 in 1977, it was difficult to judge the effect of new model introductions in any specific year.

Model Year	Worldwide Estimated Retail Sales (Units)	John Deere Production (units)
1968	85,000	
1969	255,000	
1970	425,000	
1971	495,000	
1972	460,000	12,664 – 3%
1973	450,000	36,990 – 8%
1974	435,000	26,016 – 6%
1975	316,000	18,433 – 6%
1976	243,000	33,651 – 14%
1977	195,000	14,661 – 8%

Est. retail sales courtesy **International Snowmobile Manufacturers Association**

From 1971 until 1977, industry shipments were 61 percent lower. The dramatically lower sales were like a long train wreck, with damage continuing down the track as companies failed or simply quit the business. This period was the critical first years of Deere's entry into the business. It was a tough business climate for all competitors as well. The industry shakeout accelerated as the 1970s wore on, and this put tremendous price pressure on existing manufacturers and their suppliers, who were trying to build good products and profit in doing so. While the discontinued sleds from manufacturers were absorbed in the market, it was difficult for dealers to increase market share and get price realization for new machines.

After six years, the 8 percent ratio of Deere 1977 production to estimated industry sales was disappointing. (We did not acquire annual sales for Deere, so these percentages from ISMA are yearly production divided by the Deere annual sales estimates.) The 1976 production of 14 percent was the highest ratio reached; however, the low snowfall that year forced a lower production schedule of 14,661 the next year of 1977 models to adjust for the huge carryover of Deere dealer inventory.

Another macro influence was the first energy crisis that swept across the U.S. and Canada beginning in 1973. This discouraged buyers from purchasing more vehicles that required gasoline to operate. The drop from 435,000 in 1974 to 316,000 in 1975 was a huge reduction as Deere was manufacturing their 1976 models. Another significant issue for the industry was the lack of snowfall in the snow regions of North America in 1976 and 1977 that continued to disrupt all manufacturers. All companies had to manufacture their estimate for future sales before the next snow season, ship the machines to their dealers, and hope it snowed. The huge reduction in the size of the market reinforced Deere and Company skeptics, who questioned whether Deere should be in the business. Nobody foresaw the rapid changes in the industry to the degree that occurred in that decade.

All these influences had a telling effect on both the manufacturers and their dealers. From 1970 until 1978 most of the over 100 manufacturers had gone out of business. The companies that remained were Ski-Doo, Polaris, Arctic Cat, Deere and Yamaha, and a few others who planned to exit the business. Textron had purchased Polaris and New Brunswick bought Arctic Cat. Ski-Doo, Deere and Yamaha had other businesses that helped them absorb the losses from snowmobiles.

Model Year	Estimated Retail Sales	Average Price/Sled
1971	$503,880,000	$1,020
1972	$480,900,000	$1,050
1973	$506,250,000	$1,125
1974	$543,750,000	$1,250
1975	$429,760,000	$1,360
1976	$349,920,000	$1,440
1977	$298,350,000	$1,530

Compiled from **International Snowmobile Manufacturers Association** Data

The average price realized by the industry increased from $1,020 in 1971 to $1,570 in 1977. These data are not adjusted for inflation, which was significant during those years. In the first seven years that Deere was in the business, industry volumes decreased each year, while the average price per machine did improve. However, these price increases did not cover the increased cost of needed design improvements in the drive system or for overall material price inflation. Although there are no rigorous data to support this statement, the average price increase per sled was driven more by the increased engine cost due to the power growth of engines than by inflation.

Within Deere the tragic death of snowmobile racer Roger Ebert in 1977, although not a result of racing, caused angst among the senior officers of the company. What should be done with the business of manufacturing and marketing snowmobiles? This was difficult to answer, as the justification for the decision to get into the business was still valid. Building a separate consumer products division with independent dealers was well underway by 1977 as Deere increased sales of grounds-maintenance equipment. This growth was driven by the expanded dealer network and by new models of machines from Horicon Works, the JDM products, and the Yanmar compact utility tractors. Nobody wanted to lose the capable independent consumer product dealers that were created for the snowmobiles, especially in the northern sales branch territories. In the mid–South and most of the Southern states, grounds-maintenance business was growing steadily for both homeowners and commercial markets. The distribution agreement to sell small Yanmar-manufactured CUTs in Deere dealerships increased Deere sales to the expanding grounds maintenance market, especially in the Southern and coastal regions of the U.S. where mowing and small tractor work created a year-around market. Kubota was aggressively expanding its small tractor line in those regions. Horicon PED developed a plan for new, more powerful engines and drive train components that with larger mowing decks would strengthen the market appeal of Deere products, to reach broader segments of the market.

The debate continued in Moline over what to do about snowmobiles. The Deere total business enterprise continued to grow and generate good profits. The Fortune 500 ranking for Deere in 1977 was 66th with sales of $3.133 billion and profits of $241.6 million. As early as midyear of 1977, Deere management held talks with Arctic Cat about purchasing them or selling the Deere snowmobile business to them. These discussions were not fruitful, so this was dropped as a consideration. By this time the snowmobile market recognized Deere as a strong competitor with a good snowmobile product line. With new and improved models of machines in the design stage, and with the agreement with Kawasaki engines in hand, Horicon advocated continuing snowmobiles. Horicon Works believed it was no longer necessary to build a special machine for racing. The performance and durability of the consumer sleds would satisfy that market. This position was verified by the success of the 1976 models, as Horicon consumer snowmobiles were now very competitive in racing. The snowmobile products could be sustained with a significant reduction in resources. These engineers could be used to accelerate design of new products for the rapidly growing mowing tractor markets. With no other alternative apparent for the snowmobile business, Horicon proceeded with its plan to operate with less snowmobile engineering effort, and to utilize those resources to expand the mowing tractor business.

8

Racing Snowmobiles

Racing is inborn to the human race. From the early Greeks to modern-day Olympians, humans love to compete to find who is fastest, most durable or most skillful. Racing snowmobiles is no different from cars, motorcycles or horses. Racing is entertainment, and with modern communications it became big business. It is used to promote marketing of the consumer version of ground vehicles. Components are frequently modified for race machines to achieve superior performance. Race associations set different rules every year, as was done for the WSP I-500 cross-country races. Opinions vary on the amount of racing technology that is transferable to consumer machines. The racing metric is performance, but in contrast with consumer machines, durability is measured by the distance or time of a race — not seasons of use. Within Deere the pros and cons of racing snowmobiles were debated as Horicon Works prepared to enter the business. R.J. clearly was wearing the marketing and engineering hat when he pushed for racing. By 1970, when JD was preparing for snowmobile production, the industry was involved in all types of racing: oval, drag and cross-country.

Although confined to the snow-belt areas of the U.S. and Canada, snowmobile racing generated a large following of participants and audience. Both Arctic Cat and Polaris considered it an essential part of the business. In their experience, racing led to rapid improvement of production snowmobiles. Since cross-country races required sleds with performance and durability, Deere selected cross-country as their target for racing. Market leader Ski-Doo and fast-growing Polaris and Arctic Cat were racing with front-engine chassis slide-rail suspension machines. Yamaha, a new entrant to this market, as well as some of the smaller volume manufacturers like Rupp, Mercury and Scorpion, were involved in racing. The Deere decision to build a mid-engine chassis consumer snowmobile was consistent with the conservative company culture to minimize risk entering a new market; however, as discussed in earlier chapters, their decision to pursue cross-country racing with the mid-engine chassis machine soon handicapped the marketing of high-volume consumer sleds.

After the WSP I-500 race in January 1972, John Orvis recalls, Horicon designed a front-engine machine in hopes of racing it the next year. This was during the hectic preparation underway at Horicon Works to produce the first year's JD 400 and 500 sleds. John Orvis, Tom Newhouse and Roger Tesch completed the design during the winter of 1972 in the J6 test building. "This was the first front-engine snowmobile chassis designed at Deere," John said. He did the strength calculations and the overall concept geometry of the machine. Dale Eeckoff from the factory service department made key contributions to the project. He had written the first Operators Manuals and Field Service Manuals for the 1972 models and was a savvy snowmobile enthusiast. The sled was powered with a Kohler 295cc engine. John made several trips to the PEC to work with Lee Hardesty on calibrating the engine. The Horicon Works PED May 1972 monthly report described the test results: "A front-engine machine was designed and built with help from the PED experimental shop employees." John recalls the shop employees were very cooperative in doing the work. When people believe in something, work gets done quickly. Test mechanics Eddie Kruel, Bill Borth and Bobby Hoffman did most of the testing at Jackson Hole, Wyoming, and provided contributions to the project. Their test report recommended the design be continued and produced that year for the next race season. Because most of the engineering resources were consumed with the first production machines, this recommendation was not followed.

1972–1973 Racing: Year 1

Racing had been agreed to at the April 1971 meeting with Moline Management. Gerry Buelow, as manager of product test, was assigned the additional duty to prepare to race in the WSP I-500 in January 1973. Eight drivers were selected on the first race team and were sponsored by eight John Deere grounds care and recreation products dealers from the U.S. and Canada.

The members of this team were as follows:

John Orvis from Horicon, Wisconsin
Jon Carlson from Moline, Illinois
Bobby Enns from Winnipeg, Canada
Marv Zimmerman from Nisswa, Minnesota
Ernie Meunier from Ste. Cecile-de-Milton, Quebec
Junior Pederson from Hatton, North Dakota
Ron Commo from North Ferrisbury, Vermont
Gary Munsee from Corry, Pennsylvania

Parts support for the team was provided by Horicon Works PED to modify the JD 400 snowmobile to install the Kohler 295cc engine, the size mandated by the race association rules. When the WSP I-500 race was called after the third day, John was in the middle of the group. He was an experienced race driver who knew how to operate his machine so it would survive the severe pounding when riding the rough trails on the race route. Pyrometers installed on the exhaust manifold measured the EGT (exhaust gas temperature) that was displayed in gauges mounted on his handlebars so he could avoid overheating the engine. John had success racing Polaris sleds for a number of years before he started to work at Horicon. "The major durability problem was blowing up the clutches. The Salsbury primary clutch would not last through one hard day of racing," Gerry said.

1973–1974 Racing: Year 2

The Horicon factory produced the JD 295/S in 1973 as a race model. The PED Advanced Products Division under Martin Berk was assigned the responsibility for race machine design and development. The 295/S was built on the JD 400 chassis with some improvement in the drive train and bogie wheel in the suspension. The seat was modified to provide a large fuel tank on the rear with padding for the rider's back. Horicon Works PED designed an optional slide-rail suspension and engine engineering at PEC developed a more powerful 295cc Kioritz engine. PEC engineer Lee Hardesty went to Japan to verify performance of the more powerful engine.

A factory general supervisor, Don Bischoff, was chosen race director for the team who assembled at Horicon in the fall of 1973 to condition, test and continue to develop

John Deere race team 1973–1974 (courtesy Bob Enns).

the JD 295/S for racing. The team members were the same drivers from the previous year, except Ernie Meunier was replaced with another driver from Canada. Drivers sponsored by dealers also were an important part of racing. Many independent racers are featured in videos on the Web and can be seen on JD Sleds.com. The factory team raced in several cross-country races before the WSP I-500 in January 1974. John Orvis finished in 10th place, and Tom Otte, as an independent driver, finished in 9th place, just ahead of Orvis from the factory team. Deere dealers sponsored race drivers in different racing venues across the snow belt. Racing was definitely important to dealer snowmobile marketing. Finishing in the top ten was considered good performance, even though the high center of gravity of the JD 295/S made handling more difficult than the front-engine machines. Orvis and Otte were experienced race drivers who contributed to their success. But in racing there is only one desired outcome—that is, to win.

1974–1975 Model 340/S: Year 3

This was a pivotal year for design of a Deere race sled. The success or failure of the JD 340/S in racing would have a major effect on the future snowmobile programs. As discussed in Chapter 6, the decision to build the improved 1974 consumer mid-engine models again as 1975 models provided Horicon Works a full winter to prepare the 1976 model front engine sleds for production while the Advanced Products engineers designed the JD 340/S.

A smaller Horicon Works race team included drivers Dale Cormican, Roger Jansen, Bobby Enns, Jon Carlson and Craig Knudsen. The team worked out of Dale Cormican's shop at Crookston, Minnesota that was near many of the major races. Dale was designated as the team leader and Chuck Phelps from Horicon engineering served as the factory liaison to provide parts and technical support. On balance, this was a very talented race team, as all were experienced racers. Jon Carlson had gained experience with the first two race teams and now was prepared to challenge for a place in the winner's circle. In November 1974, while Horicon PED was testing the first 1976 model prototype front-engine chassis, the new race team assembled at Dale's shop to ride and calibrate their new JD 340/S. This went well, and the drivers' enthusiasm was high as the racing season began. During their testing of the JD 340/S they encountered some problems with scoring pistons and belt/clutch failures. These were normal experiences for race drivers in severe terrain and weather conditions, but fixing problems helps to win races. The race team required support from the Horicon PED engine and drive train engineers to fine-tune the calibration of the engine and drive system. The JD 340/S acceleration and its ride and handling were significantly better than the Deere mid-engine chassis machines.

Before the race season began on the mainland, all the manufacturers were invited to Brant's Lake Lodge, Alaska, to race. There were many different classes so each manufacturer could choose where to race their machines to prepare for the upcoming race season in the lower 48. Jack Hoffman published an internal memo at Horicon on November 18, 1974, that described some of the first results of racing in Alaska: "Dale Cormican and Roger Jansen entered the stock 340cc class on the same course along with Craig Knudsen who finished first and Dale finished second after overturning behind a Mercury sled that won. Jon Carlson and Craig Knudsen both entered a modified stock class on the final day. Jon finished first and Craig was second." These were encouraging results, so enthusiasm was high as the team returned to Crookston to prepare for the cross-country season. The drivers liked the outstanding ride and handling of the JD 340/S and were eager to race. Jon Carlson recalls that he put 2500 miles on two JD 340/S snowmobiles and thought they were excellent. The early race results in North Dakota and South Dakota were mixed. Several machines experienced piston failures. These failures were caused by a number of calibration mistakes that resulted from the lack of time to test in snow and in different outdoor temperatures before releasing the design for production that summer. Horicon Engineering worked with the race team to further refine the calibration so the engines and sleds could perform to their capability.

In the WSP I-500, the JD 340/S driven by Jon Carlson finished 3rd and Craig Knudsen was 4th. These were considered to be very excellent results. Dale Cormican was leading after the first day but was flagged (disqualified) for an infraction on the course. Craig and Bobby went out with machine breakdowns.

The last day of the WSP I-500, the majority of the sleds that started in the lead flight were JD 340/S models. Independent drivers rode many of those sleds. This created a stunning impression among the followers of the race. The JD 340/S and Deere team drivers and independents were very competitive with the best in the industry; however, Deere intended to win that race.

Bobby Enns said, "The JD 340/S ran fast, was lighter in weight, and handled well. I think it was the best race snowmobile Deere made." Deere won or placed well in other cross-country races. This news spread quickly across John Deere land. So instead of being squeezed out of the cross-country racing season, Deere had a very competitive front-engine race sled on their first effort. In eight months, Horicon Works had designed and manufactured an all-new chassis powered with the new drive train components. Equally important, the Horicon factory had done an outstanding job to meet the production deadline with very short lead times, producing 1,200 high-quality sleds by the October 31 deadline. And of greater importance was this project verified the thesis that it was imperative to define the specifications for all projects with input from consumer users in the market.

Brian Nelson raced the JD 340/S as an independent that year. Brian describes how he got started in racing: "Willmar had a corporation of businessmen who promoted the town by providing money to people to advertise the town with the theme Spirit of

Willmar. Brian, Hubert Fixsen and Larry Swanson were given a grant from them to race in the winter of 1974–75. The grant helped to buy the JD 340/S sled and defray some of the costs associated with racing." The three were high school buddies who liked to ride snowmobiles. Larry and Hubert were enrolled in college and Brian was devoted to racing. Brian said:

> I had some good rides on the 340/S. I lost the Sauk Center cross-country 150-mile race by one second. On the JD 340S in Park Rapids that year I was leading the race when the throttle cables broke. I had a spare and changed it on the course and still finished third. At the WSP I-500 I was in the top ten for the last leg but about 30 miles from the finish the skid frame broke. It failed because of the repeated pounding that resulted from jumping over the numerous culverts in the road ditches. If I had the same kind of support in 1975 as Enduro Team Deere had in 1976, I would have won most of those races. Things like parts to change out every night weren't in our budget.

With the success of the JD 340/S in the WSP I-500, it was clear that Deere fielded a competitive race machine and team. Immediately after the I-500, the focus turned to the 1976 new front-engine consumer sled test program and the race sled. The 340/S race team sleds were modified at Cormican's shop by replacement of the fan-cooled 340cc stock engines with liquid-cooled 340cc Kioritz engines. This required cutting an opening in the hood to direct air to the radiator. They tested the engine installation by loading each engine with an airplane propeller that served as a dynamometer. The team then raced the rest of the season in modified classes and the sled was very competitive with all competitors' machines. Jon Carlson won the Park Rapids race with the liquid-cooled JD 340/S in the modified class. With 3rd in the WSP I-500 and success in the modified class, he "arrived" that season as a competitive race driver. The 1974–75 race season was a turning point that demonstrated to customers, dealers and competition that John Deere could design high-performance sleds that were competitive with the best in the industry.

Where did the liquid-cooled Kioritz engine come from? The industry had begun to design liquid-cooled engines as they provided more power and better durability than free air- or fan-cooled engines. The high-volume 2-cycle engine producers were designing liquid-cooled engines that were used in motorcycles and outboard motors. Liquid-cooled engines enabled the manufacturers to obtain more power in the same displacement and were a logical next step for snowmobiles. After Lee transferred to Horicon in April 1974, Kioritz was directed to design a liquid-cooled 340cc engine for racing. The specifications called for 50hp, which had never been achieved in a 340cc snowmobile engine. Lee's experience with developing high-horsepower engines for tractor pulls convinced him that to win, Deere needed to have more powerful engines than anyone else. Lee was at the Kioritz factory in August and September of 1974 to work on development in the laboratory with Hori-san, the Kioritz engineer. During ten years Lee made over 100 trips to Japan to work on engine development for Horicon projects.

Kioritz had been unable to reach the 50-horsepower level, which was higher than the power in the Kioritz fan-cooled 440cc engine. Lee recalls working for several days, and when they reached 49hp, Hori-san believed they couldn't reach 50hp. Lee convinced him to try again the next day. That night Lee worked out an approach that he thought would work, and this design change produced the desired 50hp. Kioritz continued design and development of the 340cc liquid-cooled engines while Lee returned to Horicon to help calibrate the production of JD 340/S sleds. By the end of the I-500 race, Kioritz had made prototype engines from sand-cast tooling. This type of tooling was lower in cost and satisfactory for low volumes of prototype engines. After the design was stable, the manufacturer made permanent dies for the high-volume production parts. These prototype engines were durability tested in the Kioritz test cells in December and shipped to Horicon in January of 1975. A small number were available to install in the JD 340/S race team sleds at Cormican's shop in February.

Steve Braun describes an interesting experience while working at the Donaldson factory in Canada with one of the prototype 340cc Liquidator engines. He was there to develop a new muffler with Donaldson engineers with the only engine allocated for this work. They were under time pressure to finish the new exhaust muffler, and on the last day of testing the engine scored and was unusable. There were no spare parts to repair it so they couldn't complete the test. Steve was scheduled to fly back to Horicon the next day. They disassembled the engine and discovered that the engine crankshaft case caused failure of one crankshaft bearing. They attributed this to a thin wall from the sand casting—just another one of the small hurdles that happen during new design and development work. Steve decided to take the failed engine back to Horicon rather than wait for it to be shipped.

Steve arrived at the Toronto airport carrying a 90-lb. box containing the engine and his luggage. Customs opened the box and refused to let him check it. He attempted to carry it on, but Air Canada refused. He found another airline that sold him two seats so he could strap the box in a passenger seat rather than checking it. He dragged the box to the other end of the terminal only to find there was no jet-way; therefore he had to push the heavy box up the steep steps. In Chicago he transferred to a Republic flight to Milwaukee, and the airline checked the box, no questions asked. By itself this story illustrates the dedication and extra effort that was repeated over and over by many engineers who worked on snowmobiles. Time was always short and there were more things to do tomorrow.

The 1975–1976 Race Season: Year 4

Enthusiasm and expectations were high as Deere prepared for the next season. The success racing the JD 340/S in stock and modified classes demonstrated to the industry that Deere was competitive with the best machines. The modified JD 340/S sleds served as the first test vehicles for the 1976 race machine, the Liquidator. The plan for 1975–1976 race season consisted of two components: a new approach for a race team, and how the Liquidator was designed for manufacture.

Planning a Company Sponsored Race Team for 1975–76 Racing

Jon Carlson recalls after the JD 340/S race season, R.J. convened a meeting at his home in April to plan a new direction for the race effort. It was attended by Director of Consumer Product Marketing Don Carl, along with Don Schuberg on Don's staff, and Jon. The race team would be operated under the direction of Deere Marketing at Moline as part of Don Carl's marketing organization. This separated racing from the factory and focused it as part of the Deere marketing efforts. R.J. was enthusiastic about the future based upon the success of racing the JD 340/S in stock classes, as well as the results in the modified classes with the liquid-cooled engines. The Cyclone and Liquifire 1976 consumer models would have many improved features and a new front-engine chassis. Horicon had communicated these new models were on schedule and production would start as scheduled in May. They would outperform the current Deere consumer models and be competitive with the best sleds in the industry.

The marketing plan for the next race season started immediately as R.J. directed Don Carl to tour the snowmobile dealers that summer with the JD 340/S that Jon had raced. This would help not only to generate orders, but also would link racing to consumer sled marketing in a major way. A new fall marketing advertising campaign was planned that would integrate race machines with consumer sleds. R.J. wanted a new design of race gear (clothing) that would be distinctive but reflect the Deere image. The consumer clothing was to be styled exactly like leathers for the race team. The marketing plan for the 1976 models included publication to every dealer of a weekly newsletter named *Green Streak*, that would show the latest point standings of a yet-to-be-created new racing association. The *Green Streak* Race News and Views from December 9, 1975, through February 8, 1977, are included in the appendix.

Don Schuberg was assigned the task of forming the new race association by contacting all the major race associations and inviting them to join. For Deere drivers, points would be awarded based on their finish from the most recent races. At the end of the year, the driver with the most points would receive a significant cash award. This program was open to anyone riding a Deere sled. For Enduro Team Deere, the driver with the highest point total would receive a diamond-studded ring on a par with a Super Bowl ring. At the end of the season, a banquet was planned for Deere drivers to recognize the season winners. The new association was to represent all manufacturers and drivers, not just Deere. R.J. identified eight race locations to invite to join the new association. They were familiar names like WSP I-500, Park Rapids, Sauk Centre, and the North and South Dakota Governors Cup. Just as the meeting was breaking up, he thought of one more race location. He asked Don Schuberg to contact the people at

Balsam Lake to set up a new race between Christmas and New Year's so R.J. could race in it and have some fun himself.

Where to locate the team was discussed at length. After some debate, Jon recommended that the place should be centrally located to minimize the travel time. Travel consumed precious time that all the racers needed to get ready for the next race. R.J. asked Jon to identify the biggest obstacle to overcome with the drivers. Jon answered that they needed to be in excellent physical condition, to eat right, and stay mentally focused on racing. The matter of who should manage the team caused considerable discussion. Jon suggested it should be someone who could manage a group of young guys. After thinking more about it, he suggested they select someone like Al Andersen, the coach at Balsam Lake High School. R.J. seized that idea. This meeting continued with discussion on how to select the team members. This task was assigned to Don Schubert. R.J. outlined some of the key considerations. He didn't want professional drivers; they should be younger people, and preferably racers who were independents or who raced for Deere dealers. None of the previous factory team members were necessarily excluded. Enduro Team Deere (ETD) was formed that summer, consisting of six drivers and six mechanics. The team headquarters was at Breezy Point, Minnesota, and Al Andersen was appointed the team coach and race director.

1976 JD Liquidator race sled (courtesy Roger Tesch).

Design of the 1976 Liquidator Race Sled

While organization of the new race association and selection of ETD was underway in Moline, at Horicon the engineers and factory were busy preparing for production of the race sled. Horicon PED had completed the design of the new front-engine chassis for the 1976 consumer sleds that were to be marketed as Cyclone and Liquifire. These machines were already being released for production when the JD 340/S race season ended. With the success of the modified JD 340/S powered by the prototype liquid-cooled engine, the question was how to build the 1976 race machine. By mid-year 1975, the Horicon factory was on pace to again lose money. Ray Gregg announced that a trip to Moline to request investment capital money for another all-new race machine was unsuccessful. This triggered a study to determine the lowest-cost way for the factory to build the Liquidator race machine, those choices being major revision of the JD 340/S or the new Liquifire chassis. Factory layoffs of salaried and wage personnel to reduce the cost in the entire factory operations were significant considerations in the decision.

The major criteria in the decision were schedule, cost and performance. Revising the JD 340/S chassis for production would require numerous changes to accommodate the liquid-cooled engine with a different air intake, exhaust system and cooling system. The opening cut in the hood of the JD 340/S for the liquid cooled engine not only provided air to cool the radiator, but also enough airflow to cool other components under the hood. The sound reduction to the 82 dBa required for a stock machine also made it certain that more cooling capacity was needed. Making extensive changes to the JD 340/S chassis would require many different new production parts versus making the necessary change to install the 50hp 340cc race engine in the newly tooled Liquifire chassis; therefore, Horicon Works decided to build the Liquidator using the new, longer production chassis rather than redesign the JD 340/S. This reduced the time and work for PED and the factory, and would lower the total investment and direct costs. Building a Liquidator race sled on the Liquifire chassis was the lowest-cost way to get the Liquidator into production.

The tunnel-mounted heat exchanger used on the Cyclone and Liquifire chassis did not provide sufficient cooling for the more powerful 340cc 50hp Liquidator engine. The cooling extrusions for the Liquifire engine were mounted under the tunnel on the production machines, but could not be used for the Liquidator because the race machines needed clearance for studs mounted on the track. Therefore a different hood was required for the Liquidator to provide room for a large radiator. All of the 1976 model machines, including the Liquidator, used the new design secondary clutch manufactured by Horicon with the improved Comet primary clutch. Stress tests of the Liquidator were driven by the reliability history of failures on Deere snowmobiles. The Liquidator gained 30 pounds over the JD 340/S chassis that had run in the modified class with the liquid-cooled engine. It was longer and heavier than any sled JD had made up to that time. The production Kioritz liquid-cooled engine, 15 pounds heavier than the fan-cooled engine, accounted

Liquidator race engine (Richard Teal collection).

for half of the additional 30 pounds. As with the JD 340/S the previous year, there was limited time for performance or durability testing of the Liquidator final design in different snow and temperature conditions before production. The WSP I-500 race association rules required factory production of 600 sleds to be completed by the end of October.

How Enduro Team Deere (ETD) Was Formed

Al Andersen recalls his job interview and work as the ETD race director. Al said, "I was teaching and coaching at Balsam Lake High School in '74 and '75. Our son had become friends with Jon and the Carlson family during visits there." In the summer of 1975, R.J. called and invited Al and Linda to come to his house for cocktails. During that evening, R.J. asked Al to work for Deere as the race team director. He reviewed the plans made with his staff at the meeting at his home after the 1975 race season ended. Al recalls that R.J. linked the formation of the ETD to a recent plane ride with Executive Vice-President Bob Hanson, when they agreed to have a Deere and Company sponsored team rather than a factory team. R.J. asked Al how much money he made teaching. "I answered $14,000 and R.J. told me I would be well paid working for Deere. My Deere business card job title was Competitive Engineer," Al said.

Making Their Bodies As Durable As Their Machines

By Henry Fiola

With snowmobiles becoming so dependable, are the drivers who race them, particularly on long cross country courses, durable enough to take full advantage?

At least one company, John Deere, which is staking so much of its reputation on cross country racing, isn't about to take a chance. The result is what Deere calls the "first organized snowmobile race readiness program." Call it, if you will, a training camp for factory drivers and mechanics.

No one who has ever seen Eastman, Lindblad, Duhamel, Coltom, Trapp or any other top driver in action questions the athletic condition of professional drivers. In fact, most of them maintain rigorous training programs much of the year.

But at Breezy Point Resort in Minnesota, Deere has opened what may be the first formal snowmobile driver training camp. And what "Enduro Team Deere" members are doing to get themselves in shape may, on a more limited basis, help the average rider eliminate a few aches and pains.

The daily schedule at the Breezy Point camp is tight: 7:00 a.m., out of bed; 7:15, jog and shower; 8:00 breakfast; 8:30, squad meeting; 9:00, shop; 10:15, break; 11:00 calisthenics; 11:45, body building, etc. Every day, rigid schedules.

Along with spending three or four hours each day learning more about the sled and working to improve it, physical exercise and body conditioning make up the major portion of the training camp. The purpose, says Al Andersen, a former football coach who is program director, is to "develop the physical endurance capabilities of race drivers ... to work with the endurance properties of the sled."

Some of the exercise programs used at Breezy Point are those the average snowmobiler would likely never need or even want to consider — sprinting, push-ups, sit-ups, rope jumping, isometrics, weight lifting, etc. But Andersen has developed what he calls the "S/7" exercises involving a snowmobile that can help alleviate riding problems from sore legs to tired thumbs.

This isn't to suggest these exercises are for everyone, because they aren't. They could, in fact, do more harm than good for most of us. But all are designed to simulate some type of activity most snowmobilers incur on the trail, and to strengthen the appropriate muscles and joints.

These are the seven exercises that make up the program:

THE S/7 PROGRAM

Rear Lifts: Using legs (not back), lift back of sled 10 times to point where arms and legs are straight each time.

Seat Bounces: Bounce 25-30 times while sitting on sled in normal riding position. Each bounce 4-6 inches up from seat and back to touching seat, but do not place weight on seat.

Steering: Turn handlebars all the way to the right and back, all the way to the left and back 10 times while sitting in normal driving position.

Sled Tips: Tip sled right with one foot on floor and one foot on footrest until center of gravity of sled is beyond its base. Then quickly jump to the other side of sled and do the same 10 times.

"Coach" Al Anderson points to a high point of the schedule after training camp.

Team member Brian Nelson does rear lifts.

Revs: Fully rev the throttle (engine is off) with right thumb 25-30 times while holding rear of sled off the ground with left hand. Throttle should have additional resistance added.

Leans: Sitting in driving position with feet forward, lean to the right as if in a sharp right turn until right knee touches foot rest and left arm is fully extended. Quickly move body to left and do the turning to left 10 times.

Front Lifts: Using legs (not back), grasp front bumper and carefully lift the front of the sled until arms and legs are straight. Start with two or three lifts, and work gradually up to five or 10.

If you are 25 years old or younger, and are trying out for a factory racing team, you might also try doing these in a steam room with the temperature and humidity over 80. That's the way Enduro Team Deere does them.

For those of us who aren't, however, maybe we can just go to the refrigerator for a beer and put up with the minor aches and pains.

Physical fitness program for Deere race team (courtesy Larry Swanson).

Al was directly involved with Don Schuberg in the selection of a resort for the race team headquarters. "I suggested they contact Breezy Point," Al said. In July 1975, R.J., Don Carl, Don Schuberg and Al went to Breezy Point and made a deal that day with inn manager Dave Grabdahl to house the team there. ETD stayed in the eleven-room lodge building named the (Farrah) Fawcett House. The folklore about the house was that it had been used by famous personalities like Bob Hope and Hedy Lamarr.

A conference room at the resort was converted into a shop for the team. The resort removed the furnishings and equipped it for assembly of six snowmobiles with air for the pneumatic tools and other shop equipment. Breezy Point hired a special cook to prepare team meals so they could all eat together. Since physical fitness was part of the new race program, the resort provided the team a room where they gathered every morning to work out. Conditioning involved the normal calisthenics of running outdoors in the early morning and then working out in the weight room, skipping rope, pushups, stretching, etc. Al's 82nd Airborne P.T. Instructor experience served him well in his role as the race director. In October, Al and the team assembled at Breezy Point to begin conditioning, using the special snowmobile exercises Al had devised before the Liquidators arrived.

Al recalled some of the challenges to establish the new race association: "After securing the race team headquarters Don and I began a series of meetings to create the new cross-country race association. During the meeting with Arctic Cat we did not get a positive reception. The Arctic Cat engineering manager spoke out strongly against the new association and said it was ridiculous. However, at the end of the meeting the Arctic president agreed they would join. We also met with Polaris, who agreed." When the round of meetings with the industry sponsoring companies was finished, Al and Don contacted the eight race directors from the major cross-country race associations to get agreement on the new association, named the International Cross-country Snowmobile Federation, or ICCSF. The proper contacts were made with local people at Balsam Lake to add a new race there that was scheduled to take place during Christmas week. With that finished, Don and Al began the selection process for the new race team. Al recalled their names: "Those selected were Bobby Enns, Jon Carlson, Brian Nelson, Craig Knudsen, Willie Ensue, and Ron Reimer." These drivers followed R.J.'s general direction to get young non-professional but experienced snowmobile drivers on the team.

Enduro Team Deere
1975–1976 Season

Driver	Mechanic	Parts/Chasers
Willie Anseeuw	Doug Oster	Dan Paterson
Jon Carlson	Phil Simon (Crew Chief)	Jeff Erdman
Bob Enns	Larry Swanson (Crew Chief)	
Craig Knudsen	Joel Hultquist	
Brian Nelson	Hubert Fixsen	
Ron Reimer	Doug Hough	

Dick Teal recalls his first trip to Breezy Point:

After the race team was formed, and they were preparing for the season, I was asked to give a school on how to set up the torque converter and maintain it. I reviewed each component of the torque converter with the entire team and discussed what options they had to adjust the clutch (torque converter) to individual preferences to optimize the performance of the sled in different terrain or weather conditions. This was followed with a question-and-answer session on anything they wanted to discuss. Thirty-two years later, at R.J. Carlson's induction into the Snowmobile Hall of Fame in 2007, one of the team members made a special point to thank me for the advice discussed at Breezy Point. Dick added, "Whatever I said made a difference in his life and it made me feel like I accomplished something. I remember being impressed with the way Breezy Point was being run and thought that maybe we had a chance in the race tour." After the team's conditioning period and their familiarization with the new Liquidators, the machines were shipped to Brandt's Lake Lodge in Alaska in late November. During operation before racing there, the sleds experienced an unusually high number of piston failures. The engine was operating at the highest power level to date for a Kioritz engine. Mechanics and drivers were making adjustments to the engine and carburetors but were unable to eliminate the problem.

Al describes the first competitive results from Alaska:

The races were held on the lake at Brant's Lake Lodge located about 72 miles northeast of Anchorage. There were seven classes for different sleds and several drivers of different manufacturers' sleds. Deere drivers were entered in most of them and won three races. This was quite an accomplishment, as the Liquidator weighed 512 pounds compared with much lighter competition oval-race sleds that were 350–380 pounds. The team discovered the weight was an advantage on the curves, as they could just pull over and bang the lighter sleds off the course. Overall it was a very good day for Deere and the other manufacturers protested the results. I had timed all of the Deere sleds and compared my results with the official posted final times and discovered an error. Somehow the calculations for some race results had confused the math, using 100 seconds in a minute instead of 60. Correcting them would be unfavorable to the ETD results. I called R.J. and told him of the official posted results and of my slower times. There was silence before R.J. replied let's be honest and do the right thing. This change was unfavorable to some of the initial posted results; however, *USAA* magazine gave Deere a good write-up so it all ended well.

Horicon engineering sent two engineers to Brant's Lodge to observe the Liquidator's performance. Dick Teal describes his first experience at the Alaska race:

I remember that the place was really cold and there was minimal snow so the races were being held on a frozen lake. The race team stayed at the motel next door to the restaurant and lake. Carl Firehammer and I stayed in a converted railroad boxcar that had one light bulb and no heat. We slept in our snowmobile clothes on bunk beds the first night. Carl complained about the lack of heat but wanted the light shut off so he could sleep. I told him that we better leave the light on for what little heat it provided. The temperature was below zero that night.

Race day turned into a big surprise for me. I considered the Liquidator to be too big and heavy for it to have much success. We won the race easily because we were fast. Lee Hardesty had done his magic with the engines and I had calibrated the torque converters to match the engine and the sled characteristics and each team had done their work so we were ready. During breakfast the next day R.J. Carlson called and asked to talk to me. He wanted my assessment of how good we were and if he should turn the race program on full bore. Evidently

> a number of Deere dealers were ready to go but he wanted to tell them if we had something special. I remember hesitating and told him that although we were fast I wasn't sure how we would fare on rough cross-country courses. I thought we would probably do well on fast icy oval tracks. I remember that I didn't want to paint a rosy picture but I must have helped, because we headed hell-bent into the season with all barrels firing.

After returning from Alaska the team went to West Yellowstone, where Doug Hough won that race. Then ETD returned to Breezy Point to prepare for the North Dakota Governor's Cup Race on December 19 and 20, 1975 and the Balsam Lake Classic on December 28, 1975.

Meanwhile, extensive engine testing at Horicon PED demonstrated the piston-scoring problem required reshaping the piston to better fit the cylinder shape caused by the high temperatures. It was normal for the combustion heat to cause some unequal expansion of the cylinder and piston at the high operating temperatures; however, these results were different from what Kioritz had observed in testing of the engine in their test labs in Japan. According to the ICCSF rules, no sled could use parts out of the tolerance range of those in the production Liquidators. Any new parts had to be at dealers by December 31 so that all competitors would have access to them before the WSP I-500 race. Horicon PED tested engines 24 hours a day to determine the optimum piston

R.J. Carlson at Balsom Lake Classic (courtesy Bob Enns).

shape. When the piston and cylinder bore expand at different rates, the piston may transfer metal to the cylinder wall. This causes the engine to stall or run much slower with less power. The engine lab testing at Horicon determined the optimum piston shape, but it was mid–December and there was not time to get newly manufactured parts from the supplier. The testing then shifted to determine how much material to remove from the production pistons within the original tolerance specification.

The standard piston manufacturing method was to finish the pistons by precision cam grinding, which produced a non-circular shape. Horicon Works bought a large quantity of the oldest shaping tool that Lee Hardesty termed a German milling machine — hand files. An aggressive effort was launched to reshape the pistons by hand filing to remove material in the correct location. To locate where to file, Lee drew an outline with a black marking pen on the piston. Since the factory had produced 600 machines, 1200 original pistons had to be purchased from the supplier, shipped to Horicon, reshaped and distributed to dealers before December 31. By working throughout the normal factory shutdown between Christmas and New Year's Day, the factory and PED personnel finished before the deadline. Modified pistons were shipped daily to the respective sales branch locations. The ICCSF was notified of the change, and the information was distributed to Deere dealers so they could contact all owners to supply them the new pistons. These modified pistons were made available to ETD, who used them in the Balsam Lake race on December 28, 1975.

Al recalls more of the season's race results by ETD: "Bobby Enns was leading one of the Dakota races when he wrecked due to hitting a frozen deer in the road ditch. Doug Hough won the oval race in Yellowstone. Of course, Brian Nelson won the WSP-I500 and Jon Carlson finished third in it. Other drivers had successes as well." Al continued:

> Enduro Team Deere entered six sleds in the WSP I-500 that began that year in St Paul. By the end of the third day, at Walker, I had Brian's time and thought it was good. When the official times were posted, Brian's listed time was ten minutes more than mine. My timing of all the ETD sleds in the races starting with Alaska was good, so I was confident there was an error in the official results. I had used a stopwatch to time track races as a coach. I sought a friend to help me get to see Herb Howe, the WSP I-500 race director. When I finally saw him, I asked to see Brian's time card for this leg of the race and I showed him my time for Brian. I noticed a simple math mistake in totaling Brian's time for two days; therefore, if it was corrected it would agree with my stopwatch. The director agreed they had made a mistake and moved Brian's position for the final day to start in 10th place.

Al describes his experiences during the last day of the race:

> Some Enduro Team drivers were equipped with helmet radios so they could stay in contact. Brian was passing Polaris sleds throughout the last leg of the race. One Polaris racer broke his leg. Once Brian hit a big bump and it nearly threw him off the sled but he hung on with his right hand on the throttle and the left on the bumper. At the finish line I recorded Brian with the best time, 32 seconds ahead of the second-place Polaris. Of course in racing nothing is official until the tech inspection is completed. Polaris entered a protest that required posting $100 bond. I-500 director Herb Howe was very friendly with Polaris as some of his close rel-

atives worked there. So the teardown was a long, drawn-out affair. Herb was hovering over Brian's mechanic Hubert Fixsen, who was removing parts at the request of an inspector. I went to Herb and protested that he was interfering with my mechanic doing the teardown. Finally the result was made official and Brian was announced as the winner.

This took several hours, but R.J. still hosted a party at a Winnipeg hotel to celebrate the results. It was a festive occasion with large numbers of Deere personnel, along with independent Deere race drivers. A Deere sled and driver winning the WSP I-500 was then part of snowmobile history.

During their return to Breezy Point, Al and some of the team stopped at a restaurant. When they got inside, the waitress noticed they were wearing JD jackets. "Did you hear that Deere won the race by hiring a helicopter to lift one of the sleds forward twenty miles to get ahead?" she asked. This illustrated the intense emotion some locals had about Deere upsetting the cozy competition that Polaris and Arctic Cat had enjoyed for many years. Some people were willing to believe any rumor like this.

Al summarized the outstanding results from the first ETD race season. "The team won a total of seven races and in several others had top-ten finishes. Ron Reimer's wife raced as an independent and won three races that year riding Liquidators." The history of ETD was a team effort from start to finish. Mechanics Hough, Oster and Hultquist raced in one or more events. Every race driver and his mechanic prepared for each race as if they expected to win.

RON INTERVIEWS BRIAN NELSON ABOUT HIS EXPERIENCES WITH ETD

RL: What did Enduro Team Deere mean to you?

BN: It was a tremendous opportunity for a young guy like me. It provided all the backing that I needed to be successful in racing.

Why were you the most successful driver in ETD?

I was there to win races. That meant that I had to be better prepared and ride better than everyone in the race and that included my teammates. My attitude was to win races, not be there as a social time or like in a club where you viewed the others as acquaintances or relatives. In racing you have to perform. Do your best to beat everyone, including the others on the team.

How did you get to be a member of ETD?

Don Schuberg contacted me during the summer of '75. I said OK on the condition that they take Larry Swanson and Hubert Fixsen as well. We had raced the JD 340/S sponsored by Wilmer, Minnesota. I had some good rides on it.

Compare the Liquidator to the 340/S.

The 340/S needed to be liquid-cooled. The Kioritz Liquidator engine caused problems from the beginning. Larry had observed right away that the cold water on the manifold was directed to the hot side of the piston. From the beginning, Brian and Hubert started honing the cylinder bore to provide more clearance. They polished the top of the heads and retarded the timing 2 degrees to compensate for the detonation during combustion. We lost from 2 to 4 hp on the dynamometer as a result.

[On the weight of Liquidator versus the 340/S]: I felt there must not have been good communication to the design engineers after the 340/S race season. However, the power of the Liquidator engine was excellent, so when the pistons didn't seize we could run really fast.

What were your Liquidator race results in the nine association races?

Three firsts, two seconds and one fifth: 1st North Dakota Governor's Cup; 2nd at Balsam Lake Classic, leading with two laps to go but had to pit to install a new pipe; 2nd at Eagles Heartland that Bobby won. In that race I was really fast, up to 94 mph, and blew the rubber off the rubber wheels in the suspension and that slowed me down. 1st in the Minot, North Dakota, race, and 1st in the WSP I-500. I also won the West Yellowstone race after we returned from Alaska."

What did your mechanic contribute to your success?

Hubert had a phenomenal mechanical mind. He understood what caused failures and how to fix them. One example, was we changed the gear ratio by running a smaller sprocket on the top shaft (higher ratio) but with the aggressive hard riding that I did the loads were too high, so we never did that again.

What did Al Andersen contribute to ETD?

He held it together, no friction, good travel planning and execution, vehicles, etc. The big thing was the physical conditioning. Al was very good at that. All six drivers ran every morning, and then from 10:30 until noon we were in the weight room. We rode sleds in the afternoon until 5:00, then went back to the weight room until dinner. This conditioning really paid off in each race and for the entire season.

What was R.J.'s influence on the team?

His idea for the team was great, the psychological feeling that he was behind us and the support helped the team focus on their roles. The diamond ring to the top Deere driver was nice.

How would you summarize the entire experience?

It was a tremendous opportunity for me to do something I always wanted to do: race. It launched me to further success in racing. The current state of the industry is down. EPA emissions rulings have hurt the sport. The four-stroke engines with fuel injection, etc., are making the machines more expensive. This year [2011] I am running the special race of the final leg of this year's WSP in the vintage sled class riding an Arctic Cat as a way to give back something to the industry.

[The John Deere Liquidator that Brian Nelson rode to win the 1976 WSP I-500 race is now displayed in the Snowmobile Hall of Fame, Saint Germain, Wisconsin. Brian Nelson left the team after that season to race for Arctic Cat. Roger Ebert replaced him.]

1976–1977 Racing Season: Year 5

With the 1976 successes, EDT was continued for the 1977 race year. There was no new race sled manufactured as a 1977 model by Horicon. Dealers had sufficient quantities of the Liquidators to use for their race teams. Deere believed that the Liquidator along with JD 295/S and JD 340/S sleds would fare quite well in the 1977 race season. ETD raced Liquidators again with updated parts from field modification parts kits made available to the dealers for all of the 1976 sleds. Of course, Enduro Team Deere had these installed before the 1977 race season began. The kits included a lighter weight hood, aluminum slide rail, lighter engine mounting plate, and other weight reduction items. The team was extremely successful in that they won the first three races of the year.

The team members for the 1976–1977 Enduro Team Deere were:

Drivers
Bob Enns, Jon Carlson, Willie Anseeuw, Roger Ebert, Craig Knudsen and Tom Otte

Mechanics
Terry Norguard, Doug Oster, Jerome Kretzman, Steve Tabor, Doug Hough and Joel Hultquist

Ron's interview with Al Andersen about this race season focused on Roger Ebert's accident after the third race. Al recalls how he learned about it:

> I left Breezy Point for the weekend and was having dinner at a restaurant with my wife in Balsam Lake when our daughter, who had taken the call, came to tell me about an accident. Of course the news was shocking when I learned that Roger Ebert was killed accidentally when riding a competitive sled. Roger's home was about ten miles from Breezy Point. On that Saturday afternoon he and Tom Otte decided to ride over to Roger's place. Roger checked out a Polaris sled that the team used for comparison with their Liquidators. This track was not equipped with carbide studs that were commonly used when running on ice. It was dark when they began the return ride back to Breezy Point. Since both were race machine drivers they obviously rode hard on the snow-packed gravel road. Tom Otte stated that after a short time he could no longer see Roger's headlight. He turned back and looked carefully for where he had missed a turn. This is where he found Roger, who had started into the turn when the sled skidded sideways and hit an ice ridge. This caused the machine to overturn and threw Roger against a fence post. He died almost instantly due to the severity of his injury.

This news spread like wildfire throughout Deere-land. Jon Carlson remembers that R.J. flew to Breezy Point the next day to meet with the team. He told them that each team member was free to make his own decision on whether to continue racing, but Deere would continue their support if they did. He congratulated them all on their accomplishments. The team did race for the rest of the year. "To this day most of the team members keep in contact and some of us still get together on special occasions," Jon said. Bobby Enns was the other member of all Deere factory and Deere & Co. race teams. The *Green Streak* newsletters for 1977 show that he had an outstanding year with numerous wins and top ten finishes. "We all had a great time working with and racing John Deere sleds. I don't know if we knew that we had too much fun at the time, but when I look back, I wouldn't want to change a thing we did. It was an honor to race for Deere," Bob said,

Reflecting on his experience as the EDT Race Director, Al said, "I enjoyed the competition, as my life work was in competitive sports, acting as a coach. There was some resistance because I was not a professional snowmobile driver, and significant personal sacrifice was required as we had long periods of absence from home. For me personally, working for JD was a very good experience." The 1977 race season was the last year that Deere fielded a factory or corporate race team. Dealers and independent drivers were using Deere production sleds that were very competitive in racing. The composite of Deere race teams contributed what they were intended to do: provide knowledge about competitive snowmobiles to the engineering department, and help Deere Marketing sell snowmobiles to consumers.

Lessons Learned from Racing

What was learned in racing that carried directly over to the consumer sled design? From the first year, racing production machines with few modifications pointed out the weakness of the torque converter and belt drive system. JD raced with the Kohler 295cc engine in the first year's model JD 400 race sled. The JD 295/S model the second year was powered with the Kioritz engine leading the way for the use of Kioritz engines in nearly all machines for the next several years. Both the Kohler and Kioritz engines were competitive with other factory sleds in the WSP I-500 cross-country race. The engine and its relationship to the clutch forced Horicon to abandon its plan to use components supplied to the industry and design their own clutch system. The float bowl carburetors used in the first years of production caused engine failures due to the extreme bouncing and twisting encountered in the highly variable terrain. The rapid growth of new engine technology for 2-cycle engines in snowmobiles later caused Deere to adopt Kawasaki to supply engines that used proven motorcycle engine technology. Tracks and suspensions were improved rapidly during the years in racing, especially when Deere moved to the front-engine machines. The races demonstrated the superior handling of the competitive front-engine sleds.

Horicon and PEC engineering resources were focused on correcting issues with poor durability and performance of engine and drive systems from the first two years of production — not in design of a new chassis. Increasing horsepower, as was done with the first JDX8 machines, only exacerbated the performance and durability problems in the original design. The benefit from racing in 1972 and 1973 was the accelerated improvement of engines and clutches in both performance and durability. The first all-new front-engine chassis for racing was the JD 340/S in 1974–1975. The new chassis was designed with help contracted from people with extensive racing experience. This was a significant breakthrough from the past by utilizing outside personnel to work directly with the design engineers. The JD 340/S established John Deere as a formidable competitor for cross-country racing with 3rd- and 4th-place finishes in the WSP I-500 race as well as wins in other races. The Liquidator followed the 340/S in 1976 powered by the first liquid-cooled engine. The power growth of the Kioritz engines was driven directly by racing. The two years of racing the Liquidator brought Deere to the top level of competition in cross-country racing. One can contend that Deere dominated the cross-country race scene in 1976 and '77. Winning seven races the second year with the Liquidator was beyond expectations. While the Liquidator was strongly competitive, the concept and physical conditioning of Enduro Team Deere contributed greatly to the overall success.

What else did Deere learn from racing that wasn't available from the feedback from consumer machines? The answer is hidden in the meaning of the word performance. In racing, the market can see readily which machines perform the best and are most durable. Horicon lacked understanding of why and how fast markets were changing when they first entered the business. Since the initial Deere target market was trail riding, the design of the JD 400 and 500 models emphasized comfort and durability. The mid-engine chassis was rapidly being abandoned as competition developed new designs of front-engine chassis snowmobiles during racing.

Being involved in racing created demanding schedules that required people to make extraordinary contributions of time and effort to meet rigid deadlines. This type of dedication was invaluable to the success of future engineering programs. At home during two Christmas dinners, the phone rang and R.J. asked Ron to round up a few of his engineers and meet the Deere plane at Juneau the next morning to help the race team resolve machine issues and concerns. The direct-drive Spitfire, as described earlier, was born out of an airplane trip to the Park Rapids cross-country race when Tom Lohr and the authors were stranded during a blizzard. Daring to think about an unconventional approach to design often leads to a breakthrough. This type of thinking is common in racing. During racing the performance metric is clear: win. Winning can occur when the driver and the machine are at peak performance. It is commonplace for people to say luck is involved. What is luck? The word is used to describe the interaction of numerous random chance variables that determine the outcome. Working on the frontiers of knowledge to achieve maximum performance in racing was a learning experience for the entire snowmobile engineering staff that was more than just luck.

The entire Horicon engineering group developed skills on how to work to achieve rapid response to correct problems and adhere to deadlines. There were shortcomings in being able to meet schedules in the early years. Although there were many reasons for this, any organization must understand how to make plans that balance expectations with the knowledge and resources available to do this work. In business, competition has the same metric: win—commonly understood to mean being a leader in the chosen industry and being profitable. Supporting race machine efforts and consumer machines in the same engineering department was a double-edged sword. Racing always took top priority. However, the lessons learned from racing contributed to the future productivity of Horicon Works engineering. Without doubt, others like sales branch marketing and Deere & Co. in Moline learned a great deal from their experiences with snowmobiles.

Dick Teal and Lee Hardesty had prior significant experience in achieving peak performance from drive train components. Dick Teal had raced go-carts when working for Fox in Janesville, Wisconsin. He won the Eagle River World's Championship snowmobile race in 1964–1965 driving his twin go-cart-engine-powered Fox Snowmobile. He also participated in the design of the Fox snowmobiles. When working at Salsbury, he calibrated the torque converters on many competitor snowmobiles to obtain peak performance from the many different engines.

Lee had worked with tractor engines to develop peak power for tractor pulls. For those engines, more air and fuel were pumped through the same displacement of production engines to achieve two to three times the power output of a customer's tractor engine, but only for a very short time. Lee helped Kioritz to develop the 295/S race engine in Japan. This was the first engine designed specifically with improved performance as the metric. After this race engine, Lee directed the design and development of every Kioritz snowmobile engine. Upon transferring to Horicon in 1974, he was responsible for all of the improvements made to existing suppliers' engines and related components for all Horicon products. Neither Dick Teal nor Lee Hardesty would have come to Horicon if Deere had not been in racing. Change in large organizations is usually driven by a pressing need. Horicon engineering needed to increase in size and in depth of skills for the challenges they faced in all consumer product markets in addition to snowmobiles.

Even with limited resources, Horicon benefited from the deep involvement with racing. JD racing was successful in doing what racing was supposed to do: win races to improve the company image in machine performance. More importantly, the experience helped Horicon engineering and the factory develop a sense of urgency in design and development that carried over to fuel the later successes that Horicon had with grounds-care products. The popular term for this work process in those years was simultaneous engineering. That described the state of the art of the Horicon organization by the end of the '70s. The legacy of learning how to respond rapidly to changing market requirements with snowmobiles was integrated into the design of new lawn and garden products. Those projects all benefited from a different approach to market research that more clearly defined the customer needs in different segments of the market.

9

Designing the New Breed of Deere

The journey to the "New Breed of Deere" front-engine snowmobiles was launched by the direct drive discussion while the authors and Tom Lohr were snowbound in Fargo, North Dakota. The Spitfire that was created from this discussion was on track to be manufactured in the summer of 1977 as a 1978 model. A Kohler 340cc free-air engine powered the Spitfire. Horicon Works had used a Kohler fan-cooled engine during production of the JD 295/S and JD 300. The piston ports were modified at Kohler under Lee's supervision to achieve the desired torque curve. Lee worked with Kohler to shape the ports to achieve the required engine torque at the lower engine RPM. When this was combined with Dick Teal's ability to recalibrate the clutch shift pattern, the vehicle that resulted performed surprisingly well. This engine and clutch combination eliminated a gearbox and the shorter chassis reduced the weight of the sled. To address any sales branch concern about the performance, Horicon Works invited R.J. Carlson to come to Horicon and ride the final design. After only a short ride he stopped and said it functioned quite well, although it obviously was not intended for larger adults or high-performance enthusiasts. The Spitfire was a much shorter and lighter-weight machine than anything the Horicon engineers had considered.

The Horicon Works manufactured 8,024 Spitfires for the 1978 model year, along with 5,995 Cyclone and Liquifire sleds, which were virtually unchanged from the previous year. This low production resulted from the huge dealer inventory of unsold sleds. The market demonstrated it was ready for a smaller, lighter-weight snowmobile, as sales of the Spitfire were good during another year of moderate snowfall. The smaller and lighter Spitfire did cost less to manufacture; consequently, it was priced lower in the market. Smaller adults and youth liked it, as it was easier for them to maneuver and control. Ice fishermen soon discovered that two people could lift it onto the bed of a pickup. The Spitfire was handy to tow ice fishing tents and related fishing gear on the frozen lakes. This was the last year of production for the Cyclone and Liquifire. A total of 62,331 had been manufactured during the three years Deere made their first front-engine consumer model snowmobiles.

Although the '76 model Cyclone and Liquifire snowmobiles were acclaimed as excellent sleds, they were still heavier than most major competition. What was lacking was weight and cost reduction on those machines and a chassis design that would excite

John Deere Spitfire (courtesy Roger Tesch).

the market as the Spitfire had done for the smaller or younger drivers. All of the major drive train components were functioning well on all models. As some of the engineering resources were assigned to grounds-care projects, Dick Teal accepted the assignment to explore a new design that would be lighter weight and lower cost. This work was successful and became a new snowmobile chassis that was marketed in 1979 as the Trailfire, along with the Spitfire, as the "New Breed of Deere." This project is discussed in some detail as it well illustrates the approach needed for all successful projects: careful definition of the goals and verification of the marketability of a concept should be carried out before doing full-scale design, development and tooling for production.

Trailfire Design by Dick Teal

Dick began this project in late 1976 along with Carl Firehammer, who had demonstrated that he was an excellent designer and a hard worker, especially on the race machines like the JD 340/S project. Their first efforts were to study every component in the Cyclone and Liquifire sleds to see if cost reduction was possible, or if they could devise a less complex design to manufacture. The first prototype was produced quickly and driven on the frozen Rock River just below the engineering building. They were not pleased with the results of their hard work, and others who rode the machine weren't impressed either. "The sled was just another snowmobile that would cost less to produce and it had a lot of bad features, including poor handling. We quickly came to the conclusion this wasn't the direction we should pursue," Dick said.

After some thought and discussion, Carl and Dick decided to make the best ride and best-performing snowmobile they could and to call it a mid-size snowmobile instead of mid-price. This simple decision totally changed how they approached the project. They divided the drawing duties, with Dick doing the suspension and Carl the front of the sled and the overall machine layout. To get the center of gravity low, they focused on positioning the engine and drive train as close to the track drive axle as possible. This meant that the ground clearance between the skis had to be reduced to lower those components. The second key objective in all parts of the sled was to reduce weight. "Carl and I developed the next prototype in record time. One big advantage was there were only two of us," Dick said. They did the design on layout boards typically used in that era with pencil and paper, as there were no computers. Additional engineers were added to the project after the decision was made to make the prototype so they could quickly evaluate the performance in typical snow areas. Sketches or drawings were completed of the parts made in the engineering shop by skilled craftsmen.

CHASSIS

Dick had used 80,000 psi minimum yield steel for the sheaves on the new Deere secondary torque converter and decided to use this high-strength steel for the front center pan and side supports, as it would take a lot of abuse without bending, yet would be very lightweight. This resulted in a front frame that was almost indestructible. Years later he observed that if the pan did get bent it required the full force of a 20-pound maul to bend it into shape or a Porta-Power hydraulic straightening tool to fix it. After discussing the merit of this material with Horicon manufacturing people, they agreed.

The tunnel material selected was mild steel because the manufacturing department had a monster-welding fixture for the aluminum tunnel snowmobiles that they wanted to use. Steel was also a significant cost savings over an aluminum tunnel. Carl opposed using steel for the tunnel and he "tested" the tunnel side rail stiffness by jumping up and down on it to see if it would bend. They reshaped the rolled edge to get the most strength with the thinnest steel that was practical. Even though Horicon Works had modern methods to test components, this was the method used to determine what went into production. Materials engineering had also expressed concern about galvanic corrosion at points where aluminum and steel were in contact. "Using steel turned out to be a bad choice due to customer acceptance, so the design was changed to aluminum after the first model year," Dick said. "The manufacturing department learned how to rivet aluminum instead of welding so the monster, costly weld fixture disappeared."

Dick chose to use a new plastic material for the front side pans then used in the auto industry for front and rear bumper covers. This thermo plastic rubber (TPR) material could handle the wide temperature swings a snowmobile experienced and would bend without breaking. This was important because snowmobiles hit trees, shrubs and numerous other trail obstructions. Tooling was inexpensive since the material could be vacuum-formed. This was another example of working with manufacturing before a firm design direction was established so a win-win situation was created with lower cost parts and less investment in manufacturing tooling. This was the correct decision, as TPR became an instant hit with customers and dealers. The front bumper was extruded aluminum that was used to attach the TPR pans to the frame. Holes were added to the bumper, and after it was fastened to the pan, a fluorescent decal covered the screws. This was simple, low-cost and effective. The emerging culture of design and manufacturing working simultaneously during design at Horicon Works was replacing the throw-it-over-the-wall method that was the heritage from long product life cycles for the agricultural products.

Rear Suspension

The goal for the mid-size sled suspension vertical travel was 4 inches, almost twice the travel of the current production sleds. The design objective was to keep the track at constant tension when the sled went over bumps and moguls. Dick selected a four-bar linkage to keep the geometry simple. Initially he started to lay out the suspension using a mechanical map-reader to measure the track length but this was cumbersome and took a lot of time. In late 1974 Horicon Works had purchased their first engineering computer, which was in a locked room in the test department. Dick and Tom Newhouse worked for several days to load the geometry Dick proposed into the program to calculate the track length with different locations of the four-bar linkage to reach the goal of four inches of vertical travel. Tom had learned how to use this analytical tool to assist the design groups with complex geometry design projects. This was the only computer in the factory other than the one in the accounting department (who were key-punching payroll cards, among other business data needs). Tom called the software company to download the program each day. Within a few years, more vertical travel became popular as the industry rapidly adopted motorcycle suspension technology to provide greater vertical suspension travel desired by the customers.

Prior JD race sleds were successfully designed with an extruded aluminum suspension slide rail, so Dick pushed the envelope a little farther, and made this design from lighter, thinner-gauge material. Since the seat also is part of the suspension, this design used the maximum possible amount of foam. The seat safety standard that Deere engineers had fostered as the company began to manufacture snowmobiles required a multi-density foam process to pass the seat test requirements in the standard. This standard was developed using the acceleration shock load data the U.S. Air Force had devised to safely eject pilots from the cockpit of an airplane. Any new snowmobile seat design had to pass the performance test specified in the SAE seat standard. Deere initiated development of this standard as they entered the business, as back injuries were too common when riding the early snowmobiles. The new suspension and seat combination provided a very stable and comfortable ride over any competition when the Trailfire was manufactured.

TRACK ASSEMBLY

The track chosen for the Trailfire was a basic rubber apron with riveted grouser bars. It was produced at the Horicon factory to reduce the cost compared to purchasing it from a suppler. This simple design was chosen for two reasons: it needed to be low-cost, and to operate better in deep powder snow. With this type of track the lightweight Trailfire would have good traction in the light powder snow. Industry suppliers were developing a molded track, but it was at least one year away from being available in high-volume production. The snowmobile suppliers were changing rapidly as they sought new markets for their improved developments with the OEMs in the industry. After the first year Trailfire models were produced, the new molded tracks were used on the higher power JD Sportfire and Liquifire models that were built on the Trailfire chassis.

ENGINE

In the agreement with Kawasaki, Horicon Works planned to introduce their 340cc and 440cc engines in production in 1978 for 1979 models—just one year after Ray Gregg signed the supply agreement with them. Lee Hardesty was responsible for developing the lightweight fan-cooled engines that used a single Mikuni carburetor. With high quality die cast manifolds, only one carburetor was needed to supply the fuel to both cylinders vs. two carburetors that Horicon had used with Kioritz to control the air-fuel mix.

SHIPPING

Dick also investigated the optimum size of machine to obtain the lowest shipping cost. To fit more machines into a truckload required focus on the sled height and length. After discussing the shipping container with Bob Pedigo, the manager of Horicon Works Manufacturing Engineering, Dick proceeded to design the sled so it would fit into a standard eight-foot-wide semi trailer. Doing this enabled the factory to ship more machines in a trailer load. The cost of shipping was a major part of total vehicle cost delivered to the dealer. The steering column needed to be eight inches lower to reach the maximum number of sleds per load. Instead of a rigid steering column and handlebar, a fold-down design resulted that a dealer could easily position and secure in place. This simple design significantly reduced the shipping costs.

Kawasaki 340 and 440 Trailfire engine (courtesy Lee Hardesty).

Prototype number 1

The first prototype Trailfire was built in the PED shop in a few weeks. The shop employees responded to the enthusiasm of Dick and Carl's project as they hastened to complete the prototype build. The chassis and most components were well underway, but the styled parts would come later, after HDA was brought into the project. Carl suggested making the hood and side pans out of fiberglass in the PED shop so they could test the concept more quickly. The sled was something that looked low and sleek that Carl said had a Cracker Jack box appearance. The prototype sled was taken to the Hurley, Wisconsin, test site and it soon became obvious that it was something special. Plant manager Ray Gregg, marketing manager Mike Heitman, and Ron Leonard were invited to the Hurley test site to drive the prototype. "I remember the first time Ray Gregg drove the sled from a par 3 tee to the green and back. He got off and said build it. We were on our way," Dick said. Soon memos started to fly around the factory and marketing manager Mike Heitman suggested that a liquid-cooled version of the sled should be named the Wildfire. He also believed this chassis would immediately replace the Cyclone.

JOHN DEERE COMPANY

701 GEORGESVILLE ROAD, COLUMBUS, OHIO 43228

16 March 1977

TO: Carl Firehammer, Ray Gregg, Jack Hoffman, Stan Kleiss, Jim Lamont, Ron Leonard, Dick Teal

FROM: Mike Heitman

SUBJECT: MID-SIZE SNOWMOBILE

Here are some thoughts about the mid-size sled.

1. Terrific - best sled I have ever driven.

2. Low profile may not be totally acceptable to less performance oriented buyers, but would be for high performance package. Be careful here.

3. Operator position is excellent - seat, handlebars, footrests, etc. Be sure women and kids are also considered.

4. Put storage in front of seat. 6+ gallons of fuel acceptable.

5. Engine and clutch performance is excellent for first proto's. Work on fuel consumption. 340 vs. 440 engine unanswerable at this time. Sounds good, but some people still like 340. We need to be careful and right with the selection.

6. Suggest two family versions the introductory year. Call them TRAILFIRE I and II, possibly

   A in 340cc (or 440cc)
   B in 440cc

   Hold down price (cost $)

7. Suggest liquid version in the second year. Call it WILDFIRE. This sled would replace Liquifire in probably one year.

8. The mid-size will definitely replace the Cyclone in the introductory year.

9. Build early as possible; in fact, a low build pilot run would be best. It would even be good to run in Pro-Stock class.

In closing, you are right on, and this sled will be just what we need to make it in this business. My only problem at this point is waiting for it.

Mike/ph

MKH/ph

Mike Heitman (Marketing Dept.) Trailfire comments (Richard Teal collection).

Styling the Trailfire

All Deere factories used the industrial styling design services of the HDA organization since President Wiman contracted Henry Drefuss to style the 1938 model John Deere tractors. The HDA influence within engineering groups at Deere factories was sometimes challenged if styling suggestions caused redesign or added cost. It was always

Original Bill Crookes (HDA) sketch of Trailfire (Richard Teal collection).

best to have HDA involved from the beginning of any project. The initial Trailfire configuration was designed without their input, but that worked well as the first requirement was to evaluate the merit of the low-profile snowmobile in order to determine if the project would proceed to production.

A slim, sleek look had always been emphasized in any styling sketches that HDA ever made for snowmobiles. Some conflict had occurred at Horicon with the JD 400 and 500 snowmobiles that were built on the mid-engine chassis. This placement caused the hood profile to be high, which made the sled look top-heavy. Whether or not HDA styling advice was followed was up to the design group and their management. All presidents or CEOs of Deere believed that the customers for Deere products wanted machines to be strong and purposeful but look neat and tidy. This had been done tastefully with the styling of the first garden tractors manufactured at Horicon in 1963 and with all the other implements and self-propelled machines made at other Deere units. Jim Connors of HDA often reminded the factory management that styling needed to reflect ever-changing consumer taste in shape and color, but Ron never had an experience when the HDA organization tried to compromise the performance of a machine with styling dictates. Their personnel always researched other products in that industry to better understand the customers' styling preferences. The styling decisions at the units were normally made with input from their marketing personnel and approved by the unit management.

It was not unusual for Deere engineering designers to take offense at what they interpreted as interference with their design. This is a good trait for a designer, but it always needs to be set aside to allow input from others who can better judge the final shape and graphics that will most likely appeal to the market. Subjective judgments are uncomfortable for those who work daily in the arena of objective measurement of performance in test and evaluation of engineering designs.

The Trailfire design was spared this controversy, as the initial design decisions on placement of machine components enhanced the sled performance in a manner that a snowmobile enthusiast would appreciate. Bill Crookes, the HDA associate responsible for the Horicon factory, was contacted to provide input to the appearance of the Trailfire. After the decision to proceed to production with the Trailfire, a copy of the full-scale layout was sent to the HDA New York office for Bill to use for styling. Horicon requested a cover over the front of the sled that emphasized the low profile. Shortly after Bill received the drawing, he was on a plane coming to Horicon. "He arrived at the PED with a fabulous colored sketch. I told him that he had met my expectations. It was some time later that I learned that he had done the sketch on the plane ride from New York," Dick said.

The Horicon engineering department clay room was purposefully built in the 1974–75 building expansion to provide a dedicated room for styling. Bill oversaw the build of the modeling clay buck built on a Trailfire chassis. With this room located in the engineering department, engineers could quickly verify that the shape provided

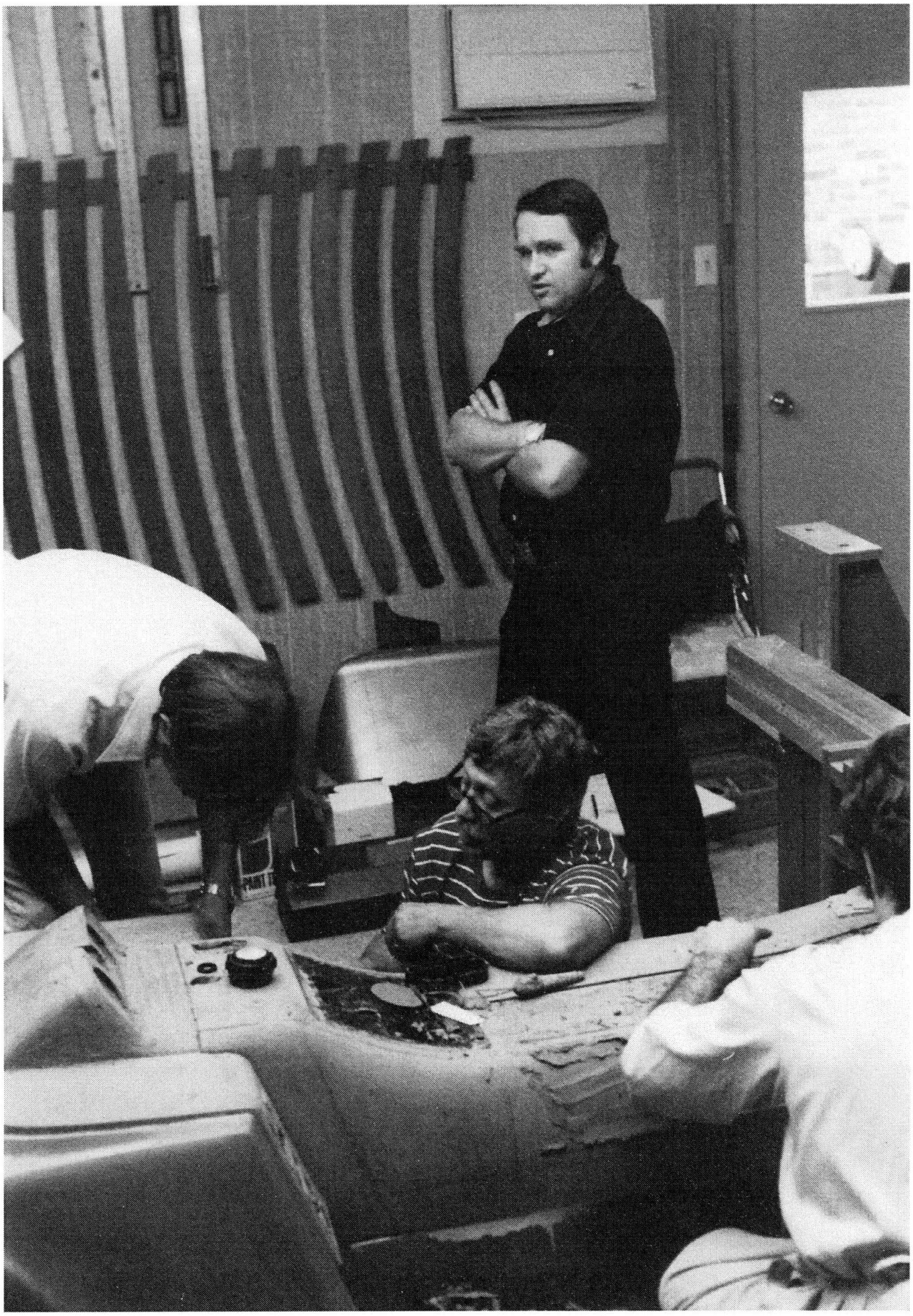

Richard Teal watching the full-size clay model development (Richard Teal collection).

the needed clearance for under-hood components. In a very short time the clay model of the hood took shape and it looked as good as the sketch Bill made.

Once the clay was roughed out with a shape that would wrap around all of the under hood components, it was sent to Detroit, where the surface was finished and a master pattern made from the clay model. The master pattern provided a means for the Horicon PED to produce fiberglass prototype hoods and covers for the pan and fuel tank. With this process the parts for the second build prototype machines were made quickly. "The prime rule for styling is 'form follows function,' and in the development of the Trailfire it actually did," Dick said. After the field performance evaluation of the first prototypes was completed at Hurley, the engineers returned to Horicon to complete the design and build of the second prototype Trailfire sleds. After operating them locally to verify they were sound, the engineers shipped the sleds to Alaska to complete a long winter of testing their durability and performance. In prior years the Horicon Works had operated test programs at Cantwell, Alaska, when the new Deere torque converter was being developed before first production.

Dick described the test location in Alaska where the Horicon Works' engineers and test drivers would operate for many weeks until the test program was completed:

> Cantwell is located at the far western end of the Denali Highway a short distance from Mount McKinley, about halfway between Anchorage and Fairbanks. When John Deere started testing snowmobiles at Cantwell, the Alaskan oil pipeline wasn't started. Upon arriving in Anchorage, they rented a large box truck with a power lift, and then proceeded to the freight terminal to pick up the snowmobiles and crates full of tools and spare parts. The test mechanics and Dick had flown out of Chicago on the same 747 that the freight was on. Anchorage only had a few paved streets and some buildings hadn't recovered or been rebuilt after the great earthquake a few years earlier and a military base was outside of town. As construction of the pipeline began, Anchorage grew and the surroundings began to drastically change.

Dick said, "We stayed at the Jack River Inn in Cantwell. The Inn was also a gasoline station, grocery store, tavern and restaurant." Electricity was provided by a large diesel engine that ran a generator 24 hours a day. Telephone conversations were sent over microwave transmission towers, so their communication was limited.

One evening after they were settled, the crew went to a bar and met some of the locals. After this the postmaster of Cantwell contacted Dick and asked him to deliver mail to a few homes on the Denali Highway. This was an unusually hard winter and some patrons had not gotten their mail for weeks. After agreeing to help, Dick went to the post office, where he learned some of the people who lived outside of town could only communicate via shortwave radio or by snowmobile in the dead of winter. The mail was sorted into packets and had instructions written on each one. This year the Denali Highway already had a base of 20 feet of snow covering it. The postmaster cautioned him to be especially careful as they approached the homes because they had dogs and guns to keep the bad guys away.

The next day he started on the mail route with another engineer. Since the test plan included exposure to many different riding conditions, this was a productive trip.

The standard test procedure was to always ride with two sleds wherever you were to minimize the danger from any unexpected event. As they approached the first house, they stopped about 100 yards away because the dogs were aroused and barking. After a few minutes the owner came outside with his rifle to see what was going on. "About the time I started to wonder if my budding career as a mailman was over, I held up the mailbag and he waved me closer," Dick said. The postmaster had radioed him that they were coming with his mail. He was really appreciative and said he would radio the next home that the mail was on the way. This scenario was repeated as they continued on to complete the mail delivery by snowmobile along the Denali Highway. Dick recalls they delivered the mail one other year when they were at Cantwell.

In remote locations it was normal for the test crews to participate with the locals in their off-work time by doing different things. In Cantwell during the winter the locals played basketball at the school gymnasium. They invited the John Deere test personnel to participate. This continued to develop over the years and became very competitive. Dick recalls that the locals had taller players delivered from remote locations by the state police cars. When the game was scheduled, the Horicon Works attempted to have the best and tallest engineers or test mechanics to make the game more interesting. The local turnout for this game was a highlight in the long winters in Cantwell. Dick recalls that the Horicon Works team was featured in one of the school publications. In the off-work hours, the test personnel looked for almost any diversion to help them endure the long absences from home.

Susitna River Experience

Another interesting experience occurred while testing the Trailfire prototypes in Alaska. The drivers rode their sleds out the Denali Highway heading east, where there were limitless locations with a wide variety of snow conditions where a customer might ride. On one of their first test rides they discovered a restaurant a long way from Cantwell that was closed, but the people staying there would open it if they wanted them to. "This worked great because the location was an ideal spot for a fuel depot. We made a gas sled by adding a pair of snowmobile skis to a pallet and towed a 50-gallon drum of gasoline out to the restaurant," Dick said.

The restaurant was located a few miles from the Susitna River. One day someone suggested they go see the river, so they proceeded to find their way. When the Horicon test crew approached the river bridge, they encountered a Yamaha snowmobile test group. They stopped to talk with them but it was obvious they had been drinking alcohol for some time. Their group leader was drunk. When Dick asked him how things were going, he started cussing out the sleds they were testing and said they were junk. Then he pulled out a pistol and started shooting at their sleds with live ammunition. "I wished them luck and suggested to our crew that we leave immediately, and that was the last time I went to the river," Dick said.

Sled in the Tree

The Horicon Alaska test crew had an unfortunate experience that is still vivid in Dick's memory. Two Japanese engineers from the carburetor or the engine supplier were working with Rob Feldman. One morning of an almost fatal day, Rob and the two guests left on three sleds to see the sites around Cantwell. The day wore on but there was no sign of them returning to the garage shop. Dick asked Horicon engineer Larry Swanson to ride down the Denali Highway to see if he could find them. It wasn't long before Larry returned with one of the Japanese engineers, then went back and got the second one. They had abandoned their sleds and were walking on the road back to Cantwell. Both were very cold but they didn't have frostbite. Larry went out one more time and returned with Rob, who was in bad shape. He had frostbite and was going into hypothermia. They placed Rob in front of a large potbelly stove in the garage. The brandy they gave him may have helped more than the stove to get his body temperature up. Rob recovered as well from what could have been a fatal experience.

By the time Larry found Rob, it was getting dark, so they decided to retrieve the sleds the next day. "What happened to the sleds is the rest of the story," Dick said. The next day they went to find them and were able to develop a clear understanding of what had happened the previous day. Rob and the two guests had ridden east into the surrounding hills. At some point Rob, who was an experienced sled rider, became separated from the two guests. They had ridden on steep slopes where Rob went one way and the Japanese went another way but couldn't follow Rob. The Japanese engineers were not experienced riders, and as they wound their way down the hill they came to a steep bank and stopped. Seeing the Denali highway in the distance, they decided to leave the sleds and walk out through waist-deep snow. Larry spotted them on the highway, nearly exhausted. "They were lucky to make it to the road where Larry found them," Dick said.

They found Rob's sled by following his tracks in the deep snow to a tree. The sled was caught in its branches, and it took about six men to get the machine freed from it. Rob had gone around the backside of a hill, but when he turned to come down he encountered a steep bank. As he rode off the bank the sled landed in a tree where the track wound around the branches, thus trapping it high above the snowbank below. Rob also decided to walk out to the highway. Larry spotted him about one quarter mile from the road struggling through waist-deep snow, just like the Japanese engineers had experienced. "Rob made it but I considered him to be lucky that he was still alive," Dick said. Next they found the two sleds the Japanese had left at the steep bank. Dick rode one and a test mechanic the other down the bank to the flat and out to the road. It ended with everyone OK and the sleds weren't damaged.

After the snow melted, the machines were loaded back into the containers and shipped to Horicon PED, where they were carefully inspected to verify the condition of every part on the machines. Safety engineers scrutinized the daily test logs from the test program and all the key data were logged into the factory Reliability data bank along with results recorded from every test program. About May 1977 the decision was taken to prepare the Trailfire for production in late winter of 1978, less than a year later. This project benefited from the proven clutch system and new KHI engines that were available from production tooling.

Jack Hoffman prepared the project production release schedule that was developed in cooperation with manufacturing and sent to Duane Trautman, who was responsible

JOHN DEERE HORICON WORKS

220 EAST LAKE, HORICON, WISCONSIN 53032

To: Trautman, Dwayne D.

cc: Kuchta, Darrell G.
Lamont, James A.
Teal, Richard D.

From: Hoffman, Jack E. Jack

Date: 1 June 1977

Subject: PILOT BUILD OF MID-SIZE SNOWMOBILE

Dwayne,

To confirm our phone conversation regarding pilot build dates for the mid-size sled.....

The new proposal is:

1 Jun 77 -- Info for AFE preparation

1 Jul 77 -- Submit AFE to Deere & Company

1 Aug 77 -- Preliminary Decision w/first group of prints

12 Aug 77 -- Final Decision w/final group of prints for JDHW Mfgr. parts and assemblies

2 Sep 77 -- Release for tooling on hood, console, etc.

7 Dec 77 -- Tool tryout starts

2 Jan 78 -- RIM parts available for test, etc.

1 Feb 78 -- Start pilot build

15 Feb 78 -- Finish build of pilot run

This schedule will provide sleds for the final test program (in northern Wisconsin), photo program and introductory Marketing meetings.

Schedule for Trailfire pilot build (Richard Teal collection).

for preparation of the tooling and assembly of the new snowmobile. The product engineers focused their efforts on completion of any needed design revisions that were finished by August 12, 1977, before the Engineering Decision released the parts for production. The pilot production machines built by the factory in February 1978 were used for the second major new dealer product introduction at West Yellowstone, held in March 1978. The AFE and production release were completed on schedule. A small pilot production run of both Trailfire models, with the Kawasaki 340cc and 440cc fan-cooled engines, was manufactured by the factory for the dealer introduction. A second benefit of the pilot run was it provided sleds for the Horicon PED to test that winter to verify that the machine performance was satisfactory before regular production.

The dealer introduction to the new sleds was held at West Yellowstone so they could experience the huge performance improvement of the new, lighter-weight Trailfire. The deep powder snow in the mountains and rough mogul trail riding there made it an ideal location to demonstrate the Trailfire compared with all major models of competitive machines. The second year's production of the Spitfire was included so both machines would be familiar to all of the Deere sales branch marketing people along with their dealers. Larry Nenneman, the Horicon marketing department snowmobile product manager, described his role in that dealer event that demonstrated both Trailfire and Spitfire snowmobiles as the New Breed of Deere: "Overall about 10,000 people were exposed to the machines during several weeks. Groups of 200 dealers from all over North America were taken every afternoon on a long trail ride following the classroom sessions in the morning," Larry said. Every night the Service Department personnel had to recondition machines that had been damaged before the next morning, when the process started all over again. This exposure, likely the largest snowmobile product introduction ever undertaken, was intended to instill confidence in the dealer that these machines were excellent performance sleds—and Deere was committed to stay in the business.

The downside of the meeting was that Larry had to explain why there was no new Liquifire that year. Carryover inventory of the 1978 model Liquifire was available at dealers, as well as Liquidators, and both were very competitive in racing. To shore up dealer confidence, they were told that a new Liquifire would be available the next year with a liquid-cooled Kawasaki engine on the new Trailfire chassis. A mockup of the proposed design was displayed high off the floor in the large meeting room. The Kawasaki 340 and 440cc fan-cooled engines powered the new Trailfire the first year of production. This was the last dealer snowmobile new product introduction by Deere.

During the West Yellowstone dealer product introduction meetings, the Horicon PED used this opportunity to refine the calibration of the Trailfire engine and clutch in the higher altitudes. The Mikuni carburetor engineer, Tosh Okabioshi, was present to assist Rob Feldman, Horicon engine engineer, with this work. Ron was nominated to take Tosh on a ride through Geyser Basin to see the geyser and return going past Yellowstone Lake via the North Highway back to West Yellowstone. Tosh was between

Horicon engineer Rob Feldman at the rear and Ron in front. Riding from the town of West Yellowstone into Geyser Basin was like a scene out of *The Wizard of Oz*. They stopped frequently so Tosh could take pictures of the amazing sights. The highway was buried under several feet of snow moguls that were caused by endless plowing. This shaped the surface of the hard packed snow above the roadway like waves. Riding slowly felt like the sensation of riding a boat in heavy seas. The endless succession of ups and downs is certain to be tiring. The fun begins when the sled is going fast enough so you skip from top to top as if you were flying, doing touchdowns and becoming airborne again. But ride slowly so you don't miss seeing the huge elk warming in the gently flowing water of Yellowstone River.

Further along toward Geyser Basin, the buffalo herds pawed away the heavy snow cover to graze. The stop at Old Faithful was a stunning contrast with its appearance in summer. After the hot water spouts from the mouth of the geyser, a cloud of steam blankets the area. The mouth of the geyser is hidden below a ring of large ice stalagmites. After stopping at the geyser, they continued on toward Yellowstone Lake to take the north road back to town. As they approached the summit, the trail was several feet deep with steep banks on each side. Occasionally a lazy buffalo chose to use the trail rather than plow a path through the deep snow. Coming up the trail close to the summit was a huge buffalo. They stopped immediately, and while pointing to the oncoming buffalo, Ron shouted to Tosh to climb over the bank and wait until it passed. A career-ending experience flashed through his mind at the thought of injury or worse to the guest. Rob and Ron both scrambled over the top of the snow-bank but Tosh didn't follow! They peered over the snow bank and saw Tosh standing on his sled removing his Japanese camera from the glove box. He ignored pleas to get out of there. Instead he waited patiently until the buffalo was alongside the first sled and began to shoot pictures. The buffalo acted as if no one was there — it just veered around the sleds and disappeared over the summit. "This was my last time as a tour guide with foreign visitors. Many years later I toured a Mikuni factory in India and to my surprise the factory manager was Tosh," Ron said.

As the West Yellowstone dealer meetings were winding down, the Horicon PED tested pilot production Trailfires at their Hurley, Wisconsin, test site. Any minor corrections that were needed were implemented immediately at the Horicon Works before high-volume production began in May 1978 of 22,286 snowmobiles: 7,000 Spitfire, 5,043 Trailfire 340, and 10,243 Trailfire 440. The market responded very well to the New Breed of Deere snowmobiles. Both machines validated the concept that customer expectations must be the first thing to verify in design of any engine-powered machine. The dealers experienced the sensation of riding on a significantly improved snowmobile chassis. The first sentence of the *Snow Goer* article sums up the general opinion in the market about the new Deere snowmobiles: "Traditionally, Deere has at best been traditional." This sled (Trailfire) changed that opinion. The industry trade press agreed that Deere had now moved into a leadership position. (The *Snow Goer* test report is in the appendix.)

It had taken several years to reshape the design and work processes for production of snowmobiles at the Horicon Works. This project demonstrated many of the different work processes that were being implemented: concurrent design with manufacturing, verification of the concept before detailed design, adherence to schedules, product quality improvement with pilot run production, and upfront departmental planning and implementation throughout the factory as the design progressed. However, many of these work process improvements came too late to help the Deere snowmobile business be profitable with the drastic reduction of the market.

More Models Built on the Trailfire Chassis:

The Horicon snowmobile engineers had matured into a very effective and productive organization. Racing contributed to understanding the performance required in extreme conditions, but many customers didn't push their machines to those limits. Finding how to balance those extremes to create a cost-effective design is the art of engineering to obtain commercially viable products. Because Horicon Works was increasing the engineering work on grounds-care machines, several of the snowmobile engineers were assigned to other projects. The remaining snowmobile design group was staffed with very talented personnel. Lee Hardesty continued to implement new higher-power engines for the Liquifire II and Sportfire that were built on the Trailfire chassis and manufactured in 1979 as 1980 models. That year the factory produced 29,898 of the New Breed of Deere that, about the same production level as the 1973 and 1976 models. By 1979 Horicon Works had produced a total of 208,616 machines in nine years of production. This year turned out to be the apex of Deere in the business.

Late in 1979, after most of the 1979 snowmobile production was built, a hurricane-like event occurred in Moline, Illinois, at Deere & Co. that forever changed the snowmobile business in John Deere. R.J. Carlson resigned from the company. This news flashed across Deere-land, as he was widely known by most of the factory management personnel, the Horicon Works organization, the sales branches and their John Deere dealers. His career in marketing had begun in the 1950s as he followed in his father's footsteps and rose to be in charge of the Deere Agricultural Equipment marketing organization. In 1971, with his appointment as senior vice-president of Marketing and Manufacturing Agricultural Equipment, he was in charge of the highest sales volume and most profitable division of the company. The impact of his resignation was devastating to the Deere sales branch marketing organization, as the 1980 production of 1981 models fell to only 7950 snowmobiles. The winter of 1980 was also another year of low snowfall that added to the impact of his resignation.

CEO Bill Hewitt planned to retire in 1982, and President Woody Curtis retired before that. To prepare candidates to advance to those positions, succession planning for replacement candidates for the executive office began in 1975 with the appointment of Bob Hanson to the newly created position of executive vice-president. Although it was not certain that Hanson would succeed Hewitt as CEO, this cast a shadow on the likelihood of R.J.'s advancing to the chairman's office. In 1970 Deere was 112th in the Fortune 500 ranking with sales of $1.043 billion and profits of $42.6 million; by 1979, that had grown to $4.155 billion in sales and profits of $264.8 million. This stunning performance improved the Deere Fortune 500 ranking to 61st from the top. During the turbulent decade of the 1970s Deere sales and profits obviously rose significantly, with the majority of that growth in agricultural products, and the smaller but increasingly profitable consumer products business was always part of the annual sales and profits. It is not the authors' intent to attribute this performance to one person, but there is no doubt that RJ's influence was very strong as he continually urged factories and sales branches to grow and expand profitably. Of equal importance during that time, R.J. nurtured the growth of the independent consumer products marketing organization that enabled Deere to locate consumer product dealers in most of the major metropolitan markets. This marketing organization was being supplied with more new products that were targeted at specific segments of the broad OPEI machinery classifications, not just garden tractors and their attachments. This fulfilled Bill Hewitt's vision of Deere getting into the consumer products market with their own independent marketing organization and the Horicon Works and JDM supplying the products.

Even with lower snowmobile production, the Horicon factory profitability was improving. Lawn and garden product sales were increasing steadily and took a dramatic turn up with the 1979 model introduction of a new line of lawn tractors: the JD 108 and JD 111. They were introduced at an agricultural dealer product introduction in Kansas City. The factory had estimated first-year volume at 5000 machines, but dealer orders poured into the factory. Finally, the factory had to cap the first year production at 15,000 machines, as Horicon and their suppliers could not ramp up production any further. This was a nice problem to have that left little doubt that the market was hungry for better quality and more productive lawn tractors. This project also reinforced the Moline management's decision to support any reasonable and profitable alternative that would enable Deere to exit the snowmobile business.

Even with less engineering resources for snowmobiles, two new models of snowmobiles, Snowfire and Sprintfire, were produced as 1982 models. The Trailfire 440 was replaced with an improved Trailfire LX that same year. In total, eight different models were made from the Trailfire chassis during the six years of manufacture of the New Breed of Deere. By this time Deere had a competitive line of snowmobiles that would compete with the best sleds in the marketplace. The Liquifire II won the 1982 *Snow Goer* Magazine Shoot-Out for Best Handling Snowmobile. (The *Snow Goer* article is in the appendix.) This was clear testimony that the performance of Deere snowmobiles was now at the top of the industry. However, Deere sales declined rapidly as dealers ordered fewer machines or took on competitive sleds, as most were of the opinion that Deere would exit the business.

The next big change would have been independent front-ski long-travel strut suspension and a longer-travel rear suspension to complement it, with even more powerful Kawasaki engines. Two prototypes with independent front suspension (IFS) were built before all snowmobile programs were canceled. They were to be named Wildfire to identify them as higher performance sleds with the new suspension. The last models put into production at Horicon were the Trailfire LX, Snowfire and Sprintfire as 1984 models. Jack Hoffman's handwritten list of snowmobiles was developed for the last major snowmobile PRM, held at Horicon in January 1981.

During the 1981 Christmas vacation the authors' families caravanned to West Yellowstone, for a week of family snowmobiling after most of the new machine work was canceled. They took one of the IFS prototype sleds with a number of other production machines. "The performance and ride of the IFS would have outclassed any of our competitors," Dick Teal said. In 1981 Dick was promoted to project engineer for mowing decks and bagging systems for the lawn and garden tractors.

In the fall of 1983 Deere announced they had sold their snowmobile business to Polaris. Ray Gregg, Jr. and Don Carl, who was director of consumer products marketing, structured the deal with Polaris. The announcement of the sale to Polaris was greeted with mixed emotions at Horicon. In the sales branches, the dealers had read the tea leaves when R.J. resigned in 1979. His efforts to merge the business with Arctic Cat in 1977 and again in 1979, as well as other overtures to competitors, spawned rumors that Deere would exit the business. This made it difficult for dealers to sell snowmobiles. Some Deere dealers began again to sell competitive brands of machines and others went out of business. These events significantly reduced dealer orders for Horicon snowmobiles in the last four years of production.

The day the snowmobile sale announcement was posted on the bulletin boards in the factory, Ray Gregg characterized as a historic day. Production of Horicon products had grown to daily shipments of fifty truck trailer loads from the factory, the highest factory production ever reached. Anthony Earl, governor of the state of Wisconsin, attended the Horicon Works parade of fifty truck trailer loads of products down Lake Street of Horicon. Horicon Works was then in the middle of what was later termed the Decade of Excellence (1976–1986). The Horicon factory achieved record production each year during that period, resulting in significant growth in sales and record profits for the company. After the sale of Deere snowmobiles to Polaris, only four manufacturers were left, who soon enjoyed higher prices and volumes that would have been welcome in the years that Deere was in the business. The last year, the factory produced only 1,705 snowmobiles. Horicon Works made a total of 233,717 sleds during the thirteen years they were in the snowmobile business.

How well did the New Breed of Deere fare? The factory produced a total of 85,310, or 36 percent of the total production. Spitfire volume was 24,173, or 28 percent of the New Breed of Deere. The other models were all built on the new Trailfire chassis. Arguably the Spitfire, at nearly 28 percent of the New Breed of Deere machines, was

23 JAN 79
JEH

PRODUCT REVIEW MACHINE LIST

① SNOWMOBILE DISPLAY IN BUILDING

1980 MODEL SPITFIRE
" 340 TRAILFIRE
" 440 TRAILFIRE
" 440 SPORTFIRE
" 440 LIQUIFIRE
} MARKETING PHOTO SLEDS

440 WILDFIRE
EXTENDED TRAVEL SUSPENSION (ALSO RIDE)

② SNOWMOBILES FOR RIDE

DEERE	COMPETITIVE
1979 MODEL SPITFIRE	SKI DOO CITATION
1980 MODEL SPITFIRE	ARCTIC JAG 3000
-1980 MODEL 340 TRAILFIRE	YAMAHA 300 ENTICER
-1980 MODEL 440 TRAILFIRE	ARCTIC TRAIL CAT
1980 MODEL 440 SPORTFIRE (2)	YAMAHA 440 EXCITER
1980 MODEL 440 LIQUIFIRE (2)	SKI DOO 440 EVEREST
1981 MODEL 440 WILDFIRE	ARCTIC PANTERA
EXTENDED TRAVEL SUSPENSION	KAWASAKI INVADER
	ARCTIC EL TIGRE
	SKI DOO 5500 BLIZZARD
	SKI DOO 9500 BLIZZARD
	POLARIS 340 TXL
	YAMAHA SRX

Last major snowmobile PRM machine list (courtesy Jack Hoffman).

long overdue in the market. In most conditions it was a fun machine to ride. During these last few years the lower cost of manufacturing made snowmobiles a profitable venture for Horicon Works; however, over the entire period, the enterprise was not profitable.

The reader is cautioned that the John Deere snowmobile production chart by Joe Wanie was developed from searching the John Deere parts data system. It is not an official Deere chart. The JD 440S?? model listed last on the left side of the chart was not a production machine; however, it is shown there to reconcile the individual model quantities to match the total produced. All other model names are accurate and the volumes are reasonably correct for most of the models. The shipment line at the bottom came from a different source and is an indication of factory inventory that was not shipped to dealers especially in years of low snowfall. The Horicon Works *Green Streak* in the appendix is another source of interesting reading. This publication has articles about racing snowmobiles for the 1976 and 1977 race teams.

The Deere snowmobile business never recovered from the initial design direction of the first model 400 and 500 snowmobiles that limited dealers to a declining segment

John Deere Snowmobile Production
1971 - 1983

	MY 1972 Totals	MY 1973 Totals	MY 1974 Totals	MY 1975 Totals	MY 1976 Totals	MY 1977 Totals	MY 1978 Totals	MY 1979 Totals	MY 1980 Totals	MY 1981 Totals	MY 1982 Totals	MY 1983 Totals	MY 1984 Totals	TOTALS BY MODEL
JD 400	7740	7348	1900	1804	2400	2401								23593 JD 400
JD 500	4924	4792												9716 JD 500
JD 600		3600	3103	1504										8207 JD 600
X-4		10353												10353 X-4
JDX-8		10897												10897 JDX-8
JD 300			5300	2614	3525	2300								13739 JD 300
JDX-4 SLIDE			4533	2180										6713 JDX-4 SLIDE
JDX-6 SLIDE			5358	1004										6362 JDX-6 SLIDE
JDX-8 SLIDE			4822	4133	3506									12461 JDX-8 SLIDE
JD 800				3267										3267 JD 800
340 Cyclone					4886	1400	1150							7436 340 Cyclone
440 Cyclone					5743	2000	1050							8793 440 Cyclone
340 Liquifire					4141	2000	1175							7316 340 Liquifire
440 Liquifire					6076	4560	2620							13256 440 Liquifire
Liquifire II									9080	2000	1086	1200	420	13786 Liquifire II
Spitfire							8024	7000	5000	2050	2099	0	0	24173 Spitfire
Trailfire 340								5043	4900	545	1860	0	0	12348 Trailfire 340
Trailfire 440								10243	5240	2135	0	0	0	17618 Trailfire 440
Sportfire									5678	1220	1510	700	371	9479 Sportfire
Trailfire LX											2670	1000	350	4020 Trailfire LX
Sprintfire											146	2400	288	2834 Sprintfire
Snowfire											175	600	276	1051 Snowfire
JD 295/S			1000											1000 JD 295/S
JD 340/S				1927										1927 JD 340/S
LIQUIDATOR					600									600 LIQUIDATOR
JD 440/S ??					2774									2774 JD 440/S ??
TOTAL	12664	36990	26016	18433	33651	14661	14019	22286	29898	7950	9546	5900	1705	0 233719 TOTAL
SHIPMENTS		12740	37302	25020	29708	17488	15205	20685	21626	18003	14640	10673		10629 223090 shipments

John Deere snowmobile production chart (courtesy Joe Wanie).

1982 Sportfire (courtesy Roger Tesch).

of the market. Well-intentioned management with no experience in this market thought this was the safest way for Deere to enter the market and therefore made the 1972 model decision they believed to be best for Deere. As they understood the market, perhaps this was the correct decision at that time. The first year production was manufactured and marketed successfully to the intended market. Product Engineering Department and factory personnel who were deeply involved had mixed emotions about getting out of the business. Deere was in business to provide great products that generated enough sales to return a profit from the invested capital and expenses. That did not happen during the years Deere was in that business. Yet the efforts made by thousands of people in the company and its dealers were not wasted. By 1981 the growth of a profitable consumer product business for Deere was well underway.

Many in Deere associated with the snowmobile business were later very successful in other business endeavors. This experience helped to develop their understanding of how to conduct business. The next two chapters will delve into lessons learned from the business that helped the Horicon factory transform itself from the agricultural model of operation into a flexible but focused team-based organization. Both salaried

1980 Trailfire (courtesy Roger Tesch).

and wage personnel contributed to the successful increase in productivity and higher-quality profitable products made at the Horicon Works. The major lessons learned from the snowmobile business prompted the factory process improvements that are discussed in Chapter 10. Collectively they drove the increased productivity of the factory that became a continuous process.

For many employees, being in a different business brought new experiences and challenges that will remain in their memories for the rest of their lives. Unfortunately these diligent efforts failed to produce the satisfaction that comes with business success. Memories of the thrill and excitement from riding a snowmobile are difficult to describe to people who never had this experience. The legacy of Deere snowmobiles is secure with those who did. Lives were changed as new experiences broadened understanding, and those lessons learned were applied with great success to the grounds-maintenance and turf-care products.

10

Horicon Works
Decade of Excellence, 1976–1986

As the 1986 fiscal year came to an end, Ray Gregg proclaimed 1976–1986 as the Decade of Excellence to recognize the Horicon Works employees for the success of the Horicon factory. As would be expected at a dealer product introduction, Ray commissioned a new cap to give to all employees at standup meetings, publicized as "Hats Off to You Day." The Horicon Works' annual sales increased about fourfold during those years, and by 1986 the Horicon factory sales were nearly three-quarters of a billion dollars. When JDM and Horicon outside manufactured products were added to the Horicon sales, the consumer products business then accounted for nearly $1 billion of annual sales. The 1976 year truly was a turnaround year, as the operations were profitable continuously during 1976 through 1986 and beyond. As the Decade of Excellence came to a close, the Horicon Works and sales branch consumer products marketing were viewed as a major contributor to the Deere enterprise. In Moline the process of organizing a separate business unit for consumer products was underway. By now you may be asking: is this just hype? The numbers reveal the answer.

John Deere's Company, about the Hewitt era (1955–1982) states:

> The consumer products division also was a substantial contributor to the company's revenues, accounting for more than one-third of $1 billion in sales in the years 1979–81; it had been profitable over a number of years, accounting for more than 11 percent of the company's operating profit in 1979 (this dropped below 8 percent for both 1980 and 1981). It was in a different posture than the other two divisions (Agricultural and Industrial), however. First, the parts commonalities, manufacturing linkages, etc., were far less substantial. Though the division produced the tractors in the lower end of the line, they were lawn and garden tractors, of a much different manufacturing configuration and product characteristic than the larger (agricultural) tractors. The other major consumer products also were unique to the division-snowmobiles, chain saws, etc.

The one-third of $1 billion in sales each year in 1979–1981 included the New Breed of Deere snowmobiles and the expanded Horicon product line of lawn and garden tractors, as well as the Yanmar-manufactured compact utility tractors (CUT). Sales growth occurred in all market segments, from lower-price machines for homeowners to higher-price commercial mowing markets that used the Yanmar CUT tractors equipped with a new 72-inch mower deck made at Horicon.

Broehl continues to describe the consumer products marketing effort:

> "A substantial percentage of consumer products marketing was done through some 1,000 independent consumer product dealers; other marketing was done through about 2000 of the John Deere agricultural dealers (sales split almost evenly between these two groups). The most substantial growth in the division was in commercial mowing products, the least in snowmobiles. The Horicon, Wisconsin, plant where the consumer products manufacturing was done, also had been involved at several stages in the development and manufacturing of the compact utility class of tractor. By 1982 Deere had about 25 percent of the lawn and garden business, but considerably less than that in snowmobiles.

The data in Broehl's book ended in 1981. From 1982 to 1986 the Horicon factory and consumer product sales continued to grow with new products from Horicon and JDM. Total sales doubled during those years.

A large number of new products were introduced to consumer products dealers at two events near Oconomowoc, Wisconsin in 1982 and 1984. During those years, for 26 consecutive months a new product began production at the Horicon Works to supply consumer products dealers with products that fueled sales growth in all market segments: rear engine riders, lawn tractors, lawn and garden tractors, and their implements and attachments. The mower deck attachments were one method that Horicon Works used to differentiate its products from competitors, as all mowing decks were formed from strong materials and the quality of cut was unequaled. By 1986 Horicon Works shipments ranked number one or two in all machine categories reported in the Outdoor Power Equipment Institute shipment data for the total industry: rear engine riders, lawn tractors, lawn and garden tractors, front mowers and compact utility tractors. Japanese manufacturers were not included in these data.

Horicon Works' unit shipments of riding mowers, lawn tractors, and lawn and garden tractors increased 52 percent from 90,106 in 1979 to 137,121 in 1985. Other new vehicles, attachments and walk-behind tillers, snow blowers and lawnmowers further increased the shipments. While snowmobile production was winding down, sale of lawn and garden machines was soaring. During this period Horicon also produced 63,024 profitable snowmobiles. This accomplishment at Horicon was a robust response to the taunt in 1975 from the Honda director who asked Lee and Ron to explain why Deere wasn't number one in the industry. In 1976, the long history of profitable operations at the Horicon Works was reestablished. After leading Deere & Company 27 years, Bill Hewitt retired in 1982. As head of the company his tenure featured new and traditional methods for "driving growth." *Fortune Magazine* data show sales in the Hewitt era peaked in 1981 and 1982, both nearly the same at about $5.5 billion. Profits were very strong in 1980 at $310 million and continued strong at $228 and $251 million in 1981 and 1982. This was a huge advance from the 1955 sales of $303 million when he took over from Wiman as president of Deere and Company. It was simply a stunning achievement. Deere now had a diversified business portfolio of agricultural, industrial and consumer product equipment and was well positioned in international markets. All equipment lines were supported by a profitable retail finance business.

The shared sales success by the traditional agricultural dealer network and the independent dealer network described by Broehl verified the successful implementation of the Hewitt strategy led by R.J. Carlson during the turbulent snowmobile years. In the authors' opinion the traditional agricultural dealer network would not have achieved half the consumer products sales without stimulus from the independent dealers who were located near large population centers. Most of the agricultural dealers became more aggressive in marketing the enhanced and broader line of consumer product machines.

All this success was about to change. In 1982 the Waterloo Tractor Works had started production of new models of their very successful tractors in a modern two-million-square-foot assembly building at a new site. These more powerful 50 Series agricultural tractors were introduced to Ag dealers in the New Orleans Super Dome. Deere forecasted more growth in market share and prepared for higher-volume, more efficient production in the new modern facility. As often happens, the business outlook changed suddenly. The agricultural market was already softening in 1982 and in fact it nearly collapsed in 1983. The daily production capacity of the new tractor facility was 200 per day. At the depths of the Ag recession daily schedules went down to fewer than 20 tractors per day. In 1983 Deere sales dropped three-quarters of a billion dollars and profits were only $52.9 million after the $251 million profit in 1982.

Robert (Bob) A. Hanson was the apparent successor to Bill Hewitt as CEO with his appointment in 1975 as executive vice-president followed by his election as president in 1978. His long career with Deere started with his first assignment under Bill Hewitt to establish a Deere presence in Mexico. Hanson was well familiar with all the growth ventures that Hewitt had initiated, particularly the international growth. When Hewitt retired in 1982, Hanson became CEO just as the storm front of the agricultural and industrial recession reached gale-force winds. His tenure as CEO was defined by this recession. Survival as the only farm equipment manufacturer without permanent financial damage emerged as his agenda. In 1982 Hanson announced an austerity program: capital expenditures were delayed, salaries frozen, employee benefits cut, and massive layoffs began in all units, except Horicon Works. The farm recession was a disaster for all of the U.S. farm equipment manufactures. Deere full-line agricultural competitors either went bankrupt or merged with others. Several of the industry suppliers were affected similarly. Deere was the only large full-line OEM agricultural equipment company to survive the recession intact. During this period Hanson urged Horicon to continue new profitable products, as this was of great help to the company and their dealers to offset some of the losses.

In the last half of the Horicon Works Decade of Excellence from 1982 to 1986, the Horicon sales and profits were vital to help Deere not only survive financially but also to keep its dealer organization afloat. The rest of this chapter describes the new products that enabled the Horicon Works to reach sales of three-quarters of a billion dollars with excellent profits. It also covers some of the growth in factory productivity and growth in quality. The ability to respond quickly to changing market needs and increase the factory productivity powered the growth in sales and profits. This was accomplished with the support and participation of all Horicon Works employees. The snowmobile business drove the factory to reinvent itself to be different from the agricultural heritage of factory operations. Work procedures were implemented to improve the quality of interaction among the factory departments and product engineering. The snowmobile annual model updates were not possible without that. Improved communication with all factory personnel was needed to implement changes in the daily operations. As was learned from snowmobiles, improved product and market planning was essential to undergird the factory success with well-designed products. This became a continuous process, not a one-time event. By 1980 the factory looked like a caterpillar turning into a butterfly. The Horicon factory that emerged from the ashes of snowmobile production was totally changed ... and for the better.

How Did Horicon Achieve These Results?

Ray Gregg transferred to Horicon in 1971 after working in marketing at the Syracuse sales branch. He had no prior experience with the operation of a factory. From his branch marketing experience Ray had acquired a good knowledge of Deere products, dealers and customers. His initial responsibility as Horicon Works marketing manager was to plan the first dealer product introduction of snowmobiles. One year later he was appointed as the general manager of the Horicon Works. His support of product engineering work was invaluable to the future of the factory. Without new marketable products, the future of the factory was dim. He was fond of saying, "Nothing happens until the dealer's cash register rings." For that to happen, the John Deere dealer needed outstanding high-quality products that were desired by the market. As described in earlier chapters, the production in 1972 of the 1973 model snowmobiles was a nightmare. The marketing effort to establish the independent consumer products dealers was disrupted as a result of this product trauma. Ray changed several key staff managers in that period, but the same basic problems remained. Without a strong base of accurate information, a factory manager's influence is compromised with senior management personnel at the corporate headquarters. Emotions often overwhelm rational thinking in those situations. Individual performance often cannot be separated from the work processes and well-intentioned but misguided directives.

In trips to the sales branches in the 1970s, Ray, Mike Heitman and Ron heard complaints about nearly every facet of the business. Product availability, poor product quality (especially paint), and products not suited to what the market needed were voiced in different ways across the broad spectrum of the Horicon products. Even though the lawn and garden products were well liked in the market, competition was aggressively supplying products that were targeted toward different market segments, for both smaller and larger area mowers. Through his participation in industry trade associations, Ray developed contacts with many of Horicon Works' competitors. His participation in ISIA and OPEI helped Martin Berk obtain broad industry support for development of safety standards for consumer products. Because most major competitors were also members of those trade associations, it was easier to arrange visits to suppliers and competitor factories. These were valuable experiences that broadened Horicon's understanding of industry work processes. The employee machine loan program provided a learning experience for Ray's staff. Every year Ray, his staff, and other key employees were loaned Horicon products to use for a season as a customer might do. The factory marketing manager and product engineering manager extended this to others in their departments. These experiences helped many Horicon employees better understand the customer's expectations from their own baseline of experience.

The customer complaints about the poor paint quality on the Horicon products were obvious, as some competitors had better paint finish and appearance when displayed on the dealer's showroom floor. Continuous efforts to improve the Horicon Works' spray paint system, which was satisfactory for the agricultural bundle goods, failed to satisfy the consumer markets. Several competitors, particularly Japanese manufacturers, had much higher quality paint finish on their machines. The lawn and garden tractors were often parked in the garage beside a shiny new automobile. Honda and Kubota were in the market with high quality walk behind mowers and lawn tractors. The market liked their easy-starting, smooth-running engines and quieter machines. Deere dealers often pointed to their products as an example of easy-starting, quiet-running engines with excellent paint finish. These products served the customers' needs very well and were sold at competitive prices. Honda and Kubota were increasing sales by selling their products through garden center and hardware store retail outlets in addition to John Deere dealerships.

Education in Japanese production processes began on the trip to Japan in June 1973 when Ray and Ron saw Japanese manufacturers firsthand. Other Horicon Works employees from purchasing and engineering began to have similar experiences. This increased awareness that the Horicon Works manufacturing operations needed to be improved. The factory manager's staff began to change with assignments of new personnel. Materials Manager Hank Martens became a strong ally of PED by staffing the purchasing department with strategic buyers who had a technical background to complement their negotiating skills. His broad manufacturing experience at the Des Moines Works before transferring to Horicon gave him a solid base of knowledge that strongly supported product engineering in their efforts to secure better parts and components. The buyer role in purchasing was still needed to maintain the supply of purchased parts to the factory assembly operations. Horicon Works' major suppliers in the U.S. as well as in Japan knew Hank well. He made valuable contributions to the ongoing effort to improve the quality and cost of the purchased content of Horicon products.

Earl Hildebrandt transferred to Horicon in 1976 as purchasing manager when Ray Allsbury retired. Earl served in that position until 1986 and was engaged in process improvements throughout the entire decade. During a long phone interview, he recalled his first trip to Japan in 1976 with Jim Lamont to explore the engine proposal from Kawasaki. This was the first official visit by John Deere to follow up on the conversations held at their U.S. office in Shakopee, Minnesota. As was customary in the Japanese business culture, they were treated to a formal dinner hosted by geisha. The business relationship blossomed after that trip and was formalized when Ray Gregg signed the contract the next summer. Earl supported upgrading the technical skills in the purchasing department. Both product and manufacturing engineering at Horicon provided engineers for two of the technical buyers on Earl's staff. "The snowmobiles made a tremendous contribution by exposure to new suppliers, new processes and new ideas," Earl said. "Changing to JIT was the most difficult challenge but it reduced inventory and helped lower our total costs."

Bob Pedigo managed the manufacturing engineering department at Horicon. This was a key function in all factories. He also had many years of experience in other Deere factories. Manufacturing engineering was responsible for administering capital investment in new processes, new facilities and new product tooling. Dwayne Trautman transferred to Horicon as his manager of process and tool and was very helpful in cooperating with PED to implement the never-ending changes required to improve the performance and quality of the early snowmobiles. The production release schedule shown in Chapter 9 for the all-new Trailfire snowmobile reveals how much progress the factory had made in implementation of new products. The preparation of the AFE for the Trailfire began June 1, 1977, and the production pilot build was finished on February 15, 1978, a period of nine months. This was accomplished because personnel worked cooperatively in all the departments in the factory to complete the pilot production as scheduled. Dick Teal's ability to design the Trailfire concurrently with the manufacturing processes increased the confidence in the factory to implement the design decisions rather than revisit them as had been done in the past.

The Horicon factory had several works managers during the first four years of snowmobile production. After John Lawson came to Horicon in 1976, his two-year stretch was the longest in the job since snowmobile production began. He transferred to Dubuque Works as the factory general manager on January 1, 1978. The next works manager accelerated the improvements in manufacturing needed at Horicon. George Elliott transferred from the Harvester Works and immediately began changes in responsibility for process outcomes as well as factory production of parts and machines. The most visible change occurred when he enlisted the help of Gene Thorn, Horicon accounting manager, to establish key metrics for all manufacturing departments. Every Friday the weekly results were discussed at a brief 15-minute standup meeting with every supervisor and staff manager. No one could opt out, so when managers or supervisors were not available they had to send a substitute. Gene and George conducted the Standard of Excellence meetings. Those departments who were below the excellent metric for that week were highly visible to everyone in the factory. In a few months there was noticeable improvement in quality, time on incentive (a Deere metric of labor productivity), meeting shipping dates, on-time schedule releases for new product design, and manufacturing engineering status for production tooling. Staff departments for product engineering, manufacturing engineering, quality, purchasing and inspection all participated and had their metrics exposed to the factory as well. Obviously this was an excellent management process that improved communication throughout the factory. Natural competitive instincts were aroused that no doubt underpinned the performance improvements.

Shortly after George came to Horicon, Ron received a phone call on Friday afternoon that had a long-lasting benefit for their relationship. George wanted the product engineering test lab personnel to work overtime that weekend to help the factory resolve a quality problem with the snowmobile ski spindle. After Ron demurred, George asked, "Why won't you support me?" The answer was that the PED test lab had worn out numerous test fixtures testing production ski spindles. Product engineering and manufacturing engineering understood why the problem occurred and what was needed to correct it. His staff could brief him well on the necessary corrective action. George slammed down the phone. The engineering lab test fixture was not scheduled for overtime that weekend.

On Sunday night Ron received a phone call from George asking to meet the next morning at the only restaurant in Horicon. About three hours later Ron and George finished their discussion and went to their offices. The result was they established an excellent working relationship from that time forward, after a frank, honest discussion of the magnitude of the obstacles to overcome in order to improve the design and manufacturing effectiveness at the Horicon Works.

In 1979 the snowmobile engineers who were familiar with short schedules for snowmobiles strengthened the engineering effort on grounds care machines. They had developed a sense of urgency and understanding of how to alter old procedures to reduce the time to develop new products. The rigid factory departmental lines began to soften into a flexible team-focused organization. New product development teams were supported with liaison personnel from the factory manufacturing departments, especially purchasing. These assignments helped to blend together the various factory staff departments. The team's understanding of designing with concurrent involvement of the method of manufacture produced huge savings of time and required fewer people to do the work; however, those involved needed to have the necessary skills and experience in order to do the job successfully. One example of this effectiveness was the work accomplished when Dick Teal was assigned as project engineer for mowing attachments. In that era, customers wanted to collect the grass clippings from their lawn while they were mowing. His assignment was to design a grass collection system for every size of mower deck and every model of riding mowers, lawn tractors and garden or compact utility tractor on which it was used. This work was completed during the next two years. Then customers who bought a new Horicon Works mowing vehicle could purchase a collection system that would function well with every mower deck and vehicle.

The improved communication among the factory departments enabled the engineers to interact more easily with the different departments. In the agricultural heritage of factory operation, each department manager exerted strong control over all activities. The days of long product life cycles with agricultural products didn't exist in the consumer products business. New product design concurrent with preparation for production requires continuous interaction between design, process engineering and purchasing for it to be successful. It has to have priority or the time lengthens before the design is final. It is like a jet plane waiting on the runway for takeoff. If the control tower has other traffic priorities, the plane just waits. Ray's staff met on a regular basis to review monthly the status of every active project; these meetings helped them to assume ownership of the concept that new products were the future of the factory. Nearly everyone will say this is obvious, but the devil is in the details. The new work processes needed to demonstrate *how* to best accomplish a goal. The general manager and his staff set the example by improving their communication processes and this was very visible to all employees in the factory.

When CEO Bob Hanson announced the austerity program in 1982, communication about the factory and Deere & Co. became a continuous process, as all employees were aware of the recession. This environment naturally aroused fear of job loss, so factual information was a virtue as rumors always were present. At the Horicon Works it was full speed ahead. The Horicon factory prepared for the manufacture of new products and modernized its manufacturing processes at the same time. Ray Gregg was fond of saying we needed to overhaul the train while it was going down the tracks. This spoke to the need to sustain high production schedules and make process improvements at the same time.

Horicon Works Learns About Shop Productivity

Perhaps the most significant process improvement at the Horicon Works during that time was replacement of the monthly production batch scheduling system. Toyota and most other Japanese capital goods manufacturers were making huge gains in productivity by workplace rearrangement and achieving reduction of in-process inventory by implementation of a new process to schedule production assembly — referred to as Lean Manufacturing or Just-in-Time (JIT). It reduced inventory by establishing a flow-through process in manufacturing for parts triggered at final assembly. The assembly line determined the hourly, daily and weekly parts needed for assembly. Implementation of JIT with the suppliers and Horicon parts manufacture destroyed the traditional scheduling system, albeit for the better. Extensive rearrangement of the factory floor was needed so parts and assemblies could be made in a continuous stream up to final assembly. Perhaps the biggest benefit of all was the involvement of factory workers in scheduling the part flow to final assembly; over time, the operators at their work stations did most of the inspection. Toyota and other Japanese manufacturers were also making quality improvements by adopting new techniques taught by G. Edwards Deming, then arguably the preeminent quality proponent in the world, to empower the shop worker with quality measurements while production was underway. Most capital goods manufacturers in Japanese industries implemented quality controls at the source rather than inspect production after it was completed. Kawasaki and Yanmar were implementing those process improvements in their factories when Horicon Works and Deere and Company personnel made their first trip to Japan in 1973. Horicon Works was using the old system of inspection after large batches of parts were made.

When these two distinct processes were integrated in a factory, huge productivity gains were possible. These were highlighted in publications about the new Toyota production system developed in the 1960s. While working there, Shigeo Shingo documented the analytical processes that determined how to implement improvements in flow of parts to assembly. He published these procedures that focused on shop floor rearrangement needed for JIT. They included providing employees with means to inspect the parts as they were made. Processes like inspection at the source (Poke-Yoke) and Single Minute Exchange of Die (SMED) were becoming widely used in the manufacturing operations in Japan, and were migrating to U.S. manufacturers. The close relationship with Yanmar, especially Dr. K., brought Shingo's work (some of which is referenced in the Appendix) to Ron's attention during his frequent visits to Kanzaki. Shingo's work was among the many process improvements discussed along with industry trends and best practices in engineering and manufacturing. Dr. K.'s entire career at Yanmar was devoted to adding new growth businesses. When doing that, he always installed more productive factory floor tools and layout. If a reasonable definition of innovation includes invention that addresses a need followed by successful implementation, then Dr. Kijiro Yamaoka was one of the most innovative people Ron had the privilege of knowing and working with during his career at Deere.

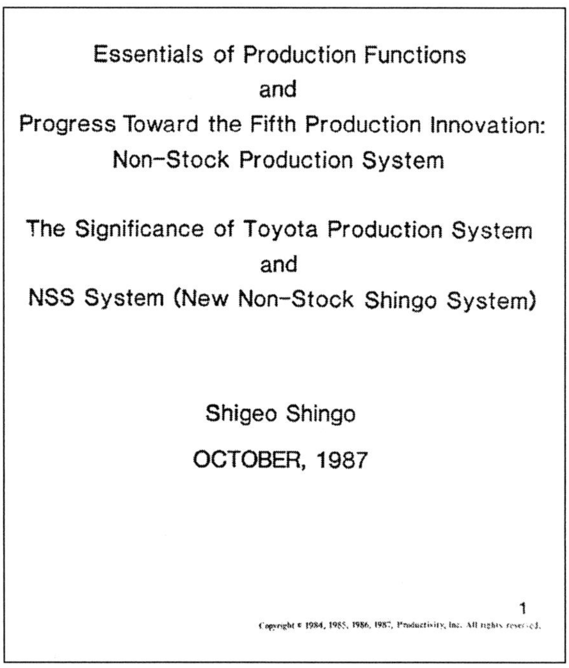
Essentials of Production Functions
and
Progress Toward the Fifth Production Innovation:
Non-Stock Production System

The Significance of Toyota Production System
and
NSS System (New Non-Stock Shingo System)

Shigeo Shingo

OCTOBER, 1987

1

Copyright © 1984, 1985, 1986, 1987, Productivity, Inc. All rights reserved.

Toyota JIT production system by Shigeo Shingo (Ron Leonard collection).

Improving Horicon Works Process Productivity

During the trip to Japan in 1977 to sign the engine supply agreement with Kawasaki, Ray and Ron visited the Mikuni factory that supplied carburetors to Horicon for snowmobile engines. After the green tea welcoming reception, the Mikuni factory manager led them on a factory tour. During that tour his people demonstrated improvements they had made to reduce the die change time in an injection-molding machine that made the carburetor bodies. Mikuni had hundreds of customers who required different sizes and shapes carburetor bodies, so the time required to change dies to make a different carburetor body caused a loss in daily production of the end product. All was quiet as the workers waited for a signal from the factory manager to start the die change. When he nodded, a large clock dial started running beside the machine. The workers descended on the injection-molding machine, made the change and stepped away, and the clock stopped. There was dead silence as the workers waited for a sign of approval or otherwise from the manager. The time on the clock was less than a minute. Since this was a new record they got a nod of approval. With daily production volumes in the tens of thousands, the seconds gained from the rapid die change increased production, but more importantly gave them flexibility to change to a different customer's order and ship completed carburetors that day.

This demonstration was a key event that sparked Horicon Works to reduce die change time in the factory press shop. The Horicon Works 101 primary part-manufacturing building was a fertile field of opportunity to reduce the time to change all of the press-shop form dies. Horicon had purchased a 2000-ton hydraulic press to form the larger metal fender and mower decks that were designed for the higher horsepower tractors. This was the largest capacity press in the company at that time. Some dies took up to a week to change before production could restart. Eventually Horicon reduced this to half a day. The Mikuni experience was of considerable help to understand the magnitude of the productivity gap at Horicon that had to be eliminated to increase productivity.

In 1980 Yanmar loaned one of their top executives to assist the Horicon factory with implementation of the first phase of JIT in lawn tractor production. Major productivity and quality improvements were made at Horicon when the batch schedule system was replaced with the JIT system. Deere CEO Bill Hewitt and his successor Bob Hanson had longstanding personal contact with Tadao Yamaoka, president of the privately owned Yanmar Diesel Company. Yanmar had installed the new Toyota production system in all of their factories. At one of the yearly management summit meetings Yamaoka-san offered to help Deere implement a JIT system at one of their factories. Horicon Works volunteered and was chosen. Tonamura-san, production manager at their engine factory, spent several weeks working directly with the Horicon manufacturing personnel to install a JIT pilot project for the welded frame of the Model 108 lawn tractor. The type and quantity of different lawn tractor frames were triggered by the daily assembly schedule. Following this successful pilot project, a plan was developed to implement JIT at Horicon for all lawn tractors, by then the highest volume production machines. Full implementation required changing the entire Horicon factory operating system. By 1983 JIT was fully implemented for lawn tractors. This work required significant relocation of the welding and sub-assembly operations before painting, and a revised assembly line. Over the next several years this system was adopted for all vehicle assembly. Jerry Hurling, one of the factory operations managers, was given the responsibility to implement JIT throughout the factory. Horicon referred to it as Waste Elimination.

The apex of factory productivity was reached in 1986 with the installation of the first automatic guidance vehicle (AGV) assembly line in Deere at Horicon. This converted most of the linear dedicated machine assembly lines to a daily mix of different models on the AGV serpentine-shaped assembly line. The AGV assembly line was configured so parts could be delivered close to or adjacent to the point of use. Earl Hildebrandt had commented about the challenge for purchasing to bring suppliers into the JIT process. Yet the installation went smoothly and productivity increased, inventory went down, and quality improved. There were two very significant productivity benefits from the AGV: first, the factory assembly workers could schedule parts needed from their work stations; and second, the daily machine mix schedule reduced the whole goods inventory. This made it much easier to build to order a mixed load of products. The Horicon Works factory personnel were justifiably proud of this accomplishment.

Associates from other factories were skeptical of the Horicon productivity gains, contending that with so much purchased content it wasn't really that hard to do. Just think about that for a minute. With 600 to 800 new parts in each product, don't they all have to be made somewhere before they are assembled in a finished machine? Horicon manufactured over *thirty* different machines. The gross number of parts in all of the different models approached 20,000. Suppliers had the same issues as Horicon had: to manufacture and deliver timely quantities to sustain the assembly operations for this many models. They had to adapt their design and production delivery to meet the Horicon Works' specifications and schedule.

The paint quality dilemma was ultimately resolved by construction of a separate building for painting, nearly adjacent to the assembly building. It was designed with filtered intake air to ensure the clean environment required for a first-class paint job. A powder paint method, the first in a Deere factory, was chosen, as it provided a more durable, high gloss-finish. An improved spray paint process also was located there. Parts and assemblies were transported on an overhead conveyor in and out of the paint shop to the assembly area. Inside the paint building, all parts went through a seven-stage washing and drying process before painting. This building and its paint system required a very significant capital investment. Ray devoted considerable time to obtaining support of key corporate people for this investment. Deere still had a restriction on capital expenditures; Horicon Works was an exception when the investments would increase sales and profits. The results were sensational in that the paint quality for Horicon products became a significant selling point for the product on the dealer's showroom floor.

Quality Growth at Horicon Works

In 1975 Harold Schofield was appointed to the newly created position of manager of reliability for the factory, reporting to the factory manager. He was responsible for implementation of a quality process that extended from the specifications for a new product until it was delivered to the customer. In 1973 he had transferred to Horicon as the PED test manager. In that work Harold became well acquainted with the product design and factory processes that determined the final product quality. The thread of quality started from the initial planning for a product, continued through design, verification, and production, and ended with a satisfied customer. New statistical analysis procedures were implemented that pointed to needed quality improvement throughout the factory. This effort helped to improve the productivity of the product engineers. The factory focus on quality improvement was aided dramatically by scheduling a production pilot run before full-scale production.

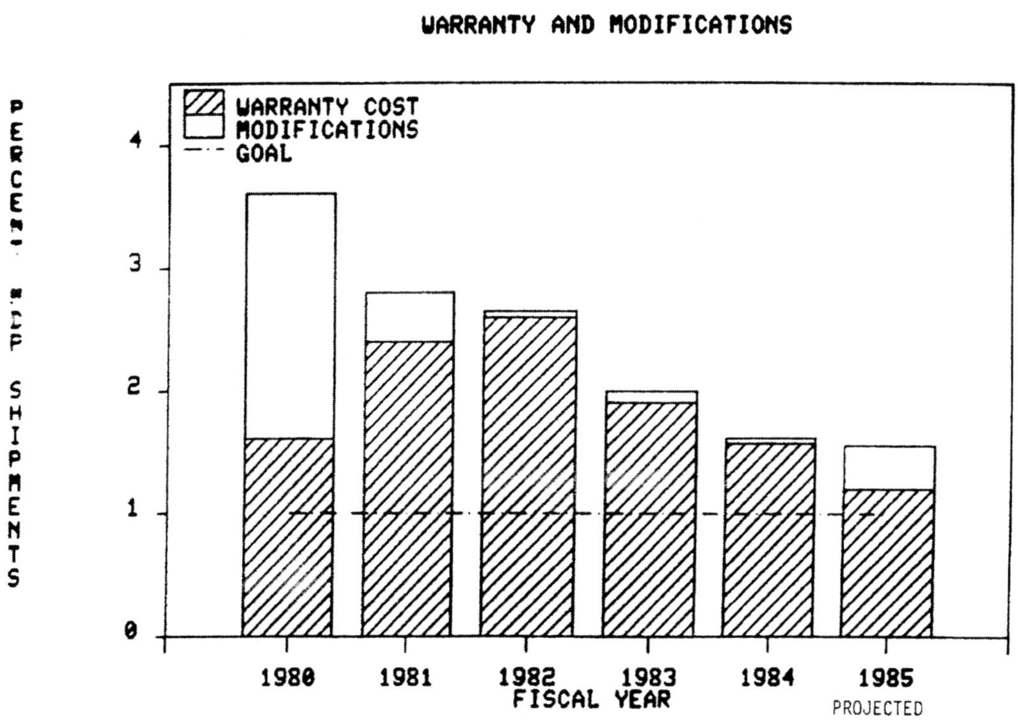

317 tractor warranty and modification costs (Ron Leonard collection).

The reliability data in the bar chart shows the result of quality improvements in dollars made from 1980 through 1985 in the total quality cost as a percent of MDP. The chart is simply a ratio of the total after-market warranty and modification program costs divided by the gross value of factory sales. In 1980 the disaster of the Kohler engine in the JD 317 garden tractors was terribly expensive and was the most significant reason for the decline of the Horicon Works' share of the corporate profit from 11 percent in 1980 to 8 percent in 1981. The high production of JD 317 garden tractors in the 1980s increased the total modification cost, but the ratio steadily declined. The cost of the after-warranty modification programs is shown by the clear space on top of each bar. Warranty costs accrue from the work done by dealers to repair and replace parts on customer machines in the normal warranty period. Continuous improvement in quality lowered warranty costs during those years, especially after Horicon PED implemented a change in direction in the use of supplier-designed and -developed drive train components. However, the biggest benefit in reducing the after-market costs throughout John Deere's long history was that it engendered greater customer satisfaction with John Deere machines.

Product Engineering Productivity

Productivity growth was also underway in product engineering. In 1981 Horicon product engineering was designing a front-mount mower for a new and growing commercial mowing market. The JD model 910 and 930 front mowers were scheduled for the Oconomowoc dealer announcement in 1984. The limit on investment capital required innovative thinking for Horicon to determine how to proceed with the freeze on capital expenditures. With little capital money for part tooling, the design needed to use different fabrication methods. The frame and structural parts were made with standard shop tools that didn't require a die, but the styling parts like the engine hood and operator's station still needed to meet the market expectations for a pleasing shape and form. Stretch-forming the engine hood eliminated a large press die. Suppliers were contacted by the purchasing department and asked to amortize their tooling costs in the production parts supplied. These data were clearly defined for the small number of new parts that required investment capital for tooling. As a result, Ray Gregg was able to show that these products would have a favorable total life cycle return to the company. Horicon margins would improve after the supplier tooling was amortized. The sales branch marketing personnel were strong supporters of Deere entering this business in the early stages. The front-mount mowers were shown as scheduled at the 1984 Oconomowoc dealer introduction and got an enthusiastic dealer response.

Throughout the Decade of Excellence, Horicon PED designed machines for mowing grass targeted for major segments of the different market sectors. As noted earlier, the production increased dramatically and the profit margins were excellent. The new lawn tractor that was introduced to dealers in Kansas City in 1979 was a stunning success. This was a landmark event for the factory and the consumer products business. The Horicon Works made 3,204 of the old model JD 100 in 1978 and 16,751 of the new lawn tractors during their first year of production. The following year, the factory production nearly doubled to 31,749. These volumes increased steadily to 45,590 in 1985. By then the market was still growing and industry lawn tractor shipments were approaching half a million units. Yet the Horicon volume in 1985 was only 8.6 percent of the total market. There were still opportunities for further growth in that market. Later model updates of lawn tractors, targeted at lower-priced and higher-priced market segments, enabled the lawn tractor to become the highest volume and most profitable consumer product line.

Horicon engineering produced new designs of garden tractors that were very successful. With a new hydrostatic transmission and improved engines in all of the garden tractor models, the Horicon production of garden tractors jumped from 34,449 in 1978 to 54,317 in 1979. The market especially liked the new JD 317 hydrostatic tractors. This tractor was the major cause of the higher production in 1979. It was powered with a new lightweight aluminum engine produced by Kohler. This new engine was part of Kohler's plan to replace the cast-iron engines they had supplied successfully to the industry in the past. They understood the threat of losing business to other engine manufacturers, especially in Japan.

The prototype engines tested in Horicon tractors operated well. However, during the first year of customer use, the Horicon service department was flooded with reports of JD 317 tractor engine failures. The engineering department performed a series of teardown inspections and tested new engines on the Horicon engine dynamometers. Inspection revealed the new engines had significant flaws in the internal engine lubrication system. Field test supervisor Elmer Quick operated them on a long hill at the Horicon Golf Course and discovered some of the engines would fail before reaching the top of the hill. The previous year this same hill had been used during the durability testing before production began. Numerous quality defects, like aluminum chips in the crankcase, were discovered in production engines. All of this was shared with Kohler, which gave assurances that corrections would be made before the next year's production.

Customers liked the JD 317 and dealer orders were high for the next year. As the production began the second year, Horicon monitored Kohler engine shipments by teardown inspections and testing new production in the PED test lab. Several of the same failures occurred as in the first year's engines. Horicon stopped production and scheduled an emergency meeting at Kohler. Ray and several of his staff attended the meeting. During that meeting, Art Kross, Kohler's engine division general manager, stated that Horicon was the only company having any problem with their engine. Ron was astonished at that comment and reminded them of the meetings at Horicon in the test laboratory that demonstrated several ways the engine would fail during normal customer operation. Harold Schofield and Wayne McClellan confronted them with the

JD model 165 lawn tractor (courtesy Bob Strassmann).

latest warranty data of hundreds of customer engine failures, along with numerous failures of this year's production engines in the Horicon test lab. Again there was a polite rejection. The most damaging comment was that none of Kohler's other higher-volume customers were having these problems. Horicon's field personnel knew this was not correct. Kohler suggested the installation in the JD 317 tractor was the cause of the engine failures. Of course, they had approved the installation before the first year of production at Horicon Works.

Ron announced he was leaving the meeting, and upon returning to Horicon would instruct the project engineers to remove every Kohler engine from any experimental test machines. They would be shipped immediately and arrive on Kohler's receiving dock by Friday of that week. And they did just that. It was many long weeks before Horicon could ship any JD 317 production tractors until both design and manufacturing process problems were corrected. Immediately Horicon product engineers began design work to replace the Kohler engines in future production with Onan engines. PED accelerated the dyno testing of Onan engines at Horicon and redesigned the tractors to install them. Horicon was not confident that Kohler would resolve the failures in the 317 engines. Even with the engine improvements for the second year's production, the Horicon engineers were convinced that this engine was not robust enough for a Deere machine.

Deere marketing was able to keep customers satisfied with their JD 317, by the warranty policy that guaranteed replacement during the first year. The market liked the machine and sales continued strong even with this problem. Any customer machine part failure rate over 1 percent was very serious, and if it grew over 2 percent it was almost certain to result in a PIP for any Deere product. The John Deere implied warranty was based on trust that the John Deere machine was better in performance and durability than most other brands. To retain customer loyalty, Deere extended the warranty for the second use season.

An interesting sidebar experience evolved from the meeting at Kohler. A few weeks later Ray Gregg got a call from Moline asking him to send Horicon representatives to meet Herb Kohler in Kohler, Wisconsin, the next evening. Apparently Herb Kohler had called Bill Hewitt about the JD 317 engine problems. Hank Martens and Ron drove to Kohler the next afternoon and met Herb in the lobby of his office building sometime after 6:00 p.m. He apologized for the problems and asked us to be honest and straightforward in answering his questions. We assured him that would not be a problem. He asked what caused the problem and we explained the design and manufacturing issues that contributed to the numerous engine failures. One of the major issues was that the Kohler engineering personnel were not close enough to the market to understand the performance requirements. Apparently Horicon was not communicating those requirements clearly to the Kohler account sales representatives who called at Horicon. Ron described some of the test failure modes that Horicon Works PED had demonstrated to his engine factory management at Horicon. None of the Kohler engine design engineers had visited Horicon to learn firsthand what was going on. We provided him answers to specific questions about his personnel as well. He was very appreciative of our input, and the next year there were numerous personnel changes made in the Kohler engine factory to address the issues that we discussed that night.

This incident with the Kohler engine prompted a significant change in our relationship with power train suppliers at Horicon. We could no longer rely on the traditional supplier base for design and manufacture of new drive train components without participating with them in the design. What was required in a John Deere product was different from other manufacturers in the industry. Most of the small U.S. engine manufacturers supplied very high volumes for lawn and garden tractors that were marketed by garden centers, hardware stores and mass merchandisers like Lowe's and Home Depot. Those products were very competitive in price and generally sold for less than John Deere products. The JD 317 engine experience was similar to Horicon Works' experience with some snowmobile supplier components, like the Salsbury clutch and the Kioritz engine. How Horicon PED altered the relationship with drive train components suppliers is discussed in the next chapter.

Horicon works had a totally different experience with the first Kawasaki engine in a new model 112L Lawn Tractor for 1985. The engine was designed by KHI to meet the specifications set by Lee Hardesty. He insisted the KHI engine provide peak torque at a lower RPM thn Honda or Briggs and Stratton. This would make the Deere mower out-perform them. Even though production of lawn tractors was about 40,000 annually, we continued to hear complaints about the Briggs and Stratton engines. The next year, with the first Kawasaki single cylinder engine in the newly redesigned lawn tractors, the factory produced about 50,000 riding mowers. Substantial market share growth was achieved in later years, as this product line became the highest volume product.

The rear engine rider production also exploded from 11,280 machines in 1983 to 58,910 in 1984. Such growth is not easily achieved in mature markets unless the machine is a standout that exceeds the customer's expectations. The Deere market share of riding mowers increased to 18.3 percent of all shipments reported to OPEI. Before this new KHI engine began production, Horicon Works had worked with Briggs and Stratton to improve their engines for Horicon products. A John Deere dealer could then easily demonstrate the difference to customers on the showroom floor. Each of the new more powerful rider mowers and lawn tractors also had new, wider mower decks that increased their productivity. All Horicon-manufactured mower decks used on the riders, lawn tractors, garden tractors and compact utility tractors had the grass collection system that was optional for dealer installation.

JD model F930 front-mount mower (courtesy Bob Strassmann).

In 1984 Deere entered the market for commercial front-mount mowers that was dominated by Toro and Jacobsen. The market for this vehicle configuration was developing rapidly. Because it virtually eliminated trimming when operated in large mowing areas, it was growing in popularity in cities for mowing parks and recreation areas, company campus grounds and some golf courses. Recalling the snowmobile chassis configuration lesson, Horicon Works didn't want to be late to this party. The first year of production Horicon made 1131 of the model 910 and 930 front mowers. The total industry shipments that year were 11,474, so Deere started with about 10 percent market share. The next year Horicon made 3419, which was 20 percent of the industry shipments. With only two competitors Deere simply had to take market share from Toro and Jacobsen. In 1986 the industry shipments were 17,486, and Deere had 40 percent of that. The market for this chassis configuration was growing rapidly and eventually spread to more price segments in the market. This was Deere's first entry into the golf and turf market.

The Yanmar/Deere compact utility tractors experienced steady growth in market share from 1979, at 12.9 percent market share, to 21.5 percent in 1985. After the Horicon Works was assigned design control for these tractors, Yanmar began to upgrade the styling, operator's station arrangement, and engine power to be competitive with Honda. These improvements, along with the Horicon mowing decks, had helped the business grow to 21.5 percent market share.

Horicon PED designed a new compact utility tractor for the market segment that preferred a hydrostatic (variable speed) transmission that began production in 1986. These tractors had approximately the same engine power level as the three smaller Yanmar CUT. The model 755, 855 and 955 tractors provided Deere dealers with a Horicon Works manufactured CUT with a hydrostatic variable speed transmission along with the Yanmar CUT with fixed gear ratio transmissions. Kubota was making rapid market share gains with a hydrostatic drive in their CUT line in the U.S. Yanmar did not have a market for this type of transmission in Japan, so elected not to design one for Deere.

The Horicon CUT was a unique design with the transmission integrated into the rear axle housing with a PTO shaft at the rear for three-point hitch machines. The new design of one housing that contained the transmission and differential axle created more room under the engine to raise the mower deck higher. The engine was positioned in front of the tractor in a traditional location. The mid-mount mower deck could be raised higher than the Yanmar CUT or competitive tractors. Ron recalls that the Atlanta sales branch manager had asked that this tractor be able to drive directly over an eight-inch curb. The drivers needed the increased clearance when mowing alongside curbs or on elevated islands in the center of a divided street. The operator could simply drive over the curb without damaging the mower deck. The 55 series tractor had a full complement of implements made for it that benefited from the new configuration of the tractor. The loader and the belly mower deck could be mounted or dismounted in minutes. There was a full line of three-point hitch attachments.

The opportunity to put these new tractors in production was nearly lost due to a last-minute dispute about the cost of the new Kanzaki transaxle. Both Horicon engineering and purchasing personnel had extensive communication with Kanzaki during the design. Kanzaki had agreed with the cost targets. Ron had discussed it with Dr. K. numerous times and was positive he was committed to supply the transaxle. As Horicon was preparing the AFE for the 55 series hydrostatic-drive CUT, Kanzaki sent a fax that advised the transaxle was much higher in cost than previously agreed. Purchasing was not successful in learning the reason for the sudden increase of nearly 50 percent in the cost. Hank called Ron and asked what we should do. We agreed to make an emergency trip to Osaka to discuss this directly with Yanmar/Kanzaki. Using our normal contacts, Horicon communicated to Kanzaki that the new quote was unacceptable and we would come to Japan to meet with them as soon as a date could be set. The next morning we received an invitation to come immediately. That afternoon they boarded the Northwest Airlines flight from Chicago to Osaka.

They arrived in Osaka late that night, and the next morning they walked a short distance from the hotel to the Yanmar Headquarters office in downtown Osaka. Tadao Yamaoka, president of Yanmar, and Dr. K. Yamaoka, president of Kanzaki, along with Oishi-san as interpreter, were the only people in the meeting. After our green tea reception we adjourned to the conference room to discuss the issue. Oishi gave a rather long explanation of the problem in English that sounded like the costs were fixed and couldn't be changed. Hank briefed them on the Horicon position with production plans already underway. Ron described the extensive communications with Kanzaki as the project developed, but it seemed that nothing was going to change as we were deadlocked.

Hank then explained that Horicon had presented this project to Deere senior management, including Bob Hanson, president and CEO. There would be huge disappointment if we returned and advised management that we would have to cancel the production of the 55 Series tractors. There was a sober pause in the discussion. Then, in what Ron realized later was a masterful intervention, Hank politely said that we had no further information to discuss. We would excuse ourselves, go back to the hotel, and let them talk privately. They could call us at our room in the hotel if there was anything else to discuss. About 2:00 p.m. the phone rang in our room, with Oishi asking us to return to their office. We speculated on the outcome as we walked back. We were welcomed warmly and Oishi apologized for any misunderstanding and said we could proceed with the original quotes. Both Hank and Ron were at a loss for any questions or comments. After thanking them, they returned to the hotel, and that night Kanzaki personnel hosted a festive dinner party. The next day they returned to Horicon with the welcome news that the flow of new and profitable products at the Horicon Works was secure. It was a nice return flight to Chicago.

Later Hank and Ron reflected often on the audacity of dismissing ourselves from a meeting with two of the wealthiest men in Japan who owned their company by asking them to think it over before we left town. About a year later we learned what had happened to interrupt the project. Dr. K. needed to buy more land to expand the Ibuki factory to handle the larger 55 Series transaxle. Investments were planned for more floor space, a paint system and a longer assembly line. Although this had been recognized from the beginning, it was on hold because T. Yamaoka wanted to spend the investment money in their engine and tractor factories. During our absence from the meeting Dr. K. called his personal banker and arranged for the investment money to expand the Ibuki factory. Without that, Kanzaki would have outsourced most of the parts and set up an inefficient assembly operation. In later visits to the Ibuki factory, Dr. K. always proudly pointed out new cost-saving work processes in that part of the factory.

With the skills and work processes necessary to manage new product design programs and implement them in the factory, the Horicon Works continued to introduce new products to sustain the growth in Horicon Works' sales and profits during the Decade of Excellence. The task ahead was to provide more new products to sustain the growth of the newly created Consumer Products Division of the company. The next chapter highlights most of the new skills, tools, and processes implemented in PED that were driven by lessons learned from the snowmobile business.

11

How the Snowmobile Changed Product Engineering

Engineering is an arcane profession. Many different activities are described as engineering, consequently its meaning is often misused or misunderstood. At its roots, engineering is based on the application of science to produce benefits to human life. The general scope of work touches nearly every aspect of human existence: water supply, waste disposal, food production, buildings, transportation, energy, communications, and the list goes on. Engineers are trained to solve problems with disciplined procedures developed over centuries of applying technology to current needs. Engineers, the people who perform engineering work, influence decisions made every day in government, academia and commercial enterprises.

Within Deere the engineering functions were well defined in product and manufacturing engineering. Product engineers with mechanical, hydraulic and electrical expertise designed and developed the products, and manufacturing engineers from several engineering disciplines designed part tooling, manufacturing machines, and factory work processes for efficient production. The legacy from snowmobiles for Horicon Works' product and manufacturing engineers was application of the lessons learned from snowmobiles to the growth of the grounds-care product line. With the additional engineers hired in 1972, 1973 and 1974, Horicon Works had adequate resources for both snowmobile and grounds-care product design and manufacturing. In 1978, Horicon Works began to assign snowmobile product engineers to grounds-care projects to accelerate design and development of new grounds-care products.

Advanced Products Engineering

When Ron Leonard transferred to Horicon in 1973, one of the most effective organization changes made in the announcement was the assignment of Martin Berk as manager of advanced products. Their work was coordinated with current product design programs as they immediately began to design racing snowmobiles as described earlier, and provided advanced technical support for safety standards and implementation of enhanced control systems for all Horicon product lines. The technical support focused on finding solutions for perplexing safety concerns with the Horicon Works products. Deere corporate management in Moline strongly urged the factories to produce the safest possible machines. HDA was responsible for coordinating the design of operator control functions for all Deere products. The advanced products engineers used human factors analysis techniques to evaluate control system design on all machines, to reduce the chance for operator error during its operation. Test reports, warranty failures and field service information all provided input into that evaluation.

In 1975 all grounds-care vehicles were manufactured with an operator's presence seat switch. The purpose of the switch was to prevent starting the machine without an operator in the seat, or if a tractor was upset on steep banks, the engine would stop when the operator weight was removed from the seat. The market reacted negatively, similar to the market reaction to mandatory seat belts required in cars in the 1960s. Customers complained to Deere dealers and some insisted the seat switch be removed. It took several years of an industry-wide effort to overcome customer objections while the seat switch remained on all the Deere machines. Advanced engineering also was responsible for Deere engineering work to develop OPEI, ISIA, ASAE and SAE standards. Noteworthy was the snowmobile seat. This seat project was a cooperative effort between Horicon Works PED, the Deere Technical Center, and industry members from a special committee authorized by the SAE Technical Standards Board.

John Orvis provided the field load data needed to develop the snowmobile seat standard. While working at Polaris, John was given the assignment to improve their seat cushions. He studied a report by a doctor in Vermont who analyzed the cause of back injuries and concluded that snowmobile riders experienced a higher frequency of injuries than riders of other vehicles. Since some of them occurred on a Polaris snowmobile, John was given the job to figure out how to improve the seat. Polaris had limited test facilities, so John looked elsewhere for help. He attended a meeting of the Society of Automotive Engineers Technical Standards Board to request an SAE committee for snowmobiles. During the first meeting of the committee, he met Martin Berk and Bob Trapp from John Deere. The SAE meeting also provided John with a connection to engineers from General Motors Corporation. They invited him to bring a Polaris snowmobile to the GMC proving ground in Detroit. GMC furnished the telemetry and high-speed photography equipment to document the G forces on the rider (John) and the compression of the seat. The seat standard that resulted was developed jointly with industry engineers.

Roscoe Pershing from the Deere Technical Center explained how the seat design and standard was accomplished:

> In late 1970, the Occupant Protection Subcommittee of SAE Snowmobile and All-Terrain Vehicle Committee worked on this problem. I worked with John Orvis, Bob Schanhals and others who were involved with this subcommittee. The SAE Paper that I authored tells most of the story and mentions the industry standard: SAE J89 Recommended Practice: "Performance Criteria for Snowmobile Seats." Of particular interest, we used the Spinal Injury Model developed by Wright-Patterson Air Force Base to predict injury probability during pilot ejection. We adapted this mathematical model to the conditions for a snowmobile rider

> hitting a bump. That work is the basis for the SAE J89 Recommended Practice and also the basis for two patents in my name:
>
> 1-Vehicle Seat Comprising Three Foam Layers (U.S. Pat. 3,833,259), 1974; and
>
> 2-Vehicle Seat Design for Minimizing Spinal Injury and Procedure for So Designing a Seat (Canadian Pat. 980149), 1975. We did construct a special dynamic test apparatus for evaluating seats and we also tested seats in cold conditions as well as at room temperature. This was a lot of work and some pretty good results for a "side bar" project at the Tech Center! Later on, I did successfully use all this information to defend the John Deere Seat in a lawsuit involving a spinal injury of a snowmobile rider.

After the seat standard was approved, some industry seat suppliers constructed a test fixture to ensure the seats supplied met the voluntary standard.

Another nagging problem addressed by the advanced products group was to learn the cause of a small number of fires that occurred during refueling garden tractors. Martin Berk researched the technology and found that Hercules, Inc., a Maryland consulting firm, had demonstrated the theory of how static electricity could ignite a fire during refueling. All known areas on a vehicle that could contribute to this were analyzed and corrective action was taken. Advanced products engineers conducted or supervised testing to certify the new products complied with all known standards. Martin chaired the factory safety committee and also was a member of all industry and technical committees for consumer products. He actively promoted participation by other industry engineers in development of new standards so the result had the best input from all companies. He often commented that the best standards defined the performance outcomes, not specific design specifications. Horicon had a dedicated test room to certify all the mower deck shields met the thrown-object performance specified in the OPEI standard. As new mower decks were designed, this test room operated almost continuously to ensure the discharge from the new mower met or exceeded the limits in the standard. During the June 1982 PRM at the Horicon Works, Martin presented to the Moline management an update on the procedures used at Horicon to ensure that a John Deere machine was the safest design the factory could produce for the market.

Test Department

Engineers were hired to expand the capacity and capability of the test department when the snowmobile projects began, and this continued throughout the Decade of Excellence. Harold Schofield, the PED Test Manager, provided the specifications for the test cells in the PED test building. Test personnel supplied critical skills for analytical evaluation of proposed designs, as Dick Teal had experienced while designing the suspension for the Trailfire track. These test laboratories provided space and test equipment for advanced evaluation of components and the complete vehicle. Since all engine-powered products at Horicon were required to meet the drive-by and operator's ear sound test regulations, the sound room saved time and money compared to doing the measurements in the field. Outdoors, small external unwanted noise compromised the vehicle data recorded by the sound meter. All of the new test facilities helped the engineers reduce the time to develop and verify their designs. This work could be done without waiting for field tests in winter to operate snowmobiles and snow blowers, or spring for operating mowers. The Horicon test department strategy that was discussed in the June 25, 1982, PSM is more fully explained in information published in the meeting PSM manual that can be found in the Appendix.

Testing in actual field conditions was still very important, as it enabled engineers to improve a machine's performance in many different conditions. Prior to construction of the Horicon test facilities, the Horicon test department obtained help from the technical center in Moline to measure force loads and vehicle load cycles during field test. This information was vital to successfully operate the test cells when the new building became available. Field load and cycle data are the soul of accelerated testing.

Competitive Review at PSM

The 1983 Product Strategy Meeting (PSM) at Horicon Works published results of an analysis of the major competition for each product line and component suppliers for Horicon Works consumer products. Horicon PED had changed the meeting name from Review to Strategy to more accurately define the purpose of the meeting. The documents described a significant change in sourcing strategy for the larger and higher-power Horicon Products. The PED planned to seek suppliers who would design and manufacture exclusive drive train components for Deere. This would enable PED to control the specifications of all power train components—engines, transmissions and axles—to ensure the Deere machines performed best in the market. This was a direct response to the unfortunate experience with the JD 317 tractor engine, as well as machine performance limitations imposed by transmission suppliers who also supplied the high-volume manufacturers. These components often limited the power or speed range in which the machine needed to operate. With the new strategy, all components would be manufactured to Deere specifications by high-quality manufacturers wherever they were located, who demonstrated their capability, and who would agree to work jointly on the specifications of each component. This approach was well received by the PRM attendees.

The experience with the Kohler engine in the JD 317 Garden Tractor in 1981 was a moment of epiphany in the Horicon Works relationship with drive train suppliers. That year Lee Hardesty completed the work for the new Liquifire snowmobile to ensure that the KHI engine installation was satisfactory. Lee had not been involved with selection of the engines for grounds-care machines. In a broader assignment, he was promoted to project engineer, responsible for the engines in all Horicon products. He would assist the vehicle project engineers to determine the engine specifications and work with the chosen supplier to design the engine. Lee was well known by Kawasaki and Yanmar engine engineering personnel and had accompanied Ron on the trip to Japan in 1976 to evaluate engine suppliers for snowmobiles. The Kohler engine debacle was the last Horicon Works' product that used OEM-supplied engines that were not designed and manufactured to Horicon Works PED specifications. This strategy was shared with all suppliers so U.S. manufacturers were not excluded from participation.

Lee Hardesty

Due to Lee's untimely death, his input was not available for this book. Rob Feldman, who worked for Lee at Horicon starting in 1975, describes some of the engine accomplishments:

> I don't think my memory is going to be a lot of help on the snowmobile engines. There were a lot of technical changes made over the course of the years, but none of them were first applications, to the best of my knowledge. Most were adaptations from racing motorcycles. Some may have been first applications by JD in snowmobile engines, but I'm not sure. The most obvious would have been liquid cooling. Others that I recall were ½ keystone L rings for the top rings, hypereutectic (high silicon) alloy pistons, cam grinding piston ODs, and applying barrel profile to piston skirts. Electronic C/D ignitions and surface gap spark plugs would have fallen into this category as well. On the L&G [lawn and garden] engines, Lee's goal was to upgrade the durability and reliability. He canvassed small engine manufacturers to try to get a vertical shaft one-cylinder engine built with full pressure lubrication. He was successful in getting Kawasaki to produce the FB460V in part because of the good working relationship between the engineering departments that started with snowmobiles. To the best of my knowledge, the KHI engine was the first high-volume L&G engine ever to have full pressure lubrication. The next step was to get Kawasaki to build an overhead valve engine family, the FC290V, FC420V and FC540V. Again, to the best of my knowledge, these were the first high-volume L&G engines.
>
> Prior to this time, most L&G engines were adaptations of generator set engines, designed to produce full power at 3600 rpm. If they weren't originally designed for generator use, the engines were still designed to develop full power at 3600 rpm, to provide the maximum in advertised horsepower. Perhaps Lee's biggest influence and impact on L&G engines was to have the Kawasaki engines listed above designed to operate with maximum power at 3000 rpm. This reduced the noise and vibration. It also allowed the engines to have high torque reserve or torque rise, as compared to the competition. Torque reserve is of little, if any benefit to a generator set engine. Increasing an engine's torque reserve restricts its maximum output, but makes it much more user-friendly in L&G applications. All of these improvements, introduced by JD, became the standard yardstick for the L&G industry engines. I believe JD was also first to introduce L&G engines with electronic fuel injection. It is still in use on JD products, but unfortunately has yet to see cost reduction benefits from increased volume.

Lee worked closely with Yanmar to install the first liquid-cooled diesel engine in the JD 430 garden tractor produced in 1983. The tractor chassis needed to be extended to provide space for a radiator, as all earlier garden tractors were powered with air-

JOHN DEERE HORICON WORKS

COMPETITIVE REVIEW

In 1982 Horicon shipped 23.6% of the value of all OPEI shipments of lawn tractors, lawn & garden tractors, riding mowers and attachments. The total OPEI industry value of these four product categories was $817 million. This is less than one-half of the nearly $2 billion value of all OPEI shipments.

Our major competitors for these product lines are:

Lawn Tractors	1. Murray 2. MTD 3. AMF
Lawn & Garden Tractors	1. MTD/IHC 2. Simplicity 3. Roper/Sears
Riding Mowers	1. Snapper 2. Murray 3. MTD
Attachments	

No Japanese company shipments are included in OPEI statistics, as the OPEI does not permit membership of foreign manufacturers.

None of the above companies, including Deere, manufacture their own engines. These components have long been produced by OEM manufacturers located in the U.S. Two companies, Simplicity and IHC (now MTD), manufacture their own tractor transmissions.

The major suppliers for transmissions and axles have been Peerless for mechanical and Sundstrand and Eaton for hydrostatics.

The major OEM suppliers are:

Product Line	Engines	Transmissions & Axles
Lawn Tractors	Briggs & Stratton Tecumseh	Peerless Div. of Tecumseh Eaton
Lawn & Garden Tractors	Kohler Onan Briggs & Stratton	Peerless Div. of Tecumseh Dana Sundstrand Eaton
Riding Mowers	Briggs & Stratton Tecumseh	Peerless Div. of Tecumseh Snapper (own design)

Competitive review of OPEI member products and components (Ron Leonard collection).

cooled engines. Since the JD 430 targeted commercial mowing markets, the large air cleaner required space to operate for long periods. This tractor with the new engine went into production in 1983 after a one-year design and test program that in earlier years would have been unthinkable. Yanmar brought a Styrofoam model of the engine to Horicon in August of 1982. From it the tractor project engineer, Frank Smith, determined how much to lengthen the tractor frame. Three months later, when the first actual engines arrived, they fit perfectly in the space allocated in the prototype tractor built in PED. Production of the JD 430 tractor started one year later in August 1983. With two cylinders in line, the engine was narrow and operated with little vibration due to an excellent internal balancer. This product quickly established the foundation for later application of the Yanmar small diesel engines in the commercial mowing products designed and made at Horicon. Deere dealers had confidence in the Yanmar diesel engines, as they powered the compact utility tractors made for John Deere. The laboratory test cells were of great help to develop the confidence in the engine and in the installation in the new chassis. Horicon Works PED had evaluated single-cylinder air-cooled diesel engines from Italian manufacturers and found them unacceptable due to excessive noise and vibration.

One of Lee's biggest accomplishments still widely used today was the narrow FB460V 2-cylinder engine made by Kawasaki. Of course, V2 engines were commonly used in motorcycles, but they were simply too wide for the garden tractor. Lee made a preliminary design of a narrower V2 engine with a 60-degree angle between the cylinders vs. the conventional 90-degree angle. This made the installation of a V2 sixty-degree engine much more acceptable in a garden tractor. He persuaded KHI to design the engine for production. This engine was used later in Deere Gators as well as the commercial mowing products. A mark of distinction for any professional is to be widely recognized for his expertise in the industry. After Horicon became so successful by using the best suppliers available worldwide, several U.S. small engine manufacturers began to plan joint ventures with Asian manufacturers. Due to his experience, most engine suppliers to the garden tractor industry frequently contacted Lee for advice. His thorough understanding of engines and work ethic magnified his influence on the success of Horicon's lawn and garden products after his successful work with snowmobile engines.

Horicon Factory Management Charts New Work Processes

During the period from late 1978 through the next several years, the Horicon factory manager's staff attended a series of offsite meetings to develop a collective understanding of how to improve the Horicon Works internal work processes and factory procedures. The experience with snowmobiles was fresh in everyone's mind after two years of financial losses. Outside resources in these discussions were provided by Lauren

Miller, Human Resources Manager. Lauren served to keep the meetings focused and documented our conclusions. The ground rule for participation was all were equals and the focus was on work processes, not individuals. The results of these off-site meetings were discussed with Ray Gregg, who did not attend until the last afternoon, when they discussed outcomes with him. The meeting conversations would have been less effective if he had been present; in his absence, it was possible to clear the air without fear of communicating the wrong message to the boss.

The Horicon Works' first efforts with new product teams were limited to designation of a person in all of the major factory departments for the project engineer to contact about new product programs. This was just another application of the Ray Gregg expression about overhauling the train while it was going down the tracks. Although the first intervention helped, the Horicon manager's staff soon agreed to a more robust process with assignments of needed disciplines of factory department personnel to new product teams, under the direct supervision of the team leader. Initially and most often, that was a PED project engineer. The team members were chosen by agreement with the department manager.

Later PED began to rotate assignments of product engineers with manufacturing engineers. In 1984 this rotation was more easily done as the manufacturing and product engineers were under Ron's direction as the manager of engineering for the factory. Salaried employees typically looked to their home department as the route for personal advancement. Some feared the team organization would threaten their career advancement as they were away from their peers. The opposite occurred as this experience enhanced their growth and strengthened their contribution to the process of market planning, design and preparation for manufacturing. The team members were responsible to keep their home department manager informed of the status of the team's project. Monthly reviews with the factory manager and his staff were scheduled for the teams to present the status of their work. These reviews kept everyone informed of critical situations so appropriate decisions could be made at those meetings. This, in turn, smoothed the path for significant reduction in time from design to production. Continuous communication was like yeast in the bread that would foster cooperation when all stakeholders understood what was required.

Shanahan study findings (described later in this chapter) stressed training team members about the importance of communication wherever needed to perform their work. In the literature of the day, this type of organization was named Simultaneous or Concurrent Engineering, with the implied meaning that the product and manufacturing processes were joined at the hip. The Horicon Works simply made changes to strengthen the teams that were fully supported by all of the factory department managers. With full participation by the factory team members, issues and concerns had the benefit of all considerations before decisions were made. During the period from 1981 to 1983, a new product started production for 26 consecutive months in the factory. Nothing like this had been done before. From market research and definition of the product on through design and testing to production is a perilous path. With the old rigid factory department control, major schedule delays occurred all too often. Departmental control yielded to a work process that enabled all key stakeholders to participate in a timely manner with the team. Adhering to the schedule was essential in every one of these projects. Finding ways to overcome obstacles made it possible to keep on schedule.

The front-mount mower that was introduced in the 1984 model product dealer introduction meeting held at Oconomowoc, Wisconsin, demonstrated the power of this focused team process. In 1982 a front-mount mower with a unique drive concept was being designed by Horicon PED. A prototype was operated in different field and weather conditions to evaluate its performance. It utilized a steering system that varied the speed of the drive wheels to set the direction of motion. A significant functional problem occurred on slopes due to wheel slip that compromised the driver's ability to maintain steering control of the mower. After an appropriate review by the factory and marketing personnel, it was agreed to abandon this approach and design a conventional rear-wheel steering vehicle to eliminate this safety risk. Marketing insisted they needed to introduce it to dealers the next year. The original schedule was met despite the time lost due to the change in direction.

New Product Introduced by model Year

1977	208 L&G Tractor 312 L&G Tractor
1978	216 WB Tiller Spitfire Snowmobile 65 Rider 21 SP Mower
1979	Trailfire Snowmobile 216 L&G Tractor 314 L&G Tractor 317 L&G Tractor 108 Lawn Tractor 111 Lawn Tractor Skid Steer Loaders
1980	Sportfire Snowmobile Liquifire Snowmobile 40 Tiller (CUD) 72 Mower (CUD)
1981	160 Mower (CUD) 272 Mower (CUD) 448 Tiller (CUD)
1982	Trailfire LX Snowmobile Snowfire Snowmobile Sprintfire Snowmobile 261 Mower (CUD) 359 Snow Blower (CUD) 111 Hydro Lawn Tractor 116 Lawn Tractor
1983	116 Hydro Lawn Tractor 318 L&G Tractor 420 L&G Tractor 260 Mower 47" Snow Blower 48" Tiller

***Above and opposite*: JD new products introduced (by model year) (Ron Leonard collection).**

The team decided to work without the formal Decision Release document that was standard procedure. It was replaced with a desk in the purchasing department. As part drawings were finished with a date of origin, a print was placed in a stack on the desk. When a change was needed, a revised print with the latest date was taken to the processing desk. Every day the involved manufacturing engineer and purchasing buyer

1984	50" Mid-Mount Mower
	38" Mid-Mount Mower
	50" 3-Point Hitch Mower
	R70 Rider
	R72 Rider
	S80 Rider
	S82 Rider
	S92 Rider
	316 L&G Tractor
	Tilt Dump Material Collection System
	Hydro Lift Material Collection System
	430 L&G Tractor
	Hydro Tiller
	F910 Front Mount Mower
	F930 Front Mount Mower
1985	R92 Rider
	46" Snow Thrower (FM)
	54" Front Blade (FM)
	112L Hydro Lawn Tractor
	160 Improved Mower (CUD)
	172 Mower (CUD)
	330 L&G Tractor
1986	130 Lawn Tractor
	160 Lawn Tractor
	165 Lawn Tractor
	180 Lawn Tractor
	185 Lawn Tractor
	F915 Front Mower
	F935 Front Mower
	47" Snow Blower for Front Mower
	900 HC Cultivating Tractor
	570 Skid Steer Loader
	575 Skid Steer Loader
	675 Skid Steer Loader
	76" Swept Spindle Mower
	Power Pack MCS for Front Mower (3-Bag)
	Power Pack MCS for CUT (Hydro Dump)
	655 Compact Utility Tractor
	755 Compact Utility Tractor
	855 Compact Utility Tractor
	50" Mower for 655
	60" Mower for 755 & 855
	72" Mower for 855
	54" Blade for 655, 755 & 855
	46" Snow Thrower for 655
	47" Snow Blower for 755 & 855
	59" Snow Blower for 855
	Power Flow MCS
1987	RX73 Riding Mower
	RX75 Riding Mower
	RX95 Riding Mower
	SX75 Riding Mower
	SX95 Riding Mower
	332 L&G Tractor
	175 Lawn Tractor
	F912 front Mower
	Improved 38" 2-Spindle Mower
	Power Pack MCS (3-Bag) (300, 400, CUT)
	Rear Discharge Maintenance Mower
	375 Skid Steer Loader
1988	RX63 Riding Mower
	240 L&G Tractor
	260 L&G Tractor
	265 L&G Tractor
	285 L&G Tractor
	322 L&G Tractor

were required to come and pick up those prints. If clarification with engineering was required, that was done immediately. The product went into production as originally scheduled without a formal Engineering Decision document. Both suppliers and Horicon Works' primary production went smoothly and production assembly of the new product was underway as planned during the 1984 Oconomowoc dealer meeting. This experience provided the confidence to simplify the formal Decision specification and drawing release process.

Market Research by Dr. Robert G. Cooper

As the snowmobile engineering work was winding down, the PED embraced the need for better market research before starting to design a new product. The necessity of this was illustrated very clearly by the mid-engine vs. front-engine chassis decisions made as Deere entered the snowmobile business, as well as for some lawn and garden products. There was more to the story than defining specifications based on competitive products, although this was useful to evaluate strengths and weaknesses of competitive machines. Several of the grounds-care products designed between 1975 and 1980 updated the original Horicon products to equal or exceed the competition, but were not new concept designs.

The Atlanta sales branch provided the Horicon Works with additional motivation to find a better way to plan new products, starting with the first redesign of the rear engine riders as 1975 models. The Atlanta sales branch sales territory was in the southeastern states, where Snapper was the main competition and held a commanding lead in market share with a basic, no-frills machine. It also was lower-priced than the John Deere riding mower. The 1975 model 66 and 68 rear-engine riding mowers were designed to meet the industry standard for lower drive-by sound levels; thus, the design required significant changes. A shroud covered the engine to absorb the sound, and similar to the experience with snowmobiles, considerable heat was trapped inside the shroud. The engineers designed the shroud to let air flow through it so the engine operating temperatures were lower than the riders they replaced.

The sales branch complained that the shroud around the engine, which was essential for sound reduction, wasn't necessary and the engines were running too hot. In a meeting at the Atlanta sales branch office, Horicon Works asked for a specific location and advised they would send an engineer with instrumentation to measure the engine operating temperatures. The branch provided the machines: an old model JD 57, a new model JD 68, and a current production Snapper. Atlanta branch personnel accompanied the Horicon Works engineer who conducted the tests. Of course, the result was the new model JD 68 had the coolest engine, and temperatures which were much lower than Snapper and the JD 57. This incident set off a firestorm of controversy with the Atlanta sales branch over riding mowers. Their customers were not used to an enclosed engine on a riding mower. They thought this was a mistake, as all engines on riding mowers were "air cooled."

The basic issue was that the sales branches and their dealers were not in support of the CPSC regulations to lower sound levels that complied with the industry developed standards. The sales branches and dealers were not fully informed about the rapid changes in regulations occurring in the industry. The Deere legal department monitored the lawsuits in the industry over hearing loss, allegedly due to exposure to high noise levels while operating homeowner grounds-maintenance products. The Horicon factory position was that all new manufactured products would meet or exceed these standards. After the temperature test of engines, the concern at the Atlanta branch was that the dealers couldn't sell the JD riders because they were too costly. The Snapper rider was priced at $1,200 and the Deere about $1,400. Division Engineer Gerry Buelow and Ron cooked up a project that would address the cost and price difference. It was quite simple. Matching the same specifications as Snapper, Deere could make a better, more durable machine that would be profitable to the factory and to Deere to sell for $1,200, and meet or exceed all known legal and safety requirements.

The PED designed a mower to those specs that became the R series of Deere riding mowers. After the AFE was approved and Deere was setting the prices for the new riders, Ray was contacted and told that Deere Marketing couldn't sell that machine because it wasn't a John Deere. What did that mean? Horicon was asked to bring a Snapper, along with the JD 68 and the R Series rider, to Moline to meet with Boyd Bartlett, then the vice-president of Agricultural and Consumer Products Marketing in Moline. During the meeting a Deere & Co. staff marketing person pointed out the Spartan specifications on the R Series that were like the Snapper, but inferior to the JD 68. Boyd supported the position that Deere marketing couldn't sell the R Series rider. The most glaring visible concern was with the semi-pneumatic front tires and bushing bearings. Their position was that Deere dealers couldn't sell a riding mower without inflatable tires and ball bearings in the front wheels because Deere dealers expected them in a John Deere product.

To no avail, Ron contended that Horicon Works marketing and engineering had an agreement to proceed with the project as long as it met or exceeded Snapper specifications. PED had tested both Snapper and Deere machines concurrently that demonstrated Deere's superior durability to the Snapper and mowing quality equal to the current model 66 and 68 Riders, as the mowing deck was the same as used on them. The pneumatic tires and ball bearings would cost $5.60 additional per machine. Adding over 1 percent to the cost, and others parts like this, reduced the margin for the company. The Horicon Works had worked hard to reduce the cost of manufacturing by about $100 in order to sell it for $1,200, the target that Horicon understood to have been set before starting the design. The meeting ended with Horicon Works ordered to use the pneumatic tires and ball bearings.

This type of experience happened often with Deere factories and sales branches over new products. Some of the sales branches would name the best-selling competition product for Deere, then advocate Deere make it with higher specifications and still sell it for the same price. In the highly competitive consumer product markets, the Horicon Works needed a better way to plan new product programs that cultivated better communication and understanding throughout the company about new projects *before* the Horicon Works invested costly engineering resources on a design that couldn't be sold because it wasn't a "Deere machine." The agricultural influence in making decisions for consumer products had exhausted its welcome in Horicon. There were others in Moline senior management who felt the same way. This experience added emphasis to the debate about the need to separate the consumer products business from agriculture at the senior management level in Moline, similar to the success that the sales branches had achieved while separating the dealer marketing of consumer products from agriculture. A separate consumer products division of Deere was beginning to take shape.

Gerry Buelow invited Dr. Robert G. Cooper of McGill University to Horicon to present a seminar on his research on companies' success with new products. His paper "Why New Industrial Products Fail" was published in 1975 in the *Journal of Industrial Marketing Management*. The introduction to the paper said: "This article reports the results of an empirical investigation into the causes of failure of new industrial products. The results, based on a sample of 114 products, point to the need for a much greater market orientation by industrial firms." Later in the paper, Cooper observes, "The most frequently mentioned specific cause of low sales was that competitors were firmly entrenched in the market and it proved more difficult to break into the market than expected." This had occurred when Deere entered the snowmobile market. Polaris and Arctic Cat front-engine chassis designs dominated new sales in a declining market and market leader Ski-Doo quickly followed their lead.

Deere did establish a good following of JD customers with the first year's JD 400 and 500 snowmobiles, but as Cooper's research revealed, it was very difficult to dislodge two strong competitors. His research included several major corporations with a diverse portfolio of products. The article continued by defining six underlying factors that influenced specific causes of low sales. Five of the six underlying factors "describe a lack of understanding of the marketplace: customers, competition and environment." After the seminar, Dr. Cooper consulted with the Horicon PED on adapting his methodology to do market research for Horicon Works. It involved extensive focus group interviews with customers. Prepared questions were designed to draw out comments about—you guessed it "the marketplace: customers, competition and environment." These discussions focused on specific customer needs for

The market research methodoloy of Robert G. Cooper helped Deere to develop a better understanding of market trends and the strengths of competititve products (Ron Leonard collection).

mowing their yard and other uses of their vehicles. The data collected were analyzed by statistical analysis procedures that linked comments from all interviews to show preference trends in the markets. Horicon Works marketing, engineering and manufacturing personnel, along with selected sales branch representatives, participated in these sessions that were held in different market areas of the country. They were usually arranged through the cooperation of a John Deere dealer. At other times they were conducted by using a speaker phone in a factory conference room. This was 1980, long before computer video and conferencing equipment were available.

Although market research methodology is more refined today, in 1980 this approach was new territory for Deere. The product planning done by the small product planning department in Moline in consultation with Deere sales branches usually produced only a carbon copy of competitors' product specifications. All too often a design engineer only understood *what* was wanted and not the *why* behind those specifications. Engineering and the factory marketing personnel needed a good understanding of the market trends and the drivers for change in all the major price segments of the market. Cooper's market research methodology was used to define product specifications for several of the new lawn and garden products, especially for new market segments which required good understanding of price and feature relationship in customer buying decisions. This market-research approach was a minor revolution within Deere as the factory assumed responsibility for product planning rather than relying on opinion information relayed from dealers to sales branches to the factory's marketing department. Discussing answers to probing questions with real customers about their needs let the sunshine in. More clarity of the market, strength of competition, and technology were needed to communicate effectively with factory and corporate management before committing to a specific schedule for a new product. This type of communication would help clarify the risk vs. the reward of alternative product design direction and schedules.

Dr. Cooper's research methodology paralleled in many ways how the Horicon Advanced Products group defined the specifications for the design of the JD 340/S race machine. Race drivers and Horicon Works' engineers worked together to set the critical sled geometry for the high-performance rider. There were no sales branch or dealer personnel present in the field experiments that set the basic machine geometry. As a result, Deere soon became competitive in cross-country racing with the first all-new front-engine chassis JD 340/S. As Deere entered the snowmobile business, the assumption that industry OEM suppliers made satisfactory drive train components was wrong. Engine power levels increased rapidly, and this pointed out the need to do an assessment of the technology required before doing the first machine design. Cooper's research was insightful in stating it was very difficult to dislodge two strong competitors when you were late to the party. The Horicon rear engine rider became very successful as a later design increased the rider production to five times the first year's production, or 58,910 machines. The Atlanta sales branch sold the most riders, as that area was the largest market for riding mowers. The market responded because the product specifications and design were right for the market.

During the years Horicon Works made snowmobiles, the model life cycle was much shorter than Deere experienced with its agricultural and industrial products. During the last part of the Horicon Decade of Excellence, Cooper's market research method helped improve the understanding of changing market trends and the quality of the communications with management as the product was developed. His research findings also pointed to the necessity to analyze the financial strength of competition along with their specific product specifications when entering a market with two or more strong competitors. There is reason to speculate that Cooper's research methodology, if it had been done before Deere entered the snowmobile business, would have changed the direction of the Deere entry into the market. Deere had formidable engineering capability as demonstrated later. It needed to be focused on the right market target and do the work in the right way.

Shanahan Study: How Yamaha Planned, Designed and Manufactured Under–40 hp Outboard Motors

Another productive outside intervention at Horicon resulted from work performed by Bob Shanahan for Horicon Works, Harley-Davidson, and Briggs and Stratton. The Horicon Works needed to shorten the time to design and prepare products for production and learned about Bob during discussions with Mercury, who had proposed selling their snowmobile line to Deere. That was not pursued, but during those meetings we discovered that Mercury Marine had contracted Yamaha to design and manufacture twelve new models of outboard motors up to 40 hp for Mercury to market in the U.S. Mercury stopped production of their under 40 hp outboard engines at Fond du Lac, Wisconsin, because they were too costly. Yamaha accomplished this within ten years, with each new engine program running 26 months from start of design to first production. Yamaha quickly made significant market share gains and eventually dominated this market worldwide. The Yamaha product engineering staff was about the same size as the Horicon PED.

Bob Shanahan had retired after serving as the Mercury-Yamaha project manager. During this time he acquired a good understanding of how the Yamaha factory functioned in market planning, engineering and factory preparation for production. He agreed to document the procedures that Yamaha had used to accomplish that work. The study cost $30,000, shared equally by the three companies. Shanahan concluded that Yamaha's success was directly related to the disciplined use of quick and continuous communication with all stakeholders involved in the game. The "aha" Bob found was quite simple and certainly not technical in nature. The conclusion in the executive summary of his report was about "communication and cooperation." The Yamaha factory included a refined level of daily communication at all levels in the organization. In the writer's (Shanahan) opinion, communication problems are alleviated by the discipline instilled in the Japanese person. To the well-disciplined worker, communication is a responsibility to be fulfilled regardless of personality conflicts and time restraints.

Shanahan's report highlighted the importance of communication in all disciplines, including management, in the factory operations. The rigid departmental barriers often found in the U.S. factories were almost seamless as the Japanese worked to design the motors and prepare for production. Marketing was deeply involved, witnessing the comparative engine testing so they could plan a strong marketing effort. At the end of each day during the 26 months, status meetings were held in standup sessions by the factory management with all the key individuals. Prior to starting a design, Yamaha completed an exhaustive detailed teardown and analysis of every part of numerous competitive outboard motors. This defined critical dimensions, materials and manufacturing processes. They conducted power tests of the competitive engines in their engine test cells. Apparently they operated as if the new product were the most important activity in the factory. It was that. Having the ability to complete all the required work in the factory for new products in a timely manner is key to increased factory productivity and market planning. There is no future without a saleable product in any business.

Horicon commissioned Shanahan to do a followup study of the Horicon new product design and manufacturing processes. That was documented in another report that paralleled the Japanese study. His methodology for the research at Horicon Works was to study the documents of a project that was recently completed, and then conduct numerous interviews with key factory stakeholders. From this he arrived at the elapsed time from start to finish. The initial reaction was shock, bordering on disbelief. The time leaks in our system were everywhere. The Horicon Works factory staff then became motivated to develop a plan to implement a new team structure to do new product design and prepare for manufacturing adapted to the Horicon Works organization. Japanese company engineers typically weren't assigned to work in design until they had spent three years in production assignments. The Japanese organization didn't have a large separate staff of manufacturing engineers like Horicon Works and other Deere factories. By careful construct of Horicon new product teams (discussed in the following section), and by transferring operational control to them, Horicon factory design and preparation for manufacturing improved dramatically. New and more effective communication with the general manager's staff developed that kept all departments equally informed of the status of each new product program.

Both Cooper's work and Shanahan's Yamaha study were the key drivers of the future direction of market planning, product design and production preparation of new product programs at the Horicon factory. These were implemented progressively during the next several years as new product projects were initiated. This subject was discussed thoroughly at the 1984 Horicon Works PSM held 19 June 1984.

There are no private offices or temperature controls in a Japanese Engineering Department.

There is one more layer of supervision/work direction in the John Deere Horicon Works organization.

My own summary of the meaning of the Shanahan study is that the Japanese company has:

1) Discipline in planning

2) Excellent communication

3) Commitment by all levels of management

In both the Japanese company and Deere, the effectiveness of Product Engineering is strongly influenced by the rest of the organization.

Another activity directed toward improving our engineering productivity is our own Horicon study of the subject. During the last several months our Engineering staff has been asked to propose suggestions for a more efficient Engineering organization.

The organization change which combined Product and Production Engineering provides a unique opportunity to evaluate some of these suggestions. Our current efforts toward improving our organization are aimed at the following goals:

o Obtain firm product specifications based upon market research conducted jointly between Marketing and Engineering.

o Involve Production Engineering at the beginning of new product programs.

o Obtain commitment to projects and schedules by all levels.

o Improve communications between factory departments by establishing clear responsibilities and eliminating overlap.

o Include financial management in the early part of project approval so that operating people are free to use financial resources at the proper time.

o Reduce development time from agreed-upon concept to saleable machine.

19 June 1984
R. K. Leonard

-14-

Future Horicon planning discussion (PSM, June 19, 1984) (Ron Leonard collection).

Yanmar/Kanzaki and Deere

Deere and Yanmar began a productive relationship in the early '70s when Yanmar started to produce 20-horsepower diesel compact utility tractors (CUT) for Deere to market in the U.S. They were needed as Kubota was growing rapidly in U.S. costal regions and Southern states. Both Kubota and Yanmar made similar sizes of small tractors for rice paddy farmers in Japan. Some modifications were needed so they would meet the needs of the small U.S. farmers who did not grow rice. The U.S. market was for mowing and small-scale farming operations. Deere no longer produced small tractors like the Model M that Wiman had manufactured at Dubuque after World War II. The U.S. market for the small diesel tractors was growing rapidly. Initially the Yanmar CUT program was managed by the PEC in Waterloo where the focus was agricultural tractors. Since the market used CUT tractors for light duty work, the design was distinctly different from heavy duty agricultural tractors. Deere & Co. elected to assign design responsibility for the CUT to the Horicon Works.

In 1975 the XR80 project of a mowing tractor of a similar size and power to the CUT was transferred to Horicon from the PEC. It was originally conceived at the Deere research center and later assigned to the PEC, where it languished behind the priority for work on large agricultural tractors. It was targeted for the small utility tractor market. After two years of evaluation of its performance and cost, the Horicon Works discontinued the project. The transfer of the Yanmar CUT to Horicon in 1979 reestablished the Horicon Works' direct involvement in this segment of the tractor market. This turned into a great opportunity for Horicon as engineering and factory personnel became more familiar with Yanmar capabilities. The PED expanded their work with Yanmar beyond the CUT to include Yanmar manufacture of components for Horicon tractors. Their diesel engine factory and Kanzaki Division transmission factory were key participants in the integrated engineering concept described in the 1984 PSM.

Yanmar had other manufacturing businesses for commercial applications in addition to tractors and diesel engines. Dr. Kijiro Yamaoka, who was a brother-in-law of the founder's son, Tadao Yamaoka, operated a separate Kanzaki division of Yanmar. As a young engineer Dr. K., as he was called by all who knew him, invented a small diesel fuel injection pump and built a separate factory to manufacture it. In addition he started a machine tool business located in Kobe. This factory was expanded to manufacture gears and small transmissions. When Yanmar decided to produce a rice harvester, Dr. K. and his engineering group created it and built another factory in the Nagahama area to manufacture it. Most of the Yanmar factories were located alongside Lake Biwa, north of Osaka. The interaction with several parts of the Yanmar enterprise provided the Horicon factory with the opportunity to make rapid market share gains in the '80s with lawn and garden tractors and commercial mowers. Sourcing diesel engines from Yanmar for garden tractors was expanded to joint engineering of transmissions and axles with Yanmar/Kanzaki that were manufactured by Kanzaki Division exclusively for Horicon Works' grounds care products.

New Machine Design Concepts

As the snowmobile effort was winding down, Horicon PED began to investigate how to design mowing machines that would offer better features and reliability. All riding vehicles that mowed grass had one common concern. Excessive vibrations contributed to operator discomfort and produced higher sound levels. How could these be reduced? The answer came by combining the transmission and final drive axle into one housing on all the machines. This provided more clearance to lift the mower and lowered sound and vibration. As a result, the machine was more appealing to the market. A new riding mower that went into production in 1984 demonstrated the value of integrating the drive components into one housing. The traditional rear-engine rider was configured with the engine mounted on the frame behind the operator's seat. One weekend Ron was moving some material with a wheelbarrow when he realized that by pushing the wheelbarrow he was like a rear-engine rider, with his body as the engine and transmission. The wheelbarrow operated without any vibration as most of the weight was supported on the ground under his feet. How much less vibration would occur in a riding mower if it were structured similar to a wheelbarrow? The rider front frame with the mower deck and the operator could be attached to the engine and drive system at the rear with vibration isolation. The engine would be mounted on the transaxle so the entire mower drive system weight and vibration would go directly to the ground and more of the vehicle weight would transfer directly to the large-diameter rear tires.

The next morning, after describing the concept to Lee Hardesty, he was enthusiastic enough to agree to do a quick mockup in the shop, with the engine, transmission and axle mounted on a plate that was attached to side frame members to support the front axle, mower deck and operator. As with earlier concept investigations, Lee had to revise the engine to run at a lower RPM to eliminate the chain drive reduction from the transmission to the rear axle. A few days later Lee called Ron to come to the shop to operate it. The concept mockup and a production rear-engine rider were parked alongside the model room wall. Lee started the production rider, then the concept mockup. The sound reduction was unbelievable. Ron called Ray and Marketing Manager Stan Kleiss to come and listen to it. They were as astonished as Lee and Ron were about the huge sound reduction. The design of this combined engine and transaxle by Kanzaki went into production. The increase from 11,280 of the old model in 1983 to 59,910 in 1984 was a dramatic verification that the market placed a high priority on vehicles that operated with much lower sound and vibration, just as the market research had predicted. This was the first riding mower in the industry to have a totally integrated drive system of the engine attached to a transaxle as one unit. This design eliminated the chain case that provided speed reduction to the drive, axle similar to what was done on the Spitfire snowmobile. Horicon Works again demonstrated that a better design concept that targeted customer needs would prevail over conventional wisdom. This design approach had been applied successfully to larger mowing tractors.

After Horicon completed a new vehicle design with the drive train location and specifications, Kanzaki and Horicon engineers held meetings to review and modify the designs as needed so they could be manufactured at Kanzaki. This was done for the design of other new model Horicon mowing products. The new components were tested at Kanzaki before installation in Horicon test machines. Yanmar/Kanzaki made the manufacturing investments for transaxles on the Horicon Works vehicles. By achieving maximum commonality with the transmissions and axles used in their tractors and rice harvester, Kanzaki was able to supply the transaxles at very competitive prices. Kanzaki was able to do rapid turnaround from design to prototypes for Horicon. They were as effective as Yamaha had been with the design of the under 40 hp outboard motors for Mercury.

The Horicon Model 755/855/955 CUT was the largest tractor configuration with an integrated transmission and axle in one housing. This optimized the vehicle configuration for the mower deck and front loader, reduced sound and vibration, and was lower cost than building it from separate components from different suppliers. It was the last major project completed at Horicon Works at the closing of the Horicon "Decade of Excellence." It opened the door for Deere to participate in the hydrostatic drive segment of the compact utility market. The CUT Yanmar produced for Deere only had a fixed speed gear transmission.

Doing concurrent design with quality manufacturers for unique components for Horicon products occurred as the lessons learned during the snowmobile era were transferred into new grounds-care machines. The snowmobiles introduced Horicon Works to a world of opportunity with manufactures in Japan and other countries. They made components and products that were much better quality than many of the U.S. suppliers to the OPEI. The new work processes in market research, definition of specifications and geometry of drive train specifications, and working concurrently with the supplier on the design, resulted in machines with the features desired by the market. The implementation of these new design and sourcing processes at Horicon Works was discussed with Moline management during the 1985 PSM.

Closing

As the Horicon Works said goodbye to snowmobiles, the factory was empowered to grow and prosper in large measure because experiences many people had from the business accelerated their personal growth and development. It would be easy to con-

Several strategic shifts are occurring which will have a long lasting effect upon our factory and our products. First is better coordination of the new layout of our factory with major new product introductions. The 100 Lawn Tractor pilot project for waste elimination was highly successful. From it our people gained a great deal of knowledge which can be applied to the manufacture of all our products.

We have integrated that knowledge into a new facilities master plan. This plan can be implemented during the five year planning period. It also includes a new paint system, which will greatly improve paint quality. Completion of the new factory layout and addition of the new paint process will improve quality and lower cost of manufacture on all our products. This plan will be implemented in stages so that normal production can continue.

The second strategic shift is the drive train components in our products. We are undergoing a transition from OEM suppliers of engines and transmissions to suppliers who will manufacture these components exclusively for us.

This process began with the Yanmar diesel engine in the 430 Tractor. Next was the KHI engine for the 112L Lawn Tractor, and now the diesel engine for the 330 Tractor. This summer all lawn tractors will begin using KHI engines. In January, production of the 240 Tractor will begin using Yanmar diesel engines and Kanzaki transaxles.

From the first 430 Tractor in 1984 until 1989, we will have made a major shift away from OEM components. Even with our past success, our marketing people have always wished for more differentiation between our products and those of competitors using the same components. Now they have it.

A third strategic shift is our people. Since June of 1984 twenty new people have begun work, helping to design our products. Twenty-five new people are at work helping plan for manufacture of these products. The quality of these people is excellent. I predict that these people will have an impact equal to what we experienced when we discontinued work on snowmobiles. That enabled us to focus our personnel on products which have created sales and profits for this factory.

New work processes at Horicon (PSM 1985) (Ron Leonard collection).

clude that R.J. was the sole driver of the snowmobile business, and it is clear that he was a strong leader during those years. The Hewitt plan to enter the consumer product business provides a framework from which to judge the snowmobile experience. Also, the agricultural emphasis of the company weighed heavily against the success of the snowmobile venture. It was a different market from anything that Deere had experienced in over fifty years. Conflict in priorities for consumer products with other units at the corporate level in the '70s was due in part to the profitable years in the agricultural division in the '70s. This soon came to an abrupt end in 1982 with a severe recession in agricultural and industrial markets.

It was always difficult for the Horicon factory to put on a false face to defend applying resources to an unprofitable business versus continuing to expand on the early success of the lawn and garden tractors. Most new businesses plan for negative cash flow during startup. However, the slow recovery to profitability in snowmobiles strengthened the resistance of those opposed to being in the business. No doubt the strong marketing voices from the sales branches in the snow regions fueled the corporate support for several years. Once the die was cast for separation of marketing from Ag, there seemed to be no turning back.

With the outstanding design of the Spitfire and Trailfire that began production as 1978 and 1979 models respectively, the factory snowmobile line was marketable and profitable. The Horicon PED had new design technology for ski and track suspensions implemented in engineering prototypes that would keep them competitive in the changing market. Racing was being done by dealer-supported and independent owners as they felt the desire to do. Racing snowmobiles did contribute knowledge about performance that was beneficial to the design for consumer markets. Racing demanded significant resources from the factory to support the effort during the startup years for the consumer market. Marketing people that we contacted said the same thing. Some dealers were enthusiastic about racing and others were not. Racing was a double-edged sword. Without doubt, racing helped build market awareness that Deere was a serious competitor in the market.

What did the snowmobile experience do for Deere? It enabled Deere & Company to grow sales by extending the scope of its business to market products different from agricultural and industrial machines—the consumer product's market. Horicon Works was assigned as the factory to manufacture those products. Until 1971 the Horicon Works products were marketed through the John Deere agricultural dealer network. With the 1000 independent dealers along with the 2000 agriculture dealers, Deere had access to a much larger market. When the annual snowmobile sales declined, Deere and Company was one of only five manufacturers that remained until they sold the business. However, Deere was not successful in dislodging strong competitors, as Dr. Cooper's research predicted.

When the product was "right" for the market, the consumer jumped on it—if it appealed to strong drivers in the fluid of changing customer expectations. The social revolution in the U.S. that began in the 1960s fueled those changing expectations. Sitting on a metal seat to mow grass on some of the early riding mowers didn't meet those expectations. Numerous government regulations reflected the political pressure by the market to protect the consumer from untoward amounts of noise and vibration. Deere embraced this as an opportunity to improve the appeal of their products in the market. Market research in a consumer product must identify those emerging trends, as Cooper's research pointed out. By identifying and embracing those trends in new product design, Deere made rapid growth in sales during the record performance of the factory that Ray Gregg proclaimed as the Decade of Excellence. Several of those new products exploded on the market similar to the Chinese firecracker welcome at the Taiwan bicycle factory. All of the products were designed and tested by a small but very talented group of engineers, designers, and engineering shop and test employees at the Horicon Works—who continued to advance and improve their products in the newly created Consumer Products Division of the company.

Personally for the authors, it was a challenging but rewarding period of our careers. The experiences and people that we met and worked with provided learning that was invaluable to later accomplishments. Lauren Miller, longtime Horicon Human Resources Manager, gave Ron this assessment of the snowmobile experience at the Horicon Works. In his normal dry wit, he said, "Don't try to do something that you don't understand." We well learned the lesson to conduct extensive market research and assess the technology required before entering a new business. For many employees, being in a different business brought new experiences and challenges that will remain in their memories for the rest of their lives. Unfortunately these diligent efforts failed to produce the satisfaction that comes with business success. Memories of the thrill and excitement from riding a snowmobile are difficult to describe to people who never had this experience. The legacy of Deere snowmobiles is secure with those who did. Lives were changed as new experiences broadened understanding and those lessons learned were applied with great success to the grounds-maintenance and turf care products.

The snowmobile was a very strenuous experience for many employees and dealers. Some employees were not well served by the stress and tension of frequent changes of priorities. Many experienced the gamut of all possible emotions during the early years. Some who were not in snowmobile markets were glad when Deere sold the business to Polaris. We, Dick and Ron, remember it as an exciting and rewarding time in our lives. We learned and played at the same time. It doesn't get much better than that.

Along with other exployees, dealers and customers, we left Deere tracks in the snow.

Appendices

I. Green Streak *Racing Bulletins*

GREEN STREAK

Race news and views from "Big John"

December 9, 1975

JOHN DEERE SWEEPS WEST YELLOWSTONE OPENER IN 440 STOCK CLASS; NEAR SWEEP IN 340 STOCK

John Deere Liquifire snowmobiles swept the 440 stock class December 7 at the West Yellowstone Opener as BRIAN NELSON raced to a first place finish in this 4-Lap, final 5/8-Mi. Banked Oval competition. JIM ALMOND, an independent from Coeur D'Alene (Ida.), came in second, followed closely by BOB ENNS in third and CRAIG KNUDSEN in fourth -- all piloting 440 Liquifires.

Placing second, third, fourth and fifth in 340 stock competition were "Big John" drivers: BOB LINDMAN, another independent hailing from Soda Springs (Ida.); HUBERT FIXEN of Willmar (Minn.), a mechanic for the Enduro Team Deere; BOB ENNS and JON CARLSON. CARLSON, ENNS, NELSON and KNUDSEN are members of the six-man Enduro Team Deere.

BRIAN NELSON, 1st Place, 440 Stock Class

BOB ENNS, 3rd, 440 Stock; 4th, 340 Stock

CRAIG KNUDSEN, 4th, 440 Stock

JON CARLSON, 5th, 340 Stock

NEXT WEEK ... A PREVIEW

Look for your Green Streak next week when John Deere brings you a preview of the North Dakota Trophy Run, as well as current news and views from the snowmobile race circuit. Meanwhile, we're looking forward to seeing you December 19 in Bismark....

JOHN DEERE

John Deere *Green Streak* newsletter (courtesy Larry Swanson).

THE DEERE CROSS-COUNTRY RACE TEAM LINEUP

Whether you're gearing up to enter the cross-country circuit, or planning to enjoy the snowmobile races as an armchair or on-the-scene enthusiast, we're sure you'll keep an eye on your fellow Deere drivers. Looking to the first race -- the North Dakota Trophy Run on December 19--20 -- here's the Enduro Team Deere and John Deere sales branch team lineup:

STEVE ANDERSON, age 26, Princeton (Ill.), Team Deere Moline. Top 20 finishes, '74 North Dakota Trophy Run and '75 South Dakota Governor's Cup.

WILLIE ANSEEUW, 21, Manitoba (Canada), Enduro Team Deere. 11th place, '75 I-500; 1st/Mod Stock 340 and 440, 3/8-Mi. Flat Oval, Nov. '75, Alaska.

JON CARLSON, 21, Moline (Ill.), Enduro Team Deere. 3rd place, '75 I-500; 2nd, Mod Stock '75 Park Rapids Race.

ROGER EBERT, 27, Nisswa (Minn.), Team Deere Minneapolis. 7th place, '75 I-500; 9th, '70 I-500.

BOB ENNS, 24 Manitoba (Canada), Enduro Team Deere. Former Canadian and Manitoba champ, Stock 400 and 440.

CRAIG KNUDSEN, 21, Kandiyohi (Minn.), Enduro Team Deere. 1st, Mod Stock 340, '74 Alaska.

BRIAN NELSON, 22, Willmar (Minn.), Enduro Team Deere. 1st/Mod Stock 340, 3rd/Stock 340, 2nd/Mod Stock 440, 3/8-Mi. Flat Oval, Nov. '75, Alaska.

ERNIE MEUNIER, 24, Quebec (Canada), Team Deere Canada. 5th place, '74 South Dakota Governor's Cup.

TOM OTTE, 20, Randolph (Minn.), Team Deere Minneapolis. 9th, '74 I-500; 1st, 0-Stock 340 and fastest time, '74 North Dakota Governor's Cup.

STACY REDMOND, 35, Mason City (Ia.), Team Deere Moline. Top 20 finish, '74 I-500; current season marks 5th year in I-500, first as John Deere driver.

RON REIMER, 24, Manitoba (Canada), Enduro Team Deere. 2nd, Mod Stock 340, 3/8-Mi. Flat Oval and 4th, Stock 340, 10-Mi. Closed Course, Nov. '75, Alaska.

GLEN WASMUTH, 29, Saskatchewan (Canada), Team Deere Canada. Top 20, '75 I-500; 3rd, '75 Regina-Minot International 250.

More information will be published about the entire field of "Big John" drivers who race to top ten finishes as the '75 -- '76 cross-country season progresses.

WIN SHARE OF DEERE PURSE PLUS BONUS CASH IN ADDITION TO REGULAR RACE PRIZE MONEY

More than 150 independent John Deere snowmobile drivers are now in the running for a share of Deere race prize money and bonus point cash amounting to $67,500 for nine designated cross-country races. Race win money will be issued by Deere & Company immediately upon receipt of official results as follows:

FINISH	ST. PAUL/WINNIPEG 500	EIGHT OTHER RACES	YEAR-END BONUS MONEY*
1st	$ 6,000	$ 2,000 ea.	$ 6,000
2nd	3,000	1,000	3,000
3rd	2,000	750	2,000
4th	1,000	500	1,000
5th	500	250	500
6th--10th	250	100	250

* To be distributed at the end of the season.

Official entry blanks for the John Deere Racing Program are available at local dealerships throughout the snow belt USA and Canada.

GREEN STREAK

Race news and views from "Big John"

December 16, 1975

ENNS WINS 400 SUPER STOCK COMPETITION IN IRONWOOD; ANOTHER VICTORY FOR 340 LIQUIDATORS

IRONWOOD, MICH., Dec. 13: BOB ENNS, an Enduro Team Deere driver from Manitoba (Canada), raced to a 1st place victory/400 Super Stock in Saturday's seven-mile cross-country race at Ironwwod. Also placing in that class were Team Deere Minneapolis driver TOM OTTE, Randolph (Minn.), in 4th followed closely by Enduro Team driver JON CARLSON of Moline (Ill.) in 5th. Of the four other cross-country classes entered by Deere drivers, CRAIG KNUDSEN, Kandiyohi (Minn.), took 2nd/440 Super Mod Stock and 7th/340 Super Stock; Enduro teammate ENNS placed 3rd in that class as well. Taking 3rd/340 Mod Stock and 340 Open Mod, respectively, were DOUG HOUGH of Forest Lake (Minn.) and CARLSON. All competed on 1976 John Deere high performance Liquidator sleds which they will drive in the next nine major cross-country events..

TOM OTTE, defending champ in this weekend's North Dakota Governor's Trophy Run, took 4th/400 Super Stock last Saturday in Ironwood.

MATCH DEERE CHAMPS AT NORTH DAKOTA GOVERNOR'S TROPHY RUN

Team Deere Minneapolis driver Tom Otte will defend his 1974 championship in this year's two-day race. The 1975 North Dakota Governor's Trophy Run covers 250 miles, 90% of which is ditch from Bismarck to Carrington to Grand Forks. Also in the offing is $100-$2,000 in excess of regular race prize money to all "Big John" drivers who finish in the top ten. John Deere will issue race prize money by check immediately upon receipt of official results. See you in Bismark....

Issued periodically by the Advertising Dept., Deere & Co., Moline, Ill. 61265

JOHN DEERE

THE BONUS POINT SCOREBOARD

Starting next week with the North Dakota Governor's Trophy Run, all John Deere snowmobile drivers who race to a top ten finish in any of eight designated events or to a top 20 finish in the I-500 will be assigned bonus points which will qualify them for additional cash prizes as well as trophies to be awarded by John Deere at season's end. Chicago model Michele Joann is pictured here with a sample of the trophy that will be presented to each of the top ten point getters.

An updated tally of bonus points will appear weekly under the Bonus Point Scoreboard section of your Green Streak. The point system works as follows:

International 500		Other eight races	
Place	Points	Place	Points
1	60	1	30
2	40	2	20
3	30	3	15
4	20	4	10
5	16	5	8
6	12	6	6
7	8	7	4
8	6	8	3
9	4	9	2
10	3	10	1
11-20	2	--	--

GREEN STREAK

Race news and views from "Big John"

December 22, 1975

NELSON TAKES JOHN DEERE TO VICTORY IN NORTH DAKOTA GOVERNOR'S TROPHY RUN

John Deere took the North Dakota Governor's Trophy Run for the second consecutive year as Enduro Team Deere member BRIAN NELSON piloted his Liquidator 340 to 1st place with best overall time of 5 hours, 24 minutes and 54 seconds. Nelson, from Willmar (Minn.), also won 340 Mod Stock and 440 Stock competition this year in Alaska and West Yellowstone, respectively.

The 1975 North Dakota race was a two-day event covering 115 miles of rough course and strong headwinds from Bismarck to Carrington, followed by 130 miles of biting cold from Carrington to Grand Forks. Of the 185 sleds to start, only 41 crossed the finish line Saturday afternoon. The top five places were well spread among different brands of sleds, with Nelson leading Kevin Furth (Devils Lake, N. Dak.) on a Yamaha in 2nd, Ronnie Zutz (Warren, Minn.) on a Polaris in 3rd, and brothers Kirt and Rex Hibbert (Driggs, Ida.), each driving Arctic Cats to respective 4th and 5th place finishes.

$14,000 BALSAM LAKE CLASSIC -- START AND FINISH AT "PARADISE"

Are you ready for the Balsam Lake Classic? It starts at 9:00 A.M. ... and ends about 4½ hours later at the finish line in front of the Paradise Supper Club. We'll see an estimated field of 130 snowmobiles ... the number presently scheduled to run the 250-mile shoreline around Balsam Lake. Entrants to date represent at least eight states and three Canadian provinces. Expect a Grand Prix-type course consisting of approximately 50% straight-aways in combination with sharp corners, bends and moguls to pit the best of drivers against his or her machine. Victors take $14,000 in prize money, with $5,000 to the winner and another $2,000 if that winner pilots a John Deere sled to 1st place. John Deere puts up a total of $5,000 in excess of regular race prize money plus bonus points (worth extra cash at season's end) to John Deere drivers placing in the top ten. Deere cash awards will be issued by check upon receipt of official results; winners are, however, invited to accept regular race money ... and trophies to the top four ... at an Awards Banquet starting at 7:00 P.M. at the Paradise. Good luck!

Issued periodically by the Advertising Dept., Deere & Co., Moline, Ill. 61265

JOHN DEERE

- More -

THE BONUS POINT SCOREBOARD

BRIAN NELSON earned 30 bonus points as the winner of the first cross-country event in a nine-race circuit. Points, worth additional money from Deere at season's end, can be accrued by John Deere drivers who race to top ten finishes in any or all of the next eight major races designated by Deere & Company.

JOHN DEERE DRIVERS -- PLEASE LET US KNOW WHO YOU ARE

All John Deere drivers who have not yet returned the drivers information form are requested to submit it as soon as possible. If you have not received this form, please notify the Advertising Department, Deere & Co., Moline, Ill., 61265 (309-792-4613). Information noted on your form will make it possible for us to publicize your wins as a cross-country snowmobile race drivers. Thanks for your assistance and cooperation.

DEERE CHAMPIONSHIP RING

A 14-carat gold championship ring with 32-point diamond inset in green sapphire will be awarded by Deere & Company to the John Deere snowmobile race driver who accumulates the most bonus points under the Deere Racing Program for '75--'76. Nine identical rings without the center diamond also will be presented at season's end to the next nine runners-up.

The Deere ring design was created by Josten's Inc., designers of the classic Super Bowl champion rings.

GREEN STREAK

Race news and views from "Big John"

December 29 1975

NELSON AND OTTE TAKE 2ND AND 3RD IN BALSAM LAKE CLASSIC

Enduro Team Deere driver BRIAN NELSON and Team Deere Minneapolis driver TOM OTTE piloted their 1976 Liquidator sleds to 2nd and 3rd place finishes last Sunday in the Balsam Lake Classic. Only 55 drivers out of a field of 150 finished the 250-mile, 12-lap course; more than half that number were driving John Deere snowmobiles. In the lead on a Rupp with 3 hours, 22 minutes and 19 seconds to finish was winner Jay Sperry of Minneapolis, followed by Nelson (Willmar, Minn.) with 3 hours, 26 minutes and 15 seconds, and Otte (Randolph, Minn.) in 3rd in 3 hours, 27 minutes and 13 seconds. Of eight John Deere drivers to place in the top 20, two independents from Illinois -- PAUL YOUNG, Erie, and HAROLD McQUEEN, Manteno -- took 7th and 8th, respectively.

BRIAN NELSON

TOM OTTE

THE BONUS POINT SCOREBOARD

Three more snowmobile race drivers are now on their way to cumulative points worth bonus money from John Deere. An updated tally shows BRIAN NELSON in the lead with 50 cumulative points, TOM OTTE with 15, PAUL YOUNG with four, and HAROLD McQUEEN with three points toward bonus cash prizes at season's end.

START NEW YEAR WITH SOUTH DAKOTA GOVERNOR'S CUP

ERNIE MEUNIER

STEVE ANDERSON

Saturday, January 10, marks the start of the two-day, 250-mile South Dakota Governor's Cup. And it could be tough! Nearly two-thirds of the field never even made the first leg from Pierre to Mobridge in the previous race. Moreover, of 60 sleds to start in that race last February, only 20 crossed the finish line Sunday in Aberdeen. Five of those 20 were John Deere drivers, however, with independent SCOTT SIMONSON from Grand Forks (N. Dak.) driving 5 hours and 57 minutes for 3rd place, Team Deere Canada driver ERNIE MEUNIER of Hamilton (Ont.) in 7th, and independent RALPH GAST, Steamboat Rock (Ia.) in 9th; also in the top 20 were Team Deere Moline driver STEVE ANDERSON and independent SAM MADONIA, of Moline and Bridgeview (Ill.), respectively.

Issued periodically by the Advertising Dept., Deere & Co., Moline, Ill. 61265

- More -

-- A CANDID LOOK AT THE ENDURO TEAM DEERE WINNER'S CIRCLE --

1) BRIAN NELSON, in 1st, crossing the finish line at Grand Forks (N. Dak.)

2) WILLIE ANSEEUW, in 1st/Mod Stock 440 and Mod Stock 440, Alaska

3) Enduro Team "coach" AL ANDERSEN, keeping time in a job well done

4) BOB ENNS, taking 1st/400 Super Stock at Ironwood (Mich.)

GREEN STREAK

Race news and views from "Big John"

January 12, 1976

TWO JOHN DEERE DRIVERS TAKE TOP 20 FINISHES IN SOUTH DAKOTA GOVERNOR'S CUP RACE

Weather conditions notwithstanding, the four-inch snowfall that blanketed the South Dakota Governor's Cup race course early Saturday morning really made it tough going for 158 machines. The first sleds out had to break trail both Saturday and Sunday on different runs, first from Aberdeen to Mobridge and then back again from Mobridge to Aberdeen on the second leg. Drivers were faced with a mixed bag ranging from deep ruts and heavy four- to six-foot drifts to minimum powder snow cover, resulting in a slower-paced race than the usual cross-country fare. But, 101 sleds came in the first day and 65 did finish in Aberdeen in an average two-day total time of 7½-8 hours. 26 of those finishers were piloting John Deere sleds, with Canadian Enduro Team Deere driver BOB ENNS of Oak Bluff, Manitoba, finishing in 12th and independent driver ROBERT SCHUMACHER of Bismarck, N. Dak. taking 18th place.

(Right) BOB ENNS starts the second leg in Mobridge, finishing 12th in Aberdeen in 7 hours, 14 minutes.

ARE YOU READY FOR THE ST. PAUL-WINNIPEG INTERNATIONAL 500 -- THE FOUR-DAY GRANDADDY OF 'EM ALL

An approximate field of 400 snowmobile race drivers from all over North America are planning to enter the January 19--22 St. Paul-Winnipeg International 500 -- the longest major cross-country race in the '75-'76 circuit. Frigid temperatures are expected again this year on a truly tough 500-mile course from St. Paul to Alexandria to Walker to Thief River Falls and across the border into Winnipeg. Of the 377 sleds that started in Winnipeg last year, only 22 sleds finished, 12 of them John Deere. Two of those John Deere drivers -- JON CARLSON of Moline, Ill. and ROGER JANSSEN from Crookston, Minn. -- took third and fourth, respectively, in a photo finish. Carlson plans to beat his time along with his five fellow members of the Enduro Team Deere and six John Deere sales branch team members. As in the past, the I-500 is held in conjunction with the St. Paul Winter Carnival.

MORE JOHN DEERE RACE PRIZE MONEY AND BONUS POINT CASH FOR I-500 THAN FOR EIGHT OTHER RACES

A $13,500 purse in excess of regular race prize money plus double the number of bonus points toward cash awards at season's end is being offered by John Deere for the I-500. Unlike the other eight races, the Deere prize money structure for this four-day event is topped by a potential first-place win of $6,000 down to $250 each to John Deere drivers who place from six to ten. Also, as noted in the December 16 Green Streak, bonus points will be awarded to the top 20 point-getters compared to the top ten in all other races. In addition, John Deere drivers finishing in the top 20 stand to enter the Bonus Point Scoreboard with anywhere from two to sixty points depending upon his or her place of finish at the end of the St. Paul-Winnipeg run.

Issued periodically by the Advertising Dept., Deere & Co., Moline, Ill. 61265

JOHN DEERE

- More -

THE INDEPENDENT CORNER

There's a lot to be said for all those John Deere drivers who finished the first three races of the season in spite of the fact that many have not placed in the top 20. This weekend alone, there were 26 John Deere sleds that managed to finish the South Dakota Governor's Cup race under extremely rough driving conditions. Some of those that made it include: EUGENE JETVIG of Hawley, Minn.; JIM ZIMMER, a John Deere dealer from Lakeville, Minn.; BOB MENNE of Forest Lake, Minn., who finished all three races this season; 18-year-old MIKE SOWARD of Sioux Falls, S. Dak., who could have placed seventh but was disqualified; DAN AKINS of Ashton, S. Dak., another driver who looked good at the start of the second leg from Mobridge to Aberdeen; and Canadian DIANNE REIMER, the only woman to finish the race. Dianne, a licensed practical nurse from Steinbach, Manitoba and the wife of Enduro Team Deere driver Ron Reimer, was piloting a 1976 John Deere Liquifire sled in South Dakota.

The December 28 lineup at Balsam Lake saw more than half the 55 finishers on John Deere sleds as well, with eight John Deere drivers in the top 20. Eighth place finisher HAROLD McQUEEN, a corn and soybean farmer from Manteno, Ill., also entered the South Dakota Governor's Cup this past weekend and plans to enter both the I-500 and Iowa Great Lakes 300. PAUL YOUNG, the Erie, Ill. farmer who preceded McQueen in seventh place at Balsam Lake, will enter the Sauk Centre Dairyland 100, Eagles Heartland Grand Prix, and the Iowa Great Lakes 300.

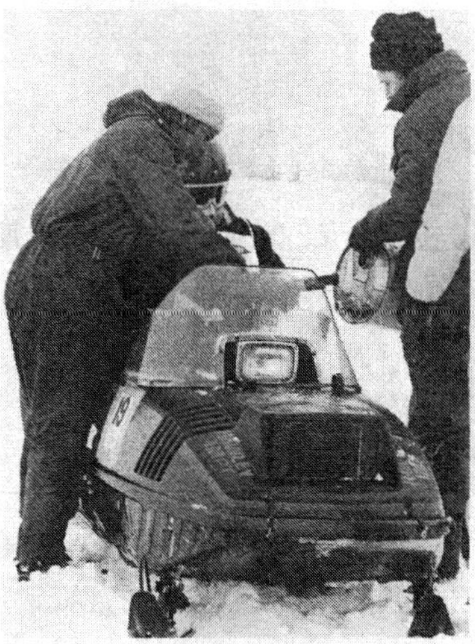

(Above) EUGENE JETVIG of Hawley, Minn., stops in the pit to refuel.

(Right) JIM ZIMMER of Lakeville, Minn., crosses an intersection at a fast clip.

More race photos on page 3 ....

(Above) DIANNE REIMER of Steinbach, Manitoba, one of two women entered and the only one to finish the race, shows great form as she barrels her 340 Liquifire along the race route.

-- THE CANDID CORNER WITH INDEPENDENT JOHN DEERE DRIVERS IN SOUTH DAKOTA --

1

4

2

3

5

1) AL BERGQUIST of Elburn, Ill., takes the rough moguls in stride.

2) BOB HUMPAL of Ft. Atkinson, Ia., drives his 340 Liquidator through a snowbank at a fast pace.

3) BRYAN HENDRICK of Isanti, Minn., is almost air-borne as he leaves the ditch at an intersection.

4) MIKE SOWARD from Sioux Falls, S. Dak., gets ready to start in 23rd place from Mobridge; he would have finished the race in seventh place.

5) RON HEMPEN of Aplington, Ia., gets ready to go in a heavy snowfall at Aberdeen.

NEXT WEEK: More News, Results and Photos from the St. Paul-Winnipeg I-500

GREEN STREAK

Race news and views from "Big John"

NELSON PILOTS LIQUIDATOR TO THRILLING VICTORY IN THE INTERNATIONAL 500

After four grueling days and more than 585 rugged miles, Enduro Team Deere driver Brian Nelson piloted his liquidator 340 to a thrilling victory in the all-important St. Paul to Winnipeg race. The 22-year-old Willmar (Minn.) native crossed the finish line with the best overall time of 12 hours, 37 minutes and 19 seconds, just 32 seconds ahead of Robert Przekwas on a Polaris.

NELSON JETS ACROSS THE FINISH LINE TO CAPTURE A WELL-DESERVED VICTORY

Nelson was among the top five finishers each of the first three days of the race (Jan. 19 - 21) but going into the final leg from Thief River Falls, Minn., to Winnipeg he had to make up 14 minutes and 11 seconds between his fourth place position and Przekwas in first. Pulling out all stops, the determined Nelson jumped ahead of the rest of the field with speeds up to 90 miles per hour to cross the finish line 14 minutes and 43 seconds in front of Przekwas.

No newcomer to the winner's circle, Nelson will add the prestigious International 500 trophy and $16,000 first prize money to the other laurels he has won this season. Including, 1st place in the North Dakota Governor's Trophy Run and 2nd place in the Balsam Lake Classic (both 250 mile cross country runs). The modest Enduro Team member gives much of the credit for his success to mechanic Hubert Fixsen and Race Director Al Andersen.

DEERE DRIVERS CAPTURE FOUR OF THE TOP 20 SPOTS AS A TOTAL OF 12 DEERE SLEDS FINISH RACE

Hearty congratulations are also in order to each of the 11 other Deere drivers who were able to finish the exhausting course. Of the 385 sleds starting the race in St. Paul, only 60 were able to make it across the finish line in Winnipeg. Top 20 finishers include: Mike Soward, Sioux Falls, S.D.; Craig Bjorklund, Isanti, Minn.; and Enduro Team member Ron Reimer from Steinbach, Manitoba. Other Deere drivers completing the race were: Abe Koop, Steinbach, Manitoba; Gene Jetvig, Clarrisa, Minn.; Floyd Beumer, St. Cloud, Minn.; Ronald Hempen, Arlington, Iowa; Keith Bylin, Adams, N.D.; Randy Stumvoll, Nissawa, Minn.; Gordon Hamm, Asquith, Sask.; Steven Cudd, River Falls, Wisc. Both Koop and Cudd were piloting Liquifires and Beumer was driving a 340 S. The other five men were on Liquidators.

Issued periodically by the Advertising Dept. Deere & Co. Moline, Ill. 61265

JOHN DEERE

THE BONUS POINT SCOREBOARD

Brian Nelson's victory in the I-500 puts him way out in front on the bonus point scoreboard with a total of 110 points for four races. An updated tally shows Tom Otte in second place with 15 points, Paul Young with 4, Harold McQueen with 3, and Mike Soward, Ron Reimer and Craig Bjorklund with 2 points each. These bonus points will qualify drivers for additional cash prizes and trophies at season's end.

An updated tally of points will appear weekly under the Bonus Point Scoreboard of your Green Streak, with five races ahead there's still ample opportunity for independent drivers to earn bonus points for cash prizes, trophies and championship rings.

"DAIRYLAND 100" - THE NEXT TEST FOR BIG JOHN

Deere drivers will have a chance to add to their bonus points and prove their individual skills January 31 at the Dairyland 100 race in Sauk Center, Minn. The action starts at 9:30 a.m. on Big Sauk Lake and follows a challenging course across 10 lakes, numerous ditches, country roads and woods before finishing back at Big Sauk Lake. Race officials are hoping for a field of 200 sleds, representing $20,000 in total prize money and a $6,000 first place purse. John Deere will also put up a total of $5,000 in excess of the "Dairyland" money to Deere drivers finishing in the top ten. This includes a $2,000 prize to any Deere sled winning the race.

INDEPENDENTS CORNER

Abe Koop of Steinbach, Manitoba gets a helping hand from a race official. Koop, sponsored by Reimer Farm Supplies of Steinbach, finished 21st on a liquifire.

Randy Stumvoll of Nissawa, Mn., discusses the rigors of the race with Enduro Team driver Ron Reimer.

Mike Soward, Sioux Falls, S.D. breathes a sigh of relief after finishing 16th.

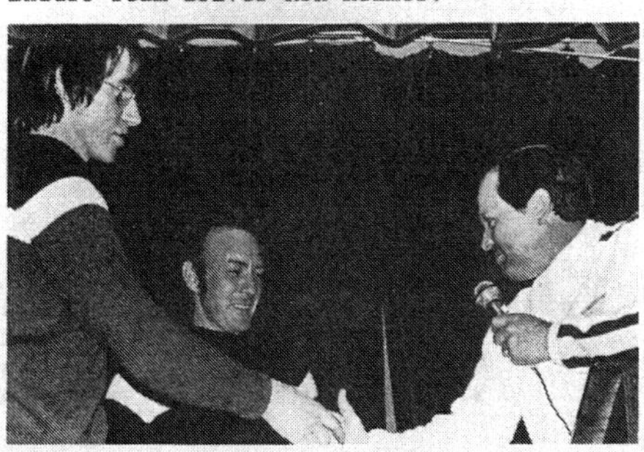

Congratulating Floyd Beumer (left) and Stephen Cudd for finishing the grueling race is Don Carl from Deere & Co. Beumer rode a 340 S and Cudd a liquifire.

WINNERS' CIRCLE

To the victor goes the spoils... Brian accepts the winners trophy and the $10,000 first place check from the Winter Carnival King and Queen as a member of the queen's court, Miss Manitoba, congratulates him.

Brian shares his victory roses with mechanic and good friend Hubert Fixsen, also of Willmar, Minn. Brian gave Hubert much of the credit for his victory.

Terry Nelson tells an interviewer just how great her husbands' win was.

Ron Reimer is met at the finish line by wife, Diane. Diane was one of five women to start the race in St. Paul.

GREEN STREAK

Race news and views from "Big John"

February 8, 1977

BOB ENNS WINS DAIRYLAND 100 BY HEART-STOPPING TWO-SECOND MARGIN! SETS RECORD FOR MOST VICTORIES IN ICCSF TWO-YEAR HISTORY.

Enduro Team Deere driver Bob Enns of Oak Bluff, Manitoba, set two records with his 2-second victory in last weekend's Dairyland 100 at Sauk Centre, MN. With a total of four firsts, he has now won more ICCSF races than any other driver in the 2-year-old circuit. And he is the winningest driver this year with three victories. Bob had previous wins this year in the Peace Garden Classic and the Willmar Eagles 200. He also won the Eagles Heartland last year.

Bob piloted his John Deere Liquidator to the finish line in 3:27:04--just 2 seconds ahead of Scott Simonson on a Polaris. James Safranski and Brian Nelson finished third and fourth on Cross Country Cats. Enduro Team Deere driver Willie Anseeuw finished fifth on a stock 340 Liquifire in 3:36:26. Willie is also from Bob's hometown of Oak Bluff, Manitoba.

There were 110 starters and 37 finishers in this 180-mile cross country race. Other John Deere finishers included Tom Otte, Northfield, MN; Cary Dehm, Chatsworth, IL; Bob Humpal, Ft. Atkinson, IA; Wayne Schmidt, Waucoma, MN; and Stan Ryman, Mansfield, SD.

Trials and tribulations on the trail. On the last lap, Bob Enns had a 4-minute lead when he met a trail rider coming towards him on a narrow section of the course. Bob "bailed out" and his sled hit a tree. The impact bent the pan, twisted the frame, and knocked the clutch off center. But Bob was able to finish ahead of the pack...with 1 second to spare.

Enns closes on Janssen in ICCSF. With 126 points Roger Janssen continues to lead the ICCSF in bonus points. Bob Enns is second with 122 points. Rounding out the "top five" are Chester Bowman, 114 points, Brian Nelson 98 points, and Willie Anseeuw, 88 points.

BONUS POINT SCOREBOARD	
Bob Enns	320
Willie Anseeuw	180
Jon Carlson	155
Doug Hough	145
Tom Otte	125
Ron Reimer	95
Craig Knudsen	90
Dave Hough	75
Bill Ryman	65
Wayne Muller	45
Stan Ryman	40
Gary Phelps	15
Myron Fast	10
Mario Hoyt	5
Jeffrey Jenson	5
Ken Lund	5
Allen Berge	5
Ray Hall	5
Orrin Behrens	5
Gene Jetvig	5
Roger Harbour	5
George Millar	5
Cary Dehm	5

ENNS WIDENS POINT LEAD

Bob Enns' victory at the Dairyland 100 last weekend ran his bonus point total to 320 points with four races remaining on the 1977 schedule. His Enduro Team Deere teammate Willie Anseeuw moves into second place with his fifth place finish, while independent Cary Dehm added his name to the board with a 29th place finish.

JOHN DEERE

COACH'S CORNER by Al Andersen

The North American Lions 250 Cross-Country Snowmobile Race is a new race on the ICCSF circuit. It will be held Sunday, February 20th, at Neenah, Wisconsin. Sonny Borchert of the Ridgeway Sports dealership is the race director.

Sonny tells us that the race will consist of 10 laps around a 25-mile lake perimeter, including some overland running. The start-finish area will be set up much like Balsam Lake and Forest Lake; however, prior to coming into the gas and lap counting area, there will be a planned figure "S" outlined to slow the sleds. The finish-line lane will be on the right and the gas stop lanes on the left. Lap counting will be done as it was at Forest Lake.

The total length of the race is set for 250 miles. It is scheduled to begin at 10:00 a.m. with a 4:00 p.m. finish cutoff. Sleds will be started in heats of 15 to 20, and heats will be spaced 2 to 3 minutes apart, depending on the weather. Sonny indicates that although there is a drivers' meeting the evening before the race, sleds need not be impounded nor engines sprayed prior to the race.

There will be an awards banquet following the race. We hope there will be a large turnout of both drivers and fans for this new ICCSF race.

IDAHO INDEPENDENT TEAM WINS "150" ENDURO TEAM RACE ON FLAT TRACK

A three-man Independent team drove a 440 Liquifire to victory in a 150-mile endurance race at Idaho Falls, Idaho. The team was composed of Paul Fife, John Deere Dealer at Rigby, Idaho, and Jim and Jerry Noble of Idaho Falls. The only other John Deere team in the 30-team field finished sixth. That team also driving a 440 Liquifire, was sponsored by Gem Equipment Lawn and Leisure, Twin Falls.

BOB ENNS . . . three firsts in six ICCSF starts!

John Deere *Green Streak* newsletter (courtesy Larry Swanson).

II. Trailfire Test Report, Snow Goer *magazine*

JD Trailfire

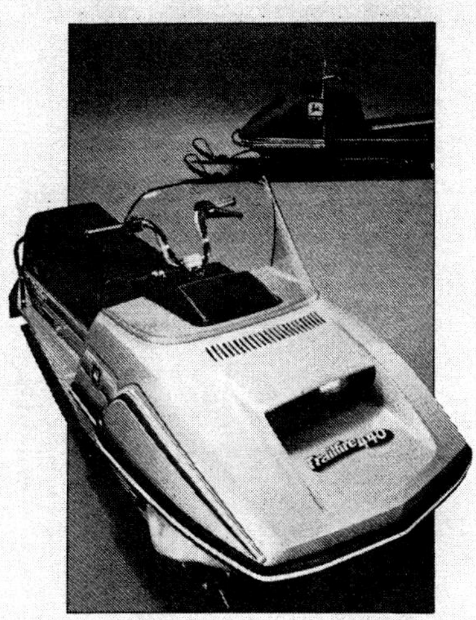

The better idea from John Deere

SNOW GOER TEST REPORT

Traditionally, Deere has at best been traditional. Trailfire is anything but traditional. From the long travel rear suspension to the lower profiled shroud, Trailfire is revolutionary for the Horicon, Wisconsin, based company. It took years to develop and test but was worth the wait.

Comments from the test drivers at the SNOW GOER tests conducted at Cable, Wisconsin, were generally positive, describing the Trailfire: "I think it (Trailfire) may be the finest machine that John Deere has ever built." Other driver comments: "The trail riding characteristics of this machine are excellent, the overall comfort of the machine is second to none. The clutch response is positive. This sled is clean, the way John Deere usually builds their sleds." The comments about the 1979 Trailfire went on raving about the new sled from the company that built its reputation on farm implements.

Lighter and sportier, the all new John Deere Trailfire features a lower center of gravity and all new colors for 1979. Trailfire is a family sled that's a noticeable change from any other John Deere. Equipped with a Kawasaki fan-cooled twin that's mounted lower than any other sled on the market, Trailfire '79 is Deere's idea of the perfect family trail sled. It's a new breed of Deere.

Design is the most noticeable feature of the '79 Trailfire. John Deere engineers mounted the 440 twin cylinder three inches lower in the chassis than any other sled they have designed to date. They moved the engine closer to the tunnel by some two and a half inches for better overall weight distribution and a near perfect pivot point.

Trailfire's fan-cooled 436cc powerplant, complete with capacitor discharge ignition, has a bore-stroke of 68mm x 60mm, a perfect combination for the family trail sled image Deere hopes to convey. A single VM34 Mikuni carburetor has been added to supply the 440 with exacting fuel.

Consistently, John Deere has produced a durable product. Trailfire not only appears durable but is lightweight to boot, about 40 pounds lighter than the 1978 Cyclone. Weight reduction was accomplished by a diet of materials such as aluminum and steel. Special high strength, low alloy steel like that used in the auto industry's construction of

34 SNOW GOER

JD Trailfire *Snow Goer* test report (courtesy *Snow Goer* magazine).

bumpers, supports, door beams and other places where strength is crucial, was used where deemed necessary. Trailfire uses steel, for example, in the center section of the pan to provide a tough shield against rocks, stumps and other trail debris that would easily dent or rip holes in aluminum. The outer edges of the pan are made of thermoplastic rubber which is both tough and flexible at low temperatures. TPR is riveted to the steel center pan to give the Trailfire strength and flex.

John Deere engineers even cut down the weight of the sled by making the exhaust chamber lighter. They did it by making it smaller. About four to five inches shorter, the new exhaust chamber has a reversed internal cone which makes the system compact and provides both the power and silencing of the old system.

Trailfire's suspension has changed. The only part of the system that has not changed is the aluminum slide rail. The rest of the system is all new for 1979. John Deere's engineering people doubled the travel of the rear suspension to nearly five inches, which has increased the riding comfort of their top line sled. The chance of bottoming out has been reduced substantially due to the shock absorber assisted rear suspension system. Deere's unique multi-layer foam seat is incorporated into the suspension system of the Trailfire, maximizing comfort. The seat is the trend setter of the industry.

Even SNOW GOER's test drivers, who've been sticklers for mechanical detail, couldn't help noticing the unique styling that went into Trailfire. "Trailfire has a super unique color (Winterfrost) which is a combination of silver and gold with just the right application of greens and reds and a little yellow. It looks great!" Another commented: "I haven't seen a better looking sled out here."

Other features which made Trailfire 440 a hit at SNOW GOER's perennial test session were its ski suspension with mono-leaf shocks and a shock absorber, mounted to give the new Deere a 30-inch stance. In addition, a large 7.5 gallon fuel tank located in front of the seat gives the Trailfire long range riding capabilities. To monitor the fuel, Deere has given Trailfire a fuel gauge. Rounding out the features that are standard for '79 are yoke-type handlebars, which are fully adjustable, and a high windshield that keeps the wind out of the driver's face and his hands warm.

Accessories available on the Trailfire are: speedometer, tachometer, carbide wear rods, track studs,

SNOW GOER 35

JD Trailfire ***Snow Goer*** test report (courtesy ***Snow Goer*** magazine).

MODEL: JOHN DEERE TRAILFIRE 440
Suggested Retail Price: $2099

Engine / Drivetrain
Engine Position: Front
Manufacturer: Kawasaki
Displacement: 436cc
Cylinders: Twin
Cooling: Fan
Horsepower @ RPM: N / A
Compression Ratio: N / A
Bore / Stroke: 68mm x 60mm
Carburetor(s) Type: Single VM34 Mikuni
Drive Clutch: John Deere

Vital Statistics
Weight (dry): 370 lbs
Weight (wet): 429 lbs
Fuel Capacity: 7.5 Gals
Snowmobile Length: 102 in
Snowmobile Width: 37 in
Snowmobile Height: N / A
Ski Stance: 30 in

Suspension / Track
Suspension Type: Slide Rail
Ski Suspension Type: Mono-leaf spring
Track Length: 116 in
Track Width: 15 in
Track Material: Riveted grouser bar

General Information
Brake Type: Disc
Chassis Material: Ultra form 80 steel
Cowl Material: Fiberglass
Ignition Type: CDI

Trailfire is all new for 1979, with an all new twin cylinder, fan-cooled power-plant (above left) providing the excitement. The 436cc twin is mounted low to the ground to carry off the image of a low profile sled.

Trailfire's suspension (left) is simple. It is simple but very effective. It boasts of four inches travel and combines with a multi-layer foam seat to maximize comfort.

John Deere clutching (below) makes shifting the 440 from the lower trail speeds to higher flat-out shots a smooth transition.

handlebar heater kits, and electrical start.

Trailfire's hit with SNOW GOER test drivers coupled with its own good looks and unique personality will make definite inroads with families interested in a fresh design and moderate price ($2099 for the 440; an even slighter price tag for the 340, $1899). Winterfrost color, longer travel rear suspension, lower center of gravity, lighter profile, and highly advanced design should bolster Trailfire sales and overall appeal.

36 SNOW GOER

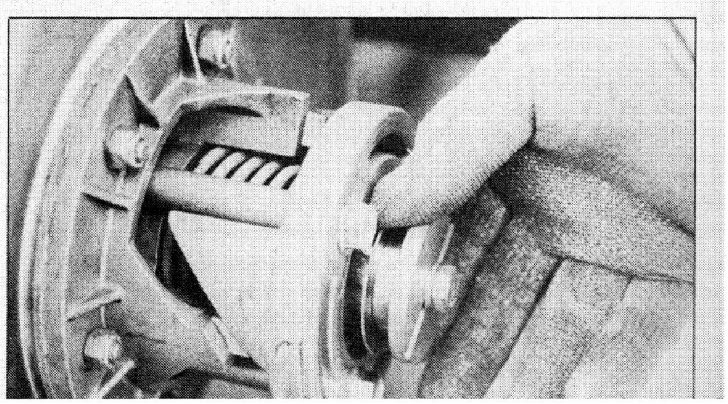

JD Trailfire *Snow Goer* test report (courtesy *Snow Goer* magazine).

III. Snow Goer *Best Handling Award for John Deere Liquifire*

BEST HANDLING

John Deere

In the handling phase, each sled had four timed attempts, of which only the best three counted. Of those three, Deere's Liquifire was first, third, and fourth best overall. The second best time was almost a full second and about half a mile per hour slower! That the Deere proved it was the "Best Handler" was no fluke. It proved it — going away!

Scoring a perfect 90 points in the handling phase, the Deere earned another 52 points in acceleration, making a total of 142, which qualified as third overall.

With a 440cc engine delivering 65 horsepower, the Deere suffered against its higher-powered, larger displacement competition. So its victory in the handling phase shows that design can win over muscle.

SNOW GOER 13

JD Liquifire ***Snow Goer*** **best handling award (courtesy** ***Snow Goer*** **magazine).**

IV. Product Safety Report from 1982 Product Strategy Meeting

JOHN DEERE HORICON WORKS

PRODUCT STRATEGY MEETING
25 June 1982

PRODUCT SAFETY

During the past several years, a number of activities have been started or re-emphasized to improve the operating safety of Horicon products.

Each new product or major revision is reviewed by a task force composed of members from various factory departments. A hazard discovery and rating system technique is used to discover and analyze safety concerns. Task force concerns are reviewed and resolved by the Product Safety Committee. Six task force reviews have already occurred in 1982.

Internal design standards are being drafted. Those covering fuel systems, wiring, and PTOs have been circulated for comment. The fuel system standard has received particular emphasis and has been successfully applied to snowmobiles, lawn tractors, and lawn and garden tractors.

An outside consultant, Hercules, Inc., is investigating the possibility of refueling fires being caused by static electricity. The final report has not been received, but current information indicates that only rarely will conditions and circumstances allow a static charge to ignite fuel vapors. We will use HERC's recommendations to minimize static electricity problems on future machines.

A system which turns off the cutting blade during reverse operation is being investigated. This system has been proposed as a means of addressing blade contact and particularly backover accidents.

Several safety training events have occurred in the past year. "Punch" Pfundsteing presented "Product Safety Technology". Jerry Duncan reviewed "Human Factors". A field comparison of skid steer loaders was conducted. Dr. Thomas Pratt of HERC presented a static electricity seminar. A continuing training effort is planned for the future.

The safety engineer is continuing to monitor daily test reports for safety concerns. These concerns are discussed with the design groups and appropriate action is taken.

A new thrown objects test which evalutes the entire perimeter of the mower is being developed with other industry members. Current ANSI tests only evaluate the discharge chute.

Requirements are also being developed for stability during turns and drive engagement on slopes to reduce riding mower and tractor overturns. The turn stability requirement will establish the relationship between the minimum turn radius and the maximum speed during a turn based on the static stability of the machine. Deere has taken a leading role in this industry activity.

Horicon Product Safety Improvements (PSM 1982) (Ron Leonard collection).

V. Horicon Works Competitive Review

JOHN DEERE HORICON WORKS

COMPETITIVE REVIEW

In 1982 Horicon shipped 23.6% of the value of all OPEI shipments of lawn tractors, lawn & garden tractors, riding mowers and attachments. The total OPEI industry value of these four product categories was $817 million. This is less than one-half of the nearly $2 billion value of all OPEI shipments.

Our major competitors for these product lines are:

Lawn Tractors	1. Murray 2. MTD 3. AMF
Lawn & Garden Tractors	1. MTD/IHC 2. Simplicity 3. Roper/Sears
Riding Mowers	1. Snapper 2. Murray 3. MTD
Attachments	

No Japanese company shipments are included in OPEI statistics, as the OPEI does not permit membership of foreign manufacturers.

None of the above companies, including Deere, manufacture their own engines. These components have long been produced by OEM manufacturers located in the U.S. Two companies, Simplicity and IHC (now MTD), manufacture their own tractor transmissions.

The major suppliers for transmissions and axles have been Peerless for mechanical and Sundstrand and Eaton for hydrostatics.

The major OEM suppliers are:

Product Line	Engines	Transmissions & Axles
Lawn Tractors	Briggs & Stratton Tecumseh	Peerless Div. of Tecumseh Eaton
Lawn & Garden Tractors	Kohler Onan Briggs & Stratton	Peerless Div. of Tecumseh Dana Sundstrand Eaton
Riding Mowers	Briggs & Stratton Tecumseh	Peerless Div. of Tecumseh Snapper (own design)

Competitive Review (PSM 1982) (Ron Leonard collection).

During the past few years, several foreign manufacturers of engines have attempted to sell their products to U.S. vehicle manufacturers.

1) Honda was prepared to supply engines to Snapper for a walk-behind mower.

2) Ducati, Ruggerini and Lombardini have attempted to interest tractor people in their air-cooled diesel engines for garden tractors. Ducati supplied some production engines to Bolens for tractors.

3) Japanese engine suppliers began calling on U.S. companies trying to sell water-cooled diesel engines and air-cooled gasoline engines. It is rumored that MTD has bought 3,000 diesel engines from Kubota.

Most of these efforts have had little commercial success. The Japanese companies entered the aftermarket to try to secure a reputation. Honda and Kawasaki have enjoyed some success in doing this. This has enabled Kawasaki to sell engines to some small manufacturers of commercial mowers.

Some companies, like Kubota, Yanmar, Shibaura and Honda set about to supply end product vehicles to compete with the U.S. manufacturers. To date the major efforts have been as follows:

Lawn Tractors	Honda	Announced for 1984
Lawn & Garden Tractors	Kubota Yanmar	G Series for 1983 YM12 & YM14 for 1983
Riding Mowers	Honda	Announced for 1984

We believe that the Japanese will alter the fundamental nature of this business. Vertically integrated companies will design and manufacture the entire vehicle, including engines and transmissions. Some of these companies will make the components available to U.S. manufacturers in order to increase their volume base. This is in sharp contrast to the OEM supplier situation that has existed in this industry for the past twenty years.

From this information several observations follow:

1) Japanese tractor manufacturers will attempt to capture most of the quality end of the lawn & garden tractor business.

2) Honda will challenge Briggs & Stratton for leadership as the major engine supplier for lawn tractors and riding mowers while aggressively marketing their own vehicles.

3) Kawasaki will compete with Honda as an engine supplier.

4) Transmission suppliers from Japan will compete with Peerless and Sundstrand.

Competitive Review (PSM 1982) (Ron Leonard collection).

A key part of any company's future is its engineering capability. We have made an assessment of the relative engineering strength of some of the Japanese companies.

In a recent visit to Honda's U.S. facility in Gardena, California, we learned that they employ 400 engineers in their Outdoor Power Products Group. About 250 are new since 1981. Nearly half of them are researching new markets for Honda engines. Their current products are power plants, roto tillers, walk-behind mowers, generator sets, water pumps and outboard motors. Pending new products are lawn tractors and riding mowers. Honda's most recent success was with small portable generators. From nearly nothing they now sell about 4.5 million units annually. Honda's announced goal is to become the number one producer of small engines worldwide.

Yanmar employs 1300 engineers. About 500 of the 1300 work on diesel engines. At their Technical Center in Kyoto half of the 400 people are working on diesel engines. Each vehicle factory has its own Product Engineering group which includes engine and transmission engineers. The Kinomoto Tractor Factory employs 130 engineers.

Kawasaki has an engineering group of 130 people working in their agricultural engine section, which is separate from motorcycles. Currently most are working on new engine programs. About 10% are supporting their transmission effort. Kawasaki produces intermediate size transmissions for Isuzu 1.5 and 2 ton trucks, axles for Club Car golf carts and front wheel drive axles for Iseki tractors. Their engine business is mostly for Iseki rice combines and for small air-cooled pumps and generators. This group also does their snowmobile and Jet Ski engine work.

For comparison, Briggs & Stratton has about 60 engineers.

Kubota and other Japanese tractor manufacturers have significant engineering staffs to support their product lines which include agricultural and utility tractors as well as recent efforts on garden tractors. Kubota said they spend 4.5% of agricultural sales on engineering. Agricultural sales total about $1 billion, worldwide sales are $2.5 billion, and employment is 17,000. They employ 3,000 people at the Sakai factory where they produce engines, B&G Series tractors, and agricultural equipment. They stated 200 engineers work on engines and they have 800 people in Research & Development.

John Deere Horicon Works Engineering has 77 salaried people, of which 50 are working as engineers. Can we remain competitive while using OEM components in our vehicles and with our small engineering effort?

The answer is yes or no, depending upon what we do.

Yes, if we secure high technology components sourced from the best companies worldwide and if we can secure unique designs for our products.

No, if we stay with the likes of Kohler and Briggs & Stratton who have not perceived that the Japanese products are superior in performance and quality.

Competitive Review (PSM 1982) (Ron Leonard collection).

Japanese small engine manufacturers are desirous of aligning with U.S. companies to tap the large outdoor power market in the U.S. and Canada. We have an excellent opportunity to obtain the best suppliers before any major alliances are formed, since we currently enjoy major success in the lawn & garden tractor and lawn tractor markets.

To be successful with our limited engineering resources will require us to direct the major engineering efforts of certain high technology manufacturers for engine and transmission components like Kawasaki and Yanmar. In effect, this will enable us to pit one Japanese company against another. This will help insure competitiveness of design. If we are associated with companies which have high enough volumes it will also keep our costs competitive.

Kawasaki and Mitsubishi are the major manufacturers of gasoline engines in Japan. We believe that Kawasaki will be our best choice as a supplier of both air-cooled and liquid-cooled gasoline engines. We also believe their future designs will be competitive with the latest in technology, comparable with Honda.

The Yanmar Diesel Company is our best choice as a supplier of small lightweight diesel engines for technology and cost.

Kawasaki and Yanmar are also possible suppliers of transmission components. Sundstrand will continue to supply hydrostatic transmissions although Daikin, Kayaba, Linde/Ebara and Kawasaki are also possible suppliers of hydrostatic transmissions.

As our company sets new goals for increased business in consumer products for homeowner and commercial markets, we will employ the same engineering strategy in the design for manufacture of these vehicles. In the highly competitive technological world today, we believe this global strategy will provide us the best chance of remaining competitive with our end product in features, quality and cost.

Competitive Review (PSM 1982) (Ron Leonard collection).

VI. John Deere Fortune 500 Rankings, 1955–2005

Deere ranking Fortune 500 US 4/13/12
Millions of dollars

Year	Rank	Sales	Profits
1955	104	303.4	20.6
1956	100	339.6	28.3
1957	123	313.6	20.1
1958	101	388.1	28.7
1959	81	422.6	42.1
1960	78	542.5	48.5
1961	97	468.5	17.8
1962	95	509.6	32
1963	97	541.5	36.3
1964	81	639.1	45.7
1965	71	816.6	59.4
1966	74	886.6	55.8
1967	65	1,062.10	78.7
1968	73	1,086.40	57.6
1969	99	1,030.50	42.6
1970	112	1,043.00	54.1
1971	103	1,137.70	46
1972	108	1,188.10	63.3
1973	90	1,500.20	112.2
1974	78	2,003.20	168.5
1975	74	2,495.10	164.3
1976	62	2,955.20	179.1
1977	66	3,133.80	241.6
1978	60	3,604.00	255.6
1979	61	4,155.00	264.8
1980	60	4,933.10	310.6
1981	60	5,469.80	228.3
1982	65	5,446.70	251
1983	75	4,608.20	52.9
1984	92	3,967.90	23
1985	86	4,399.20	104.9
1986	96	4,060.60	30.5
1987	111	3,516.30	-229.3
1988	108	4,135.00	-99
1989	87	5,365.00	-315
1990	66	7,221.00	34.6
1991	62	7,881.00	411.1
1992	72	7,055.20	-20.2
1993	79.00	6,960.70	37.4
1999	113	13,821.50	1,021.40
2005	106	19,916.10	1,406.10

Bibliographic Notes

A Google Internet search for John Deere history will produce 7,650,000 results. Consequently one can find a book or publication that relates the history of nearly every aspect of the company, starting with the founder John Deere and continuing with his successors, his company and the products that proudly bear his name. The name John Deere is simply an American legend that has endured for 175 years.

One can find hundreds of books about John Deere tractors and others about John Deere agricultural products. There have been no books written that describe the history of John Deere in the snowmobile business. However, there are thousands of snowmobile publications that were produced by Deere and Company while they were manufacturing and marketing snowmobiles. The relatively short 13 years in the business of manufacturing snowmobiles served as a catalyst that spurred the dynamic growth of their consumer products business as a result of lessons learned from the snowmobile experience.

One comprehensive publication is an excellent, well-documented work: *John Deere's Company, A History of Deere & Company and Its Times*, written by Wayne G. Broehl, Jr., and published by Doubleday in 1984. To write this substantial and definitive work, Broehl had access to the Deere archives in Moline, Illinois, and from this treasure trove of information and extensive research, he created a book that traced the John Deere story from the founder's ancestry through five eras of family descendants who served long periods of years as president and CEO of the company.

Product Review Manuals from 1971 to 1986: These documents contain the specifications of the machines being designed and tooled for manufacture at the Deere Horicon Works. They were produced in limited number by factory personnel from the product engineering, marketing, accounting and quality departments with limited distribution to the Moline management who attended the meetings. The PRMs also contain data reported by industry trade associations, Horicon Works sales, and market share of their products.

Deere and Company Annual Reports: These are produced at the end of each fiscal year and widely distributed to stockholders and other financial agencies.

Jack Hoffman's personal files of internal product engineering department documents, which include the engineering department's monthly reports to the factory manager, and approved Engineering Orders (EO) that authorized expenditure of time and resources on the design, development and verification before production release of a new machine.

Jack Hoffman's bound volume of internal Horicon Works factory memos from marketing and manufacturing about issues and concerns about specific machine complaints or production improvements to them.

Martin Berk's file of Engineering Orders.

Open Door, published by the Horicon Works, provided employees information about the factories' products and employees.

Shigeo Shingo's publications about the Toyota production system, translated into English by Norman Bodek, founder of Productivity Inc., in the USA.

Dr. Robert Cooper's publications about industrial products and innovation:

"Why New Industrial Products Fail," published in *Industrial Marketing Management* 4 (1975).

"The Misuse of Marketing: An American Tragedy," published in *Business Horizons* (November/December 1981) coauthored with Roger C. Bennett.

"The Performance Impact of Product Innovation Strategies," published in *European Journal of Marketing* 18, Number 5 (1984).

A Strategic Planning Institute publication "Degrees of Product Innovation," as a SPI Working Paper in 1979.

Bob Shanahan's self-published report of the Yamaha outboard motor design and production procedures and a similar analysis of the John Deere Horicon Works processes of design and preparation for production.

"Outlook of the Machine Tool Industry in the Age of Mechatronics," by Kojiro Yamaoka, Doctor of Engineering, president of Kanzaki Kokyukoki Mfg. Co. and president of Shoun Machine Tool Co. Ltd. located in Kobe, Japan.

Green Streak race news and views from Deere & Company.

Snow Goer magazine test reports for the 1976 Cyclone and Liquifire and the 1979 Trailfire.

Snowmobile West Magazine 1979 Trailfire Dealer Introduction.

The following people contributed to various parts of the Deere snowmobile story. Most were employees or family members. Their stories displayed the passion they had for John Deere and John Deere snowmobiles:

Allen, Cliff
Anderson, Al
Apple, David
Berk, Martin
Braun, Steve
Carlson, Jon
DeWitt, Roger
Dummer, Duane
Eekoff, Dale
Enns, Bob
Feldman, Rob
Firehammer, Carl
Geddes, Pat
Gregg, Ray
Hardesty, Lee
Hedburg, Lynne
Heitman, Mike
Hildebrandt, Earl
Hoffman, Jack
Kruel, Ed
Lee, Bill
Leonard, Diane
McClellen, Wayne
Miller, Lauren
Mitchell, Bill
Muenchow, Ralph
Nelson, Brian
Nenneman, Larry
Orvis, John
Pershing, Roscoe
Preston, Randy
Scholten, Steve
Stickler, Fred
Strassmann, Bob
Stricker, Dave
Swanson, Larry
Tesch, Roger
Voy, Gerry
Wanie, Joe
Wanie, Lee
Wheeler, Ron
Wreath, Wayne

Index